W9-BOL-744

WASHINGTON SENATORS' ALL-TIME GREATS

April 11, 2004

To: Rich, Mary and Family

Rich, you are the consummate innovator and I thank you for all of the help you provided me at NSA. Congratulations on your successful climb up the ladder, despite the fact you didn't make Director! Frances and I enjoyed being with you and Mary and you have a great family. I expect you to root for the Senators when we get our team in 2005! May God bless you.

C. Norman Willis

WASHINGTON SENATORS' ALL-TIME GREATS

C. Norman Willis

Library of Congress Number: 2003093600

ISBN: Hardcover 1-4010-9619-0

Softcover 1-4010-9618-2

This book was printed in the United States of America.

To order additional copies of this book, contact:

Xlibris Corporation

1-888-795-4274

www.Xlibris.com

Orders@Xlibris.com

18048

CONTENTS

This book is dedicated to the memory of longtime friend and Washington Senators fan, Robert L. Hagedorn, who retrieved baseballs and shagged flies as a teenager in Griffith Stadium, shoulder to shoulder with Senators greats during the 1930s. Bob passed away on October 27, 2001.

ACKNOWLEDGEMENTS

First, I want to thank my dear wife, Frances for her patience, understanding and encouragement while I was working on this book over the past two decades. Next, I want to express my sincere appreciation to my close friend and former colleague, Dick Hughes, whose computer expertise and generous use of his time, enabled my vision for the book to become a reality. His wife, Micki, also helped by letting me use her laptop computer for more than a three-year period. My brother, Claude, made first drafts for several of the mini-biographies, did some editing, and deserves recognition. My late friend and former boss, Bob Hagedorn, to whom I have dedicated this book, made many helpful suggestions during its formative stages. Another former work associate, Bill Cherry, deserves thanks for his meticulous editing of the text.

Many librarians at the Martin Luther King, Jr. Library in Washington, D.C., where I did most of my research, deserve special kudos, including Margaret Goodbody, Faye Haskins and Peggy Appleman. Researchers Bill Francis and Bill Burbick at the National Baseball Hall of Fame Library in Cooperstown, New York aided me greatly. The Minnesota Twins Baseball Club, Minneapolis, Minnesota was gracious in providing photographs for the book. Fran Smith, Megan Brewer and Robin Wright of United Photo in Beltsville, Maryland also provided photographs. Friends, Bill Howerton and Craig Knox, copied and processed many of the photos. Dave Wineman, one of my contacts at Xlibris, flawlessly guided me through the preliminary process and Melissa Dileonardo and her staff corrected numerous errors during the editing process. Laura Cuorato, Jen Foulk, Lisa Modica and Kerrick Jones were very helpful in producing the final product.

To all of the former Senators ballplayers who granted me interviews, to Frank Howard who willingly consented to do the foreword for the book, and to Mickey Vernon and Jim Lemon who kindly endorsed the book, I am especially indebted. Finally, I thank my Lord Jesus Christ for His sustaining power during the long and arduous process of completing the book!

FOREWORD

Washington has a long history of professional baseball dating back over 130 years. I was privileged to be a part of that scene for seven years, one of hundreds of ballplayers who wore the Washington uniform. While the Senators (or Nationals as they were sometimes called) were oftentimes not very competitive on the field, a great number of skilled players drew the cheers of loyal fans. This book does an excellent job of summarizing team performance over the years and brings alive the fading exploits of the Washington stars of yesteryear. Emphasis is placed on the on-field exploits of each hero, but the book is replete with other interesting anecdotes and personal background information.

The fans of Washington deserved a better fate in 1972 when they were left without a major league franchise after owner Bob Short moved the club to Texas. Like any other franchise, which has experienced a losing record for a long period of time, the Senators sometimes experienced marked decreases in attendance. But, records show that when the Nats were competitive and winners, the fans flocked to support them. While Washington has failed heretofore in its attempt to acquire another team, I believe that major league baseball should look kindly on attempts to bring a team to Northern Virginia or to the District of Columbia.

I enjoyed my years in the Washington area and have fond memories of the fans who treated me in a very special way. Reading the book has certainly enlightened me in many ways and given me a few surprises, one of which is the fact that Washington baseball in the Expansion Era was better than that in the Post-World War II Era. I believe that area fans and other baseball enthusiasts will find this volume a welcome addition to their libraries!

Frank O. Howard

PREFACE

The Washington Senators have been absent from the local scene for over thirty years. While most people remember them as the doormat of the American League, it wasn't always so. It is true that Washington fans didn't have much to cheer about a lot of the time but you may be surprised to learn the club had its glory days.

The Super Bowl victories of the Washington Redskins touched off wild celebrations in the nation's capital but they did not exceed the wildest celebration of local fans. The city exploded emotionally for the first time in 1924 when the Senators won their first and only World Championship. Washington capturing the American League flag and their edging the New York Giants in the World Series four games to three precipitated this. Total strangers pounded each other on the back, countless others lined Pennsylvania Avenue for victory parades and the team was received by President Coolidge.

Washington's 1924 World Championship team is honored with a parade down Pennsylvania Avenue.

While area fans are hopeful that the Redskins will gain another Super Bowl victory before too many years pass, there is presently no such hope for another World Series victory for the Senators. Since the Senators departed in 1971, there has been a real void only partially filled by the neighboring Baltimore Orioles. There is the possibility that an existing team, perhaps the Montreal Expos, will be placed in the Washington area before too long, possibly in 2005. This would ease some of the pain experienced by local fans. Locals have been disappointed many times before, however, when Washingtonians did not receive "promised franchises."

Washington not only won the 1924 World Championship but it also was champion of the American League in both 1925 and 1933. While these successes were few and far between, the Senators boasted a number of individual stars, including many enshrined in the Hall of Fame in Cooperstown. By providing sketches of some of their brightest stars, I hope that these will provide some comfort to loyal Senators fans. In addition, more than a generation of Washingtonians has grown up without major league baseball in town. Most of them know little or nothing about past glories or the professional skills of many who wore the Washington Senators uniform. Hopefully, they will gain some appreciation of the important contribution of professional baseball to the Washington scene.

Washington teams were in the American League from 1901-1971. But, it is not well known that during the nineteenth century they fielded teams in the National League for 12 years, the National Association for four years and the American Association for two years. In 1884, they had two teams, one in the aforementioned American Association and one in the Union Association. Over the 101-year period, Washington teams completed a total of 12,883 games, winning 5,669 and losing 7,214 while playing at a .440 clip.

I have selected an all-time Washington team as well as all-star teams for each of five eras—the Nineteenth-Century Era (1871-1899), Dead Ball Era (1901-1919), Post-World War I Era (1920-1945), Post-World War II Era (1946-1960), and Expansion Era

(1961-1971). A brief sketch of each player selected is included as well as certain career statistics and his performance while with the Senators. *For twentieth-century ballplayers no one was eligible for selection who had not spent at least part of four seasons with the Senators.* During the nineteenth-century ballplayer movements were much more dynamic, so *a few of the nineteenth-century picks were with Washington teams for only three seasons. Players on the all-time team were not considered for their period teams. A player was considered for a particular era if he played the majority of his major league career during that era.*

There may be considerable disagreement with my picks, but I'm hopeful they will provoke much friendly discussion and arguments in the manner of the old "hot stove leagues," when "old timers" used to gather around the local grocer's wood stove during the winter and consider the merits of various teams and players.

The author, a member of the 1934-35 "Hot Stove League" is seated immediately to Bucky Harris' left.

CHAPTER ONE

Washington Senators' All-Time Team

Introduction

The all-time Washington Senators Team could hold its own against any other city's all-time team. With Walter Johnson on the mound, the team includes six Hall of Famers! Further, if Bucky Harris had been picked for second base, Heinie Manush for the outfield and Harmon Killebrew for third base instead of designated hitter, only first base would have been without a Hall of Famer.

To demonstrate the proficiency of the selected all-time and period players, one need only examine the following table which shows that many of them are among the top 100 players of all time in important hitting and pitching categories. (See the glossary for an explanation of the abbreviations used throughout the book). Rankings are taken from official major league records as of the end of the 2002 season.

Batting

	AB	R	H	2B	3B	HR	RBI	BB	SB	TB	BA
George Case									99		
Joe Cronin				32	99		51	74			
Goose Goslin	75	59	46	39	22		23			42	72
Dummy Hoy		65			95			91	17		
Frank Howard						43					
Joe Judge				88	42						
Harmon Killebrew						7	28	13		55	
Heinie Manush			75	44	39					94	33
Clyde Milan									36		
Buddy Myer					81						
Sam Rice	45	52	26	41	14				98	65	47

	AB	R	H	2B	3B	HR	RBI	BB	SB	TB	BA
Kip Selbach					52						
Roy Sievers						85					
Cecil Travis											77
Mickey Vernon	70		79	45	96		79			90	
Eddie Yost								9			

Pitching

	W	W/L PCT	ERA	G	CG	IP	SO	SHO	SV	H/9IP	BB+H /9IP
Nick Altrock			62								47
Walter Johnson	2		11	26	4	3	9	1		30	6
Frank Killen					76						
Darold Knowles				30					58		
Dutch Leonard				94		92					
Fred Marberry		52							96		
Win Mercer					77						
Claude Osteen						70		44			
Camilo Pascual							48	62			
Early Wynn	19			70	48	20	36	21			

The most difficult decisions revolved around the choices for first base between Mickey Vernon and Joe Judge, third base between Ossie Bluege and Eddie Yost, the left-handed pitcher between Tom Zachary, George Mogridge and Earl Whitehill, and it was difficult to leave Hall of Famer Heinie Manush out of the outfield. Here are my selections:

All-Time Team

Right-Handed Pitcher: Walter Johnson
Left-Handed Pitcher: Tom Zachary
Relief Pitcher: Fred Marberry
Catcher: Rick Ferrell
First Base: Mickey Vernon
Second Base: Buddy Myer
Third Base: Ossie Bluege
Shortstop: Joe Cronin
Outfield: Sam Rice
Outfield: Goose Goslin
Outfield: Frank Howard
Designated Hitter: Harmon Killebrew

All-Time Team
Right-Handed Pitcher

Walter Perry Johnson

(The Big Train, Barney)

BR TR 6'1" 200 lbs.
B. Nov. 6, 1887, Humboldt, KS.
D. Dec. 10, 1946, Washington, DC.
Hall of Fame 1936

	Y	W	L	PCT	ERA	G	GS	CG	IP	H	BB	SO	SHO
Life	21	417	279	.599	2.17	802	666	531	5914.2	4913	1363	3509	110

The incomparable Walter Johnson displaying his classic sidearm delivery.

Walter Johnson is generally recognized as the fastest and best pitcher who ever lived. The powerful Kansas farmer was one of five original members of the Hall of Fame, inducted in 1936 along with Ruth, Cobb, Speaker and Matthewson. He labored exclusively on the mound for Washington for 21 years (1907-1927). He was their "franchise" player and drawing card, keeping the club solvent during difficult times. Clark Griffith would try to arrange Walter's starts for weekends or holidays and it paid off as attendance would multiply when Johnson was pitching. He was affectionately known as "Barney" and fans all around the league loved him and appreciated his skills.

His blazing fastball was legendary and Ty Cobb said that his worst experience was facing Johnson on a cloudy day, giving credence to the Johnson legend that "you can't hit what you can't see." Another tale is that Johnson got two quick strikes on a player, purported to be the Yankees' Birdie Cree, who turned and headed for the dugout. When reminded by the umpire that he had another strike coming, he replied "it wouldn't do me any good."

Strikeout Record Endures for More than 50 Years

When the Big Train retired he had registered a record 3,509 strikeouts, a record that stood for more than a half century until Nolan Ryan broke it in 1983. He went to the mound 802 times with 531 complete games, 417 of them wins, second only to Cy Young's 511. He had a record 110 shutouts and a low earned run average of 2.17. Johnson used a full windmill windup, started his delivery three-quarters and finished it side armed. The kind, gentle and modest gentleman deliberately threw at a batter only once. When Frank "Home Run" Baker was riding him mercilessly, trainer Mike Martin urged Johnson to "knock him down." After throwing at his head, Johnson turned pale and wanted to take back the pitch. He confided in his roommate, Clyde Milan, that he was afraid he might kill a batter with his fastball. One wonders what Johnson's record might have been, if he had been more aggressive and used the "brush back" pitch as is common today.

While playing with the minor league Weiser, Idaho team, Johnson went 85 innings without giving up any runs. In one game he struck out 21 batters and in another, while pitching a no-hitter, he struck out 18. A former teammate of Washington manager Joe Cantillon kept sending him letters urging him to sign Johnson. Cantillon sent injured catcher, Cliff Blankenship, west to scout both Clyde Milan and Walter. He signed them both but before signing for $350 per month, Johnson insisted he be given a round-trip ticket in case he didn't make it. It is hard to believe that in this megabucks era, Johnson's top salary was $25,000 per year!

Hurls 3 Shutouts in 4 Days

Barney began his big league career in 1907 playing for a woefully bad team. Appearing in 14 games his ERA was a low 1.87, yet his won-lost record was 5-9. His first start was on August 7 when he lost to the Detroit Tigers 3-2. He reached the .500 level at 14-14 the next year with another fine ERA of 1.64. One of his worst years was in 1909. Bothered by a persistent cold, he lost 25 games and his ERA rose to 2.21. It would be more than a decade before Johnson had another losing season, for Walter hit his stride in 1910.That year, Johnson was the hurler on opening day in Washington when President Taft inaugurated the tradition of throwing out the first ball. Johnson responded with a 3-0 shutout, allowing just one hit. He led the league in appearances (45), games started (42), games completed (38) and innings pitched (373), while chalking up a 25-17 record with a 1.35 ERA. His league leading 313 strikeouts was his best mark ever, yet it fell 30 shy of Rube Waddell's record. But the most amazing pitching performance of all time occurred in New York against the Highlanders late in the season. Johnson pitched three shutouts in four days, winning a 3-0 five hitter, a 6-0 three hitter and a 4-0 two hitter! It's safe to say that no one will ever top that.

16 Straight Wins Sets Record

Walter was a holdout in 1911, along with Clyde Milan, and

was late signing. His first start was in Boston on April 15 when he tied a major league record by striking out four men in the fifth inning. One of the victims had reached first base when a third strike had gotten by the catcher and rolled to the backstop. Barney managed 25 wins again with an ERA of 1.89 and with a league-leading total of 36 complete games. He fashioned a sixteen-game consecutive win streak in 1912, getting his sixteenth win against the Tigers on August 23. He only required 51 days to achieve it, often pitching with only two days rest. The win streak ended shortly thereafter against the St. Louis Browns amid controversy. Johnson left the game with the score tied 2-2 and runners on first and second with one out. Reliever Long Tom Hughes made a wild pitch to move the runners up and then permitted a single, which drove in the winning runs, and the loss was charged to Johnson. Griff appealed to League President Ban Johnson to have the loss charged to Hughes, but Ban rightfully rejected the plea. Late in the season, Walter won two games in extra inning relief stints against the Philadelphia A's to preserve the Senators' second place finish. He won 32 games that year and led the league with a 1.39 ERA and began an eight-year stretch (1912-1919) atop the league in strikeouts with a total of 303.

Posts 56 Consecutive Scoreless Innings

The Big Train's banner year was in 1913 when he posted a record of 36-7, including 12 shutouts, five one-hitters, and winning streaks of 10, 11 and 14 games. From April 10-May 16, he pitched 56 scoreless innings over eight starts and relief appearances, breaking Jack Comb's record of 53. Walter's jinx club, the St. Louis Browns, ended the streak in the fourth inning when Gus Williams doubled and Del Pratt singled to drive him home. His league leading ERA of 1.09 was second only to Three Fingered Brown's record of 1.04 and he also led the league in games won (36), winning percentage (.837), complete games (30) and strikeouts (243).

Walter failed to win 30 games in 1914 but had a 28-18 record with a league leading 10 shutouts and an ERA of 1.72. He also led in appearances (51), completed games (33), strikeouts (225) and wins (28). Johnson was a holdout again before the 1915 season, and Washington almost lost their star pitcher. He signed with Chicago of the Federal League for $10,000 a year, much to the dismay of Clark Griffith, who managed to pry $10,000 from Chicago White Sox owner, Charles Comiskey, convincing him that Johnson pitching for another Chicago team, would materially affect the White Sox's attendance. Griff travelled to Johnson's home and talked him into returning to Washington. His 27 wins in 1915 were tops in the league, as well as his 39 games started, 35 completed and 203 strikeouts. Occasionally Johnson would play the outfield between pitching assignments because of his long ball potential. During his career, Barney slammed 24 home runs.

In 1916, for the fourth straight year, he led the league in wins with 25. His 36 complete games and 228 strikeouts were also tops. In 1917, he only led the league in one category with 188 strikeouts. He did win 23 games, though, and had eight shutouts. The next year, 1918, his 23 victories and 1.27 ERA were tops in the league, as well as his 162 strikeouts and eight shutouts. Walter completed a string of 10 consecutive years of 20 victories or more that year with his 23 wins.

Johnson not only failed to win 20 games in 1920, but he had a losing record (8-10) for the first time since his debut in 1907. His ERA rose to 3.13 and this was attributed to a sore arm contracted after a long 18-day road trip. Despite this, he pitched his only no-hitter against the Boston Red Sox on July 1. He had been detained in Washington because of his son's illness and did not arrive at Fenway Park until one hour before game time. Winning 1-0 and striking out 10, only five pitches were hit out of the infield. It was almost a perfect game but the usually reliable Bucky Harris' error permitted the only base runner. Harris atoned for his error by driving in the only run of the game.

The following three years (1921-1923) were not typical Johnson years. His ERA for the period was over 3.00 and his won-lost record was 49-42. His only league leading stats were achieved with 121 strikeouts in 1921 and 130 in 1923.

Johnson Leads Nats to First A.L. Flag in 1924

The Big Train bounced back in 1924, leading the Senators to their first American League championship with league highs in wins (23), winning percentage (.767), ERA (2.72), games started (38), strikeouts (158) and shutouts (6). In a crucial late August series with the Yankees, Walter won the second game 5-1 with relief help from Fred Marberry. He was in the midst of a consecutive game win streak which ended in September at 13, when he lost a heartbreaker to the Red Sox 2-1 in the first game of the final series. The Nats were still a game up with three to go despite the loss and went on to win the pennant. For his great season, Walter was voted the Most Valuable Player in the American League.

Johnson had labored for 18 years before he had a chance for a World Series win. Naturally he was named to pitch the opener against the New York Giants in Washington. The entire nation was pulling for Barney, who was about to reach the age of 37. Some of the fire had gone from his fastball, but his remarkable comeback had Washington fans anticipating a World Championship. George Kelly and Bill Terry of the Giants managed cheap homers into the temporary bleachers early in the game to give the Giants a 2-0 lead in the fourth inning. Walter then reeled off seven consecutive shutout innings before Ross Youngs singled with the bases loaded in the twelfth to deny Johnson the win, 4-3. He tied a World Series record by fanning 12. His next opportunity was in the fifth game in New York but Johnson didn't have it as the Giants got to him for 13 hits during his complete game. It seemed that he was destined to end his career without a Series victory.

Johnson Win Gives Nats Only World Championship in '24

With the Series tied at three games apiece, Johnson was unable to start the seventh game with only one day's rest. With the score tied in the ninth inning, Walter was brought in to relieve Fred Marberry.

Washington fans went wild! With Frankie Frisch on third base and only one out, Barney struck out George Kelly and then got out of the inning. With the Giant's tie-breaking run on second in the eleventh inning, he struck out Kelly again. Moreover, in the twelfth, he struck out the dangerous Hack Wilson after he had failed to sacrifice a runner into scoring position. Then, in the bottom of the twelfth, McNeely's famous pebble hit made Johnson a World Series winner. There was bedlam in Washington and joy around the nation!

Walter was slow rounding into shape in '25 but finished the season 20-7 with a 3.07 ERA. He had three shutouts during the year and two came at opportune times. The first was against the Philadelphia A's on June 30 and it elevated the Senators into first place, and the other was a 1-0 victory over the Cleveland Indians in late August putting the Nats back into first place on their way to their second consecutive American League Championship.

Pittsburgh Defeats Washington in '25

Johnson took the mound in the first game of the World Series against the Pirates in Pittsburgh and checked them on five hits, striking out 10 while winning 4-1. He was the Johnson of old with a blazing fastball, sharp-breaking curve and the only run given up was Pie Traynor's home run. In the fourth game, he blanked the Pirates 4-0 on six hits in another sparkling performance to give the Nats a 3-1 Series lead. After the Pirates later tied the Series three games each, the fate of the Senators was placed in the hands of Johnson for the seventh and deciding game. The weather was atrocious, with a cold rainy afternoon putting a damper on the Series. Many writers believed that the umpires should never have started the game, but the players had to perform in a steady pouring rain, a field thick with mud and fielders barely visible to the fans. Under the circumstances, Johnson didn't have it and the Nats lost 9-7, with Walter allowing the Pirates 15 hits. Washington fans and most of the nation were deeply disappointed.

In 1926, although 38 years old and beginning his twentieth

year in the majors, Johnson began the season with a classic 1-0, 15 inning win over the Philadelphia A's and Ed Rommel. But, as the season wore on, the fading Big Train dropped under .500 with a record of 15-16 and an ERA of 3.61.

His last year on the mound was 1927, when he appeared in only 18 games and had a 5-6 losing record with an ERA of 5.10. No one will touch his career record of 110 shutouts, and his 416 victories are second to Cy Young's 511. He pitched in sixty 1-0 games, winning 38 of them, an all-time record.

Johnson Pilots Senators and Indians

Washington fans were saddened in 1928 when Johnson asked for his unconditional release to pursue other offers. He then served as manager of the Newark minor league team. His team was only able to finish seventh but drew a record 300,000 fans. But, despite his lack of success, Griffith rewarded his friend in 1929 by signing him to pilot the Senators. That year they wallowed in the second division all season and finished in fifth place. But, he led them to second place and two-third place finishes before being replaced in 1933 by Joe Cronin. Walter went to Cleveland as manager for the '33-'35 seasons, leading the Indians to fourth, third and fifth place finishes. His seven-year major league managerial record was not bad, as he posted a .551 winning percentage. On one occasion when Johnson brought his Indians to Washington, local fans had a "Walter Johnson Day" to honor their beloved player.

The Big Train then retired to his Maryland farm in the Washington suburbs except for a brief stint as a radio announcer for Senators ball games and an unsuccessful attempt to win a seat in Congress.

He died December 10, 1946, leaving grieving and grateful Washington fans with a record of achievements that will be impossible to duplicate!

All-Time Team
Left-Handed Pitcher

Jonathan Thompson Walton Zachary

(Tom)

BL TL 6'1" 187 lbs.

B. May 7, 1896, Graham, NC.

D. Jan. 24, 1969, Graham, NC.

	Y	W	L	PCT	ERA	G	GS	CG	IP	H	BB	SO	SHO
Was.	9	96	103	.482	3.74	273	211	93	1589.0	1764	472	336	10
Life	19	186	191	.493	3.73	533	409	186	3126.1	3580	914	720	24

Tom Zachary tossing a few for photographers during spring training.

Tom Zachary is best remembered as the pitcher who served up Babe Ruth's record setting sixtieth home run on September 30, 1927. But the "Old Country Boy" from Graham, North Carolina was probably the best left-handed pitcher Washington ever had. He labored in the big leagues for 19 years for seven different teams and although his won-lost record was under .500, he was a terrific "clutch" pitcher. He was undefeated in three World Series and played a major role in bringing Washington its one and only World Championship.

Much has been written about the pitch Zachary made to Ruth on that fateful day. One version is that it was high and inside and that Babe connected as he was falling away from the plate, while another version has it low and outside with Ruth using a golfing stroke to send it out of the park. Francis Stann, the former Washington sportswriter, interviewed Zachary in 1960 in an attempt to settle the controversy once and for all. Tom asserted that it was one of his best curve balls that was a little low and that he was trying hard to keep the Babe from hitting one into the seats.

Zachary broke into the majors in 1918 after pitching some for Guilford College. While waiting in Philadelphia with his Quaker Red Cross Unit to be shipped overseas, he approached Connie Mack for a tryout with the Philadelphia A's. Desiring to keep his college eligibility, Mack allowed him to pitch in two games under the name "Zach Walton." He was signed by Washington when he returned to the states in 1919, appearing in 17 games using his right name. Although he was 1-5, his ERA was only 2.92, giving evidence of a promising future. Zachary defeated Connie Mack's A's during the season and Mack went into the Senators' clubhouse after the game to verify that this was the same "Zach Walton" who pitched for him the year before.

Ace of Senators' Pitching Staff in 1920

With Walter Johnson ailing in 1920, Tom took over as the ace of the Washington staff. He posted a 15-16 won-lost record and a

3.77 ERA. He appeared in more games (49) and led the other Nat hurlers in the number of innings pitched (262) and the number of complete games (18). On July 10 he stopped Tris Speaker's record string of consecutive hits at 11, a record Speaker held for the next 18 years. The next year, he was 18-16 with an ERA of 3.96 and he again appeared in more games (39) than any other on the staff. Tom had another winning year in 1922, posting a 15-10 mark with a 3.12 ERA, but he slipped in '23 when his ERA jumped to 4.49 and he won only 10 games while losing 16.

One of his biggest years was 1924, when he helped propel the Nats to their first American League flag. He lowered his ERA to 2.75 enabling him to win 15 games while losing only nine. In late September when it counted, Zachary was up to the task. He beat Cleveland on September 16 to put the Senators back into first place and later in relief he helped beat the Red Sox to put the team up by two games with only two left. With only one day's rest, he and Fred Marberry combined to clinch the pennant with a 5-3 victory over Boston.

Tom's "Shining Hour"

His "shining hour" however, was in the '24 World Series against the New York Giants. After Walter Johnson had suffered a disappointing loss at home in 12 innings in the opening game of the Series, Zachary stepped into the breach and beat the Giants 4-3 in the second game. He pitched brilliantly, shutting them out for six of the innings before weakening in the ninth. Firpo Marberry relieved to get the last out and preserve the victory. With their backs to the wall and down three games to two, Zachary rescued the Senators again with an even better performance in game six. Going all the way, Tom tied the Series at three apiece with a sterling 2-1 win over Giant ace Art Nehf. This set the stage for Walter Johnson and the Senators to bring Washington their only World Championship the next day.

Although he slipped in 1925 to a mark of 12-15 with an ERA of 3.84, Zachary did his part in helping Washington repeat as

American League champions. Late in the year, he held Cleveland scoreless as the Nats won 1-0 in 12 innings. Marberry and Johnson worked in relief to seal the victory and enable the Senators to regain first place. Zachary only saw limited service in the 1925 World Series. He hurled an inning and two-thirds in a losing cause in Game Five as the Pittsburgh Pirates took the Series four games to three.

Wins Game 3 of 1928 World Series for Yankees

Tom was traded to the St. Louis Browns for the 1926 season, but in mid-season 1927 he was reacquired by the Senators. For St. Louis in '26, he was the ace of the staff, winning 14 and losing 15 with an ERA of 3.61 while starting and completing the most games on the staff. He was second in the league in shutouts with three and first in home runs allowed with 14. After going 4 and 6 in 13 appearances with the Browns the next year, he was traded to Washington for Alvin Crowder. He didn't do much better with the Nats, posting a 4-7 record in 15 games. When his ERA soared to 5.42 in 20 games in 1928, Clark Griffith tried to slip him by waivers to send him to the minors. Manager Miller Huggins plucked him from the waiver list for the Yankees in their pennant drive. Zachary went 3-3 in seven games and Griffith lost the crafty left-hander for the waiver price of $7,500. Griff believed that Tom was nearing the end of his career. Huggins used Zachary as a surprise starter in Game Three of the World Series against the St. Louis Cardinals. Tom won 7-3, scattering nine hits and setting the stage for the Yankees' four-game sweep. He used tantalizing slow curves and his knowledge of how to pitch to hold the Cardinals at bay.

Notches Perfect 12–0 Record in 1929

Tom reached the pinnacle of his career in 1929 when he appeared in 26 games and established a major league record with a 12-0 mark; his ERA was 2.48. He began the year in a relief role, taking the mound once in April, five times in May and three times in June, but when the Yankee starters collapsed, he was inserted into the starting rotation and he started six times in each month July-September. Seven of his victories were at the expense of the Cleveland Indians and St. Louis Browns. He had only one bad outing all year, when the Senators scored seven runs in five and two-thirds innings. His teammates, however, rallied to avoid the loss. Tom's undefeated record was unparalleled at the time and his feat is all the more noteworthy because it followed four successive campaigns in which he failed to reach the .500 level, and in two of them he didn't even reach ten victories total.

Winds–up Career in National League

After playing in only three games for the Yanks in 1930, he was sent to the Boston Braves of the National League, and he remained in that league until his major league career ended. With the Braves until the first part of the 1934 season, he was able to compile a winning record despite his age. In 147 games with the Braves, Tom posted a 54-48 record, relying primarily on slow stuff and his cunning. He was sent to the Brooklyn Dodgers after appearing in five games in '34. On the mound for the Dodgers from 1934-36, he played in 48 games, winning 12 and losing 18. When Brooklyn's manager, Casey Stengel, sent him in to pitch for one inning in '36 his ERA was an astonishing 54.00, so Casey sent him to the Philadelphia Phillies where he closed out his career, appearing in seven games and failing to win. Tom called Baker Bowl the home of the Phils, a "cracker box" and a "death trap" for pitchers, so he decided to call it quits and return to North Carolina as a tobacco farmer.

Tom deserved a better fate! Not only did he give up Ruth's famous 60th homer, but also he was on the mound when Tris Speaker made his 3000th hit in 1925. Zachary died of a stroke in his hometown at the age of 72.

All-Time Team
Relief Pitcher

Fred Marberry
(Firpo)

BR TR 6'1" 190 lbs.
B. Nov. 30, 1898, Streetman, TX.
D. June 30, 1976, Mexia, TX.

	Y	W	L	PCT	ERA	G	GS	CG	IP	H	BB	SO	SHO	SV
Was.	11	117	71	.622	3.59	474	134	64	1654.0	1620	568	667	5	96
Life	14	148	88	.627	3.63	551	187	86	2067.1	2049	686	822	7	101

An imposing Firpo Marberry is warming up for the Senators.

Club President, Clark Griffith, maintained that Firpo Marberry won the 1924 and 1925 pennants for the Washington Senators. Manager Bucky Harris had made Marberry the first bona fide relief pitcher in baseball history, calling him from the bullpen 90 times in the two championship years. He was the first exclusive relief man to appear in more than 40 games a year. Senators starters knew that Fred was in the bullpen and they would pitch as long as they could without saving their "stuff" and wait for Harris to bring in Marberry to relieve them.

The big Texan was an imposing figure at 6' 1" and 190 pounds as he strode from the bullpen to the mound with a confident swagger that struck fear in the hearts of most hitters. His number one pitch was a high hard one, oftentimes used to brush back the batters and keep them from digging in at the plate, creating the false impression that he was really mean. His high leg kick seemed to put his foot right into the batter's face, giving the impression that his fastball travelled faster than it did. He would purposely make some of his warm-up tosses a little wild to make hitters think twice about crowding the plate, and catcher, Muddy Ruel would stagger a bit under the impact of Fred's throws to reinforce the feeling that Marberry was exceptionally fast.

Marberry was given the nickname "Firpo" because he was big, dark and swarthy like the popular heavyweight challenger from Argentina, "Luis Angel Firpo." The name stuck. After two years in the minors, he was brought to the Senators in September 1923 after scout Joe Engel coaxed Griffith to Little Rock, Arkansas to look Fred over personally. Firpo was an immediate success, appearing in 11 games and going 4-0 with an ERA of 2.82.

Has a Record 15 Saves in 1924

Harris used Firpo 50 times in the 1924 pennant year (tops in the league), 35 times in relief. He won 11 and lost 12 with a record 15 saves and he was a big factor in the club's stretch drive and in the World Series. With three games remaining in the season,

Marberry relieved George Mogridge to secure the Nats' victory over Boston, putting the Senators two games up on the Yankees with two games to go. The next day he relieved Tom Zachary, clinching the American League Championship with a 5-3 win over the Red Sox.

Marberry was the workhorse of the Series, playing in four games, three in relief. In the second game, he relieved Zachary with two outs in the ninth inning and a runner on first. He struck out Travis Jackson on three pitches to notch his first Series save. He was the starting pitcher the following day but lasted only three innings as Harris' error trying to start a double play led to New York Giant scores. But, he came right back the following day to gain his second save in three days and preserve George Mogridge's 7-4 win. Finally, in the seventh and deciding game, he relieved Mogridge in the sixth inning, pitched four and two-thirds of scoreless relief and set the stage for Walter Johnson to win his first World Series victory and Washington's only World Championship.

Appears in Record 55 Games

The following year, Firpo broke the major league record for relief appearances when he played in 55 games, all in relief, and he was credited with 15 saves tying his record. Lou Gehrig hit 23 grand slam home runs during his career; the first one was given up by Fred on July 23, 1925. Marberry's role in the 1925 World Series was more limited because Washington starters pitched well in most games. In game three, he relieved starter Alex Ferguson in the eighth inning, pitching two scoreless innings and notched his only save of the Series, despite Earl Smith's controversial drive which Sam Rice "caught" while falling into the temporary stands among the spectators. Fred also pitched a third of an inning in the fifth game as the Nats lost 6-3.

In 1926, he broke his own record appearing in 64 games, 59 in relief, winning 12 and losing seven, while gaining a league leading 22 saves and posting an ERA of 3.00. Marberry continued his role as principal reliever from 1927-29, averaging over 50 appearances a year and leading the league with 11 saves in 1929. His 3.06 ERA that year was second in the league. In the span 1924-1929, Firpo was on the mound in 322 games, a remarkable record!

Fred recognized that the time had come for a younger player to take over his role as principal relief pitcher. Early in his career, he could be warm and ready to pitch with only half-dozen tosses. A little "zip" had gone from his fastball and so for the remainder of his career, except for 1932, he was essentially a starting pitcher. He made the transition nicely. In 1930 and 1931, he made 47 starts, winning 31 games while losing only nine. In '31, he was second in the league with a win-loss percentage of .800. In 1932, as a reliever again, he led the league with 54 appearances and his 13 saves were tops.

Marberry was one of Griff's favorites but he reluctantly traded the veteran to the Detroit Tigers prior to the '33 season. Despite his banner year in '32, Clark believed that the right-hander was slipping. But, Firpo showed no signs of it as he was used as a starter in 32 games by the Tigers, completing 15 of them while posting a 16-11 record with an ERA of 3.29.

Big Factor in Detroit's '34 American League Flag

The trade proved a boon to Fred as the Tigers won the American League Championship in 1934 with Marberry having another fine season. He went 15-5, despite an ERA of 4.57, in 38 games (19 starts) to do his part in the Detroit pennant drive. He saw action as a reliever in Games One and Seven of the World Series. In the first game, he was roughed up in two-thirds of an inning as Dizzy Dean won the Series opener for the St. Louis Cardinals. In the seventh game, he pitched a scoreless eighth inning in a losing cause, since Dizzy and the Cardinals had earlier built an 11-0 lead.

Although he was a member of the Tigers World Championship team in 1935, he developed arm trouble and was essentially just kept around for insurance, appearing in only five games and winning none. He was not used in the World Series. He decided to quit pitching after the Series and was hired as an American League umpire in 1936. He hated the job, saying that he liked to be around the players and have companionship but not in an umpiring capacity. Before the season was over, he quit umpiring and was signed by the New York Giants who used him in only one game and then sent him to the Texas League. A compassionate Clark Griffith rescued him near the end of the season and he was 0-2 for the Senators in five games, marking the end of his major league career.

Marberry either pitched or managed in the minor leagues for the next six years in Dallas, Toledo or Fort Worth and he retired from baseball for good in 1942.

In October 1949, Fred was in a serious automobile accident and his left arm was severed above the elbow by the impact of the crash. A false rumor was circulated in the spring of 1954, claiming that Marberry had lost his left leg in another accident. Marberry denied it a few days later and the source of the rumor was not discovered. He died on June 30, 1976 in Mexia, Texas at the age of 77.

All-Time Team
Catcher

Richard Benjamin Ferrell

(Rick)

BR TR 5'10" 160 lbs.

B. October 12, 1905, Durham, NC.

D. July 27, 1995, Bloomfield Hills, MI.

Hall of Fame 1984

	Y	G	AB	R	H	2B	3B	HR	RBI	BB	SO	SB	BA	SA
Was.	8	659	2080	218	568	100	10	3	237	331	99	9	.273	325
Life	18	1884	6028	687	1692	324	45	28	734	931	277	29	.281	.363

Rick Ferrell in a catching pose during spring training with the Washington Senators.

Rick Ferrell was one of four professional ballplaying brothers, George, Marvin, Wes and Rick. Rick's brothers all wanted to pitch, so at 10 years old, Rick saved his pennies and purchased a catcher's mitt for a $1.50 to handle their practices. Wes and Rick became big leaguers, with Wes better known because of his early successes and his violent temper. Rick, the quiet and durable Ferrell, lasted much longer in the majors, a total of 18 years. He was, at the time of his retirement, number two all time in the number of games caught with 1,805 only trailing Al Lopez. He was number 10 in double plays with 139, number 13 in putouts with 7,248 and number of chances with 8,510. At the plate, his lifetime batting average of .281 is much better than most catchers. He had a good eye and compiled an excellent walk to strikeout ratio, gaining 931 free passes while striking out only 277 times. He achieved a fine .433 on-base percentage, was selected for the All-Star Game eight times and he was elected to the Hall of Fame in 1984.

Ferrell hit .333 for Columbus of the American Association in 1928 and was the property of the Detroit Tigers. Commissioner Kenesaw Mountain Landis declared him a free agent when Detroit tried to protect him illegally. The St. Louis Browns where he began his major league career in 1929 gave him a $25,000 bonus. During the course of his career, he played with the Browns and Senators twice and the Red Sox once.

Formed "Brother Battery" with Wes Ferrell

Rick never had the chance to catch his brother in the majors when Wes had his blazing fastball that won 20 or more games for Cleveland his first four seasons. When they were at last united as a brother battery at Boston and Washington, Wes' arm was gone. Wes could never accept defeat and often wrecked the locker room after a bad day, while Rick rarely raised his voice.

In his first year with St. Louis, Ferrell played behind catcher Wally Schang and caught only 45 games. His batting average was a meager .229. He became the regular catcher the following season, catching 101 games and lifting his batting average to .268. He had his first .300 season in 1931, when he hit .306 while catching 108 games. He achieved his highest batting average (.315) in 1932 and was behind the plate for 120 games.

Caught Entire All–Star Game for A. L. in 1933

After only 22 games in 1933, Rick was traded to the Boston Red Sox along with pitcher Lloyd Brown for catcher Mervyn Shea and cash. Playing against his brother Wes as the Red Sox and Indians squared off on May 9, each homered. It was the first time that brothers on opposite teams had done so. He continued to play well while with Boston and he was named to the first All-Star game along with catcher Bill Dickey of the Yankees. Connie Mack was the manager of the American League Team and unlike later managers he played the game to win. Surprisingly, he named Rick as starting catcher. At the team meeting before the game, Connie indicated that if the American League got ahead he would stick with the starters except for pitchers. He was true to his word except for removing Babe Ruth for defensive purposes in the eighth inning. Dickey didn't get in the game and Ferrell caught as Lefty Grove struck out Gabby Hartnett for the final out. Rick finished the season with a .290 batting average.

The Red Sox acquired brother Wes and the brothers were reunited for the 1934 season. They played together there for three full seasons '34-'36 with Rick recording hitting averages of .297, .301 and .312. He caught over 120 games in each of the seasons.

On June 10, 1937 both Rick and Wes along with outfielder Melo Almada were traded to the Washington Senators for pitcher Bobo Newsom and outfielder Ben Chapman. Ferrell became the regular catcher as he was behind the plate for 102 games that season, but the trade seemed to affect his hitting and his average dipped to .244.

With Washington the next three seasons '38-'40, he regained his batting eye and hit .292, .281 and .273 in successive seasons. In 1938, he was separated from his brother, when the Senators traded Wes to the New York Yankees late that season. After nine seasons of catching 100 or more games, Rick was limited to 83 in 1939 and 99 in 1940.

In 1941, Rick was traded by Griffith to the St. Louis Browns for pitcher Vern Kennedy after appearing in only 28 games with the Nats. He caught a total of 119 games that year but the trade seemed to affect his hitting again as he dropped to .256 that year. On June 8, against Washington, Ferrell pulled off one of the rarest plays in baseball: an unassisted double play by a catcher. He did not hit well for the Browns the following two years either, falling to .223 and .239.

Handled Greatest Collection of Knuckleball Pitchers

Before the 1944 season, the Browns gave up on him and traded him back to Washington. Griff realized he had made a mistake when he traded Ferrell in 1941. The "Old Fox" had acquired a group of knuckleball pitchers and needed Rick to handle them. Nearing 40 years old, in '44 and '45, he had the unenviable task of trying to catch the greatest collection of knuckleballers ever assembled. First and foremost was Emil "Dutch" Leonard who threw the pitch 75 percent of the time. Also on the staff were knucklers Roger Wolff, Mickey Haefner and Johnny Niggeling.

Ferrell used to warm them up in full catcher's regalia (except for the mask). Although the team finished last in 1944 with Rick behind the plate for 96 games, they almost won the pennant in 1945, carrying the fight until the last day of the season before the Detroit Tigers edged them. The foursome combined for 60 victories that year with Rick catching 83 games. He hit for averages of .277 in '44 and .266 in '45 to aid the cause.

Rick did not play in 1946, serving as a coach for the team. But in 1947, he returned as a player for his final year and went out in style, posting a batting average of .303 while behind the plate for 37 games.

After his playing days, he was with the Senators for three more seasons as a coach before joining the Detroit Tigers organization as a coach, scout, general manager and executive consultant. He was an integral part of that organization well into his eighties!

All-Time Team
First Base

James Barton Vernon

(Mickey)

BL TL 6'2" 170 lbs.

B. April 22, 1918, Marcus Hook, PA.

	Y	G	AB	R	H	2B	3B	HR	RBI	BB	SO	SB	BA	SA
Was.	14	1805	6930	956	1993	391	108	121	1026	735	657	125	.288	.428
Life	20	2409	8731	1196	2495	490	120	172	1311	955	869	137	.286	.428

A smiling Mickey Vernon selecting a bat.

Mickey Vernon is the choice for all-time Senators first baseman, edging the popular and capable Joe Judge in one of the closest contests for any position. Mickey was the only Senator to capture two batting titles. Only three others won one. The tall, lean left-hander had a classic batting stroke which drew praise from the best hitter who ever lived, Ted Williams. His grace around the first base bag was equally well recognized and he was also a flawless base runner. At the time of his retirement, his major league career had spanned 20 years and he was one of only nine players who played in four different decades.

After playing ball as a freshman at Villanova, he was signed by Washington scout, Joe Cambria in 1938 after the St. Louis Browns failed to give him $800 to sign. Cambria, normally known for bringing Hispanic ballplayers to the Nationals, brought Vernon to camp in '39 after Mickey hit well over .300 in the minors. After being optioned to Springfield, he was recalled by Washington and played in 75 games, hitting only .257. Griffith was enamored with the long ball potential of first baseman Zeke Bonura, so he acquired him from the Chicago White Sox and Vernon was sent back down to Jersey City of the International League in 1940 where he hit .283. Griffith quickly tired of Bonura's hapless fielding and Vernon was brought back from the minors in 1941 to take over first base again. This time he hit well, .299 in 132 games to nail down the position. He missed only three games in 1942, batting .271 and was second in the league with 25 stolen bases. He appeared in 143 games in 1943, averaging .268 and in one game during the season he made two unassisted double plays.

Mickey Wins Two Batting Titles

Vernon lost two years to military service, but he returned in 1946 with a bang! His .353 average in 147 games was enough to beat out Ted Williams for the batting title by 11 percentage points, giving Mickey his greatest thrill in the majors. Mickey also was second in the league with 587 trips to the plate. The next two years were disappointing to both Vernon and the Senators as his averages dropped considerably to .265 and .242 respectively. As a result, on December 14, 1948, Griffith made one of his worst trades when he sent Vernon and pitcher Early Wynn to the Cleveland Indians for pitchers Joe Haynes and Ed Klieman and first baseman Eddie Robinson.

Mickey regained his batting eye in 1949 with the Indians raising his average to .291. In 1950, however, he got off to a slow start, hitting only .189 in 28 games and Griffith, seeing the error of his ways, seized the opportunity and reacquired the slick-fielding first baseman in a trade involving pitcher Dick Weik. With Washington that year, he hit .306 in 90 games, raising his season average to .281. He had another good year in 1951 batting .293 in 141 games but he lost his touch again in 1952, his average dropping to .251. Despite this, he played in every game during the season.

He repeated as American League batting champion in 1953, edging out Al Rosen when he collected two hits in the final game of the season. Word arrived during the game that Rosen's game was over and Mickey was leading him by only .0011 points. He would have come up again had not teammate, Mickey Grasso, who had doubled, been picked off second base, or had not Kite Thomas been thrown out at second when he "leisurely" tried to stretch a single into a double. It appeared that Vernon's teammates were protecting his title. He had taken the lead at the start of the season and was never headed. He also led the league that year with 43 doubles and was second in hits (205), triples (11), RBI (115) and total bases (315).

President Eisenhower's Favorite Ballplayer

Vernon was President Eisenhower's favorite ballplayer and on Opening Day 1954, Ike was thrilled when Vernon's two run homer in the bottom of the tenth inning resulted in a 5-3 Senators victory over the Yankees. This triggered another good season for him as he hit .290 in 151 games, leading the league in doubles again with 33 and finishing second in total bases with 294. On September 2 Vernon got his 2,000th hit and in the same game his 19th home run, a Senators record for left-handed batters surpassing Goose Goslin's record of 20 years. He went on to hit one more before the end of the season. Vernon wore a Senators uniform 14 of his 20 years in the majors. His last season with the Nats was in 1955 and he made it a good one, hitting .301 in 150 games.

In the twilight of his career, Mickey played for the Red Sox in '56 and '57, hitting .310 in 119 games but then dropping to .241 in 102 games the latter year. Returning to Cleveland again in '58 he hit .293 in 110 games, his last year as a regular. He was with the Milwaukee Braves in '59 who released him at the end of the season after hitting only .220 in 74 games. His friend and fellow Pennsylvanian, Danny Murtaugh manager of the Pittsburgh Pirates, brought him to Pittsburgh in '60 as first base coach, but he was activated in September as a pinch hitter to help the Pirates capture the National League flag.

One of the Greatest Fielding First Basemen

At the end of his career, Mickey was near the top in many all-time categories for first baseman, particularly for his fielding. He was number two in games played (2,237), number six in total chances (21,647), number two in putouts (19,808), number two in assists (1,448) and number one in double plays (2,044). He also was number one in single season assists (155) and number six in double plays (168). One of his most impressive strengths was his ability to "put the ball in play." He struck out less than one time in ten plate appearances and no more than 66 times in a season.

Managed Expansion Senators

Mickey was modest and known as "Mr. Nice Guy," and he was one of Griff's favorites. Also, he was the ideal choice to manage the expansion Senators in 1961. The team played .500 ball the first 60 games but blew leads of five runs or more four times in Boston and never recovered. He managed them again in 1962 but was replaced in 1963 by Gil Hodges. Eddie Yost managed for one game until Hodges arrived. Making a winner of an expansion team was a near impossible task!

Later, Vernon coached, scouted and served as a minor league instructor for a number of teams. He was well suited for the tasks.

Vernon considers Washington a "second home" and he and his family had some of their best times in the Capital City.

All-Time Team
Second Baseman

Charles Solomon Myer

(Buddy)

BL TR 5' 10" 163 lbs.
B. Mar. 16, 1904, Ellisville, MS.
D. Oct. 31, 1974, Baton Rouge, LA.

	Y	G	AB	R	H	2B	3B	HR	RBI	BB	SO	SB	BA	SA
Was.	16	1643	6035	1037	1828	305	113	35	759	864	385	117	.303	.408
Life	17	1923	7038	1174	2131	353	130	38	850	965	428	156	.303	.406

Buddy Myer displaying his batting stroke for photographers in Griffith Stadium.

After attending Mississippi State University, Buddy Myer was purchased by Washington in 1925 from New Orleans of the Southern Association for two players and $25,000. He was used at shortstop for only four games that season. When third baseman, Ossie Bluege was beaned during the '25 World Series, Myer was pressed into service for three games at third base. He connected for two hits in eight times at bat and fielded the position flawlessly. The next year, 1926, he replaced Roger Peckinpaugh as the regular shortstop and batted over .300, becoming a fixture in the majors.

Myer's main weakness early on was turning the double play and in 1927 he was having difficulty teaming with second baseman Harris. As a result, after only 15 games in '27, Griffith made probably his worst trade as he sent Buddy to the Boston Red Sox for shortstop Topper Rigney whose big league career ended after playing only 45 games for Washington that year. At Boston, he was shifted to third base and he hit well, posting a .288 average in 133 games with them. The next year (1928) he led the league in stolen bases with 30 and hit for a nice .313 average. The next winter, Griff admitted his mistake and reacquired Myer, this time to play second base, by sending five players and $70,000 to Boston. He remained with the Senators for the rest of his career (another 13 seasons) hitting over .300 more than half the time.

From 1929-32, Buddy proved his durability by playing in an average of 138 games a season over the period, and he proved his value to the team by averaging more than 100 runs scored and posting an excellent strikeout to walk ratio by averaging twice as many walks than strikeouts for the four years. The left-handed batter was so adept at dragging the ball that, remarkably, he beat out 60 bunts in one season. He posted batting averages of .300 in '29, .303 in '30, .293 in '31 but only .279 in '32, although he did manage to finish second in the league in triples that year with 16. In 1931, he led the league's second basemen in fielding percentage with .984.

Myer–Chapman Brawl Sparks Nats to A.L. Flag

In 1933, Myer corrected his only glaring weakness, pivoting on the double play. He and Joe Cronin, Washington shortstop and manager worked smoothly as the Nats' middlemen. Buddy was always a threat at bat, lightning fast on the bases and clever in the field. In fact, it could be said that Myer ignited the spark that enabled the Senators to beat out the Yankees for the '33 American League pennant. On April 25 at Griffith Stadium, Tony Lazzeri, Yank second baseman, hit a double play ball to Cronin who tossed to Myer at second, but Ben Chapman sliding in hard, threw a perfect block on Buddy, breaking up the double play. Myer proceeded to kick Chapman, who had spiked him the previous year, and this precipitated a near riot. Myer and Chapman were ejected from the game, but as Chapman passed the Washington dugout, he and Earl Whitehill, the stormy Senators pitcher began fighting. This resulted in a free-for-all involving New York and Washington players, fans, and the police before order was restored.

The Yankees claimed that Myer was the roughest base runner in the league and deserved all he got. While Myer claimed that the Yankees, especially Chapman, had been out to get him for three years. Shortly thereafter on May 6, Buddy was carried off the field unconscious after being hit by a pitch thrown by Detroit pitcher Whitlow Wyatt. Fortunately for the Senators, he recovered quickly and only missed three games during the season.

Washington met the New York Giants in the World Series that fall and Myer also did his part with the bat to help propel the Nats into the Fall Classic by posting a .302 batting average. He continued his .300 hitting in the Series but his fielding hurt the Senators' cause when he committed three costly errors in the losing effort.

He did, however, play a major role in the Senators' lone victory in Game Three. Each of his three hits scored or drove in a run, providing a growing cushion for pitcher Earl Whitehill, who recorded the Series' only shutout.

Wins Batting Championship in 1935

The following year (1934) he continued with his hot bat, hitting .305, scoring 103 runs and drawing over 100 bases on balls, but that was only a precursor of what was to come. In 1935, Myer reached the pinnacle of his career when he led the American

League in batting with a .349 average, edging Cleveland outfielder Joe Vosmik on the last day of the season. He was two points behind Vosmik before the final day, but when Buddy collected four hits in five at bats in a doubleheader to Vosmik's one for four, Myer won the title. His 215 hits enabled him to finish second in the league in that category and he led all league second sackers in putouts (468) and double plays (138).

The following year (1936) was a disaster for Myer and the team as Buddy suffered greatly from stomach ulcers and was sent home on August 10 to recover from the season-long ailment. He managed to play in only 51 games and his batting average plummeted to .269. He was back in 1937 for 125 games and he regained his batting form with a .293 average. He had another outstanding year in 1938 when he hit for a .336 average in 127 games and led the league in fielding percentage with a .982. Myer followed that with another good year as he posted a .302 average in 1939, playing in 83 games. His playing time was reduced again in 1940, when he played in only 71 games as he neared the end of his career. From 1936-1940, Buddy hit .290 or better except for one season, despite suffering from stomach ulcers.

In 1941, his final year in uniform, Myer was slated to be replaced by Jimmy Bloodworth at second base. Bloodworth however, was beaned the day before the season was to start and Buddy regained his job on opening day. Playing in his 17th year, Myer was still rolling along in July, hitting .319. But, he tailed off the latter part of the season and his average fell to .255 and the veteran who had topped .300 nine of the 17 years he was in the majors was given his unconditional release at the end of the year.

After retiring from baseball, he was in the building business and later owned a mortgage company in New Orleans. He passed away October 31, 1974 in Baton Rouge, Louisiana.

All-Time Team
Third Baseman

Oswald Louis Bluege

(Ossie)

BR TR 5' 11" 162 lbs.
B. Oct. 24, 1900, Chicago, IL.
D. Oct. 14, 1985, Edina, MN.

	Y	G	AB	R	H	2B	3B	HR	RBI	BB	SO	SB	BA	SA
Life	18	1867	6440	883	1751	276	67	43	848	723	515	140	.272	.356

Ossie Bluege as an executive of the Washington Baseball Club.

Baltimore had Brooks Robinson, Pittsburgh had Pie Traynor and Philadelphia had Mike Schmidt, all Hall of Fame third basemen. But, Washington had non-Hall of Famer Ossie Bluege who was probably the greatest fielding third baseman of all time. Ossie played the shallowest of any, relying on his cat-like reflexes and swift reactions to handle hotly smashed ground balls and snare fierce line drives. He considered that the area he covered was cone shaped and the closer he was to the originating point, the narrower the areas he had to cover on each side.

Clark Griffith heard that the Philadelphia A's were interested in Bluege, who was playing for Peoria in 1921. So he dispatched scout Joe Engel to look him over. Ossie had a bad knee injury from playing basketball, so Engel had him test it in a foot race with other team members; when Bluege finished second, Engel signed him for $3,500. When Griffith first saw him sparkle in the field, he remarked that the Senators wouldn't have any problem at third base for a decade.

Became Nats' Regular Third Baseman in '23

After appearing in 19 games with the Nats in 1922, he was sent to Minneapolis for more seasoning. His .315 batting average in 44 games caught Griffith's eye, and Bluege was installed as the club's regular third baseman on April 29, 1923, where he played in 107 games and hit .245. He was tops in the league for third baseman with 29 double plays. In 1924, he hit considerably better, compiling a .281 average in 117 games and helping the Nats win the American League pennant. He also did his part in giving the Senators their only World Championship with a win over the New York Giants that year. In the first game of the Series, he scored the tying run in the ninth to send the game into extra innings but New York eventually won in 12 innings. In the next game, he made a key sacrifice in the bottom of the ninth to enable Joe Judge to score the winning run in the Senators' 4-3 victory. He also drove in two runs in the bottom of the eighth to seal a 7-4 win in the fourth game.

Beaned in 1925 World Series

He batted .287 in 1925 and although his play in the 1925 World Series against the Pittsburgh Pirates was limited, he played errorless ball in the field and hit .278. In the opening game of the Series, Bluege, Sam Rice and Joe Harris collected two hits each and drove in all of the runs in Walter Johnson's 4-1 victory. Ossie was beaned in the second game by Pirate hurler, Vic Aldrich and taken to Johns Hopkins Hospital for observation. When X-rays were taken, the doctors claimed that Bluege had the hardest skull of any ever seen! He returned to the lineup in the fifth game and had a total of 18 at bats in the Series with five hits.

In '26, he hit .271 and in '27 he continued to give fine defensive performances, leading the league in number of assists (337) and number of games (146). He led the league in assists (337) again in 1928 and had his best year, hitting when he posted a .297 average. Bluege's goal was to reach the .300 level but that was as close as he would come. He reinjured his bad knee in 1929 and was relegated to a utility role by new manager, Walter Johnson, and appeared in only 64 games, although hitting .295. He was a regular again for the 1930-33 seasons and continued to be one of the best third basemen in the league. He hit .290 in 1930 and led the other league third baseman in assists (258) and games (134). He led in three categories in '31 with 286 assists, 152 games and a .960 fielding percentage while hitting .272. In 1932, he led the league with 28 double plays but his average dropped to .258.

Bluege played in 140 games and batted .261 in 1933 as the Nats captured their third American League flag. Near the end of the season on September 9, the fans, the club management and his teammates honored Bluege on "Ossie Bluege Day" at Griffith Stadium. He received an automobile from the fans and a silver service from the players. In the World Series, Bluege did not contribute much with his bat, hitting only .125, as the Nats lost to the New York Giants in five games. His fielding, however, was steady as usual.

Relegated to Utility Role in '34

Ossie was replaced at third base early in the 1934 season by Cecil Travis, the smooth swinging, dangerous hitter and Bluege was relegated to a utility role for most of the rest of the career which ended in 1939. He was able to play in 99 games in '34 despite a .246 batting average, and in '35 he played in 100 games and hit .262. For a short time in 1936, when Travis was shifted to shortstop, Ossie was the starter at third. One day while there, Bluege fielded a bunt and fired toward first base, however, on the mound was the colorful pitcher, Bobo Newsom, whose right ear was in the way of the throw. After reeling around awhile, Bobo resumed pitching and eventually shut out the St. Louis Browns 1-0. By May, however, Buddy Lewis became the established starter at third. Later, while filling in at second base, Bluege set an American League record by playing in 37 games without an error, handling 205 chances flawlessly. He hit a nice .288 that year. In '37 he hit .283 in 42 games and in '38 his average was .261 for 58 games. His final season as an active player was 1939 but he appeared in only 18 games and hit a lowly .153.

Bluege played all infield positions and even played in the outfield for five games. He had a great arm and recalled his best play, fielding Freddie Lindstrom's bunt in the '24 World Series and nipping him at first base. He also remembered costing the Philadelphia A's the pennant one year as he started an inning ending double play with a spectacular stop. He was a clutch hitter and a team player; one of the players Griffith would not trade. He was one of the fastest base runners going from second to home but his real talent was fielding. Luke Sewell, Washington catcher, said that Bluege was one of the "best two infielders he ever saw," meaning you only needed one person on his side of the infield. Ossie had to be coaxed into taking batting practice preferring to practice fielding ground balls.

Manages Senators from 1943–47

Ossie played 18 years, hitting .272, and he, Sam Rice and

Goose Goslin were the only players on all three Washington pennant winners. After his playing days were over, he was a coach with the Senators from 1940-42 and he replaced Bucky Harris as manager in 1943. He almost brought in a winner the first year as Harris and Joe Cronin had done, but he finished second to the New York Yankees by a large margin. Again, in 1945, his club finished second, only a game and a half behind the Detroit Tigers and things might have been different if center fielder Bingo Binks hadn't lost a fly ball in the sun in a late season loss to the Philadelphia A's. Bluege managed the Nats through 1947, when Joe Kuhel replaced him after a seventh place finish.

He was appointed Director of the Nats farm system in 1948 and later comptroller of the team. He moved on to Minneapolis in the same capacity after the 1960 season, when Calvin Griffith moved the team there.

Ossie died of a stroke at the age of 84, just a few days after travelling to Washington to be inducted into the "Washington Hall of Stars" at RFK Stadium.

All-Time Team Shortstop

Joseph Edward Cronin

(Joe)

BR TR 5'11" 180 lbs.
B. Oct. 12, 1906, San Francisco, CA.
D. September 7, 1984, Osterville, MA.
Hall of Fame 1956

	Y	G	AB	R	H	2B	3B	HR	RBI	BB	SO	SB	BA	SA
Was.	7	940	3580	577	1090	242	72	51	672	466	274	56	.304	.455
Life	20	2124	7579	1233	2285	515	118	170	1424	1059	700	87	.301	.468

Senators' manager Joe Cronin, right, chatting with White Sox manager Jimmy Dykes before the game.

Joe Cronin was among the best-hitting shortstops of all time with a lifetime batting average of .301. He hit with power and upon his retirement he was among the leaders in games played, runs, hits, doubles, extra base hits, RBIs and bases on balls. Although he was considered only an adequate fielder, he was among the leaders in double plays and no one else could go as far to his right and still be able to throw out the runner. He possessed the mightiest arm of any shortstop. He was a great clutch man whether a long ball was needed or a sparkling fielding play. He was voted into the Hall of Fame in 1956, just 11 years after his playing days were over.

He was born in San Francisco and at the age of 14, he won the boys' tennis championship there. He later switched to baseball at Sacred Heart College, the alma mater of James J. Corbett and Harry Heilmann. Joe was signed by the Pittsburgh Pirates while playing semi-pro ball and sent to Johnstown of the Mid-Atlantic League. In 1926, he played 38 games for the Pirates, hitting .265 but spent part of the season with New Haven of the Eastern League. In '27, despite being with the parent club all season, he got in only 12 games, batting .227. He was released to Kansas City of the American Association for the 1928 season.

Registers His Highest Batting Averages in 1930

Joe Engel, Washington scout, signed him for the Senators for $7,500 without Griffith's permission. Griff was quite upset but the Nats needed a shortstop to back up Bobby Reeves. Cronin played in 63 games at short but hit only .242. Joe beat out three other candidates in 1929 for the regular shortstop job, playing in 145 games, finding his batting eye with a .281 average and leading the league with 459 assists. He really hit his stride in 1930, playing in all 154 games, he compiled his highest batting average of .346 and his highest RBI total (126). He was no slouch in the field either, leading the league in putouts (336), assists (509) and double plays (95). He was hailed by many as the best shortstop in the American League, was compared to the great Honus Wagner and named by the *Sporting News* as player of the year.

Cronin followed this with three more .300 seasons in 1931-33. He played in a league leading 156 games and repeated as leader in putouts (323) and double plays (94) in '31. Joe led the American League in triples (18), fielding percentage (.959) putouts (306), assists (448) and double plays (95) in '32. In '33, he led with 45 doubles and a fielding percentage of .960.

As Rookie Player/Manager, Leads Nats to '33 Pennant

It was that year that Clark Griffith tried to duplicate the success he had in 1924 with "Boy Wonder" Bucky Harris by naming Cronin as manager of the Senators. It worked, and Joe led the Nats to their third and last American League pennant as Washington took the flag from the New York Yankees. Unfortunately, the club lost to the New York Giants in the World Series four games to one but Cronin did his part, hitting .318.

In 1934, Cronin managed the American League All-Star Team to victory at the Polo Grounds in New York. But that was the game in which Carl Hubbell fanned five greats in a row: Ruth, Gehrig, Foxx, Simmons and Cronin. He failed to hit .300 that year for the first time in five years, posting an average of .284 and his season was curtailed on Labor Day when he collided with Boston Red Sox pitcher Wes Ferrell on a play at first base and broke his wrist. Riddled with injuries that year, the Nats fell to seventh place.

Sold to Red Sox in '34 for Record Price

In October '34, Griffith accepted a fabulous offer from Boston Red Sox owner Tom Yawkey, who sent Washington a quarter-million dollars and shortstop Lyn Lary for Cronin's services as a Red Sox player/manager. The record price was more than double the $100,000 price given for Babe Ruth earlier. Cronin was given a contract for five years with a substantial salary. Griff was reluctant to part with Cronin who had recently married Griffith's niece, Mildred Robertson, who was serving as club secretary. But, since he could not offer him a similar contract, he thought that Cronin deserved the special opportunity.

Clark commented that Cronin was a great ballplayer and a great manager who had given the Nats seven good years and that he was one of he finest boys he ever knew!

Joe became the regular Red Sox shortstop for most of the next decade, hitting .300 or more in seven of the next 11 seasons. In his first year with the Sox, he was involved in one of the strangest plays ever when his line drive caromed off the head of Cleveland third baseman Odell Hale to shortstop Bill Knickerbocker, who started a triple play to end the game. Cronin loved hitting in Fenway Park. Three times he registered slugging percentages over .500, with a career-high .536 in 1938, the year he led the league in doubles again with 51. He hit a career-high 24 home runs in 1940. Despite hitting .311 with 16 homers and 95 RBI in 1941, he took himself out of the regular lineup in 1942 to make room for newcomer Johnny Pesky.

In the twilight of his career, Cronin was noted for his pinch-hitting ability, leading the league in the number of pinch hits (18) in 1943 and setting a major league record with five pinch homers, including one each in both ends of a doubleheader. He delivered several game-winning home runs as a pinch-hitter. His playing career ended early in the 1945 season when Cronin broke his leg, ending a career spanning 20 years in the major leagues. He was selected for the American League All-Star Team seven times.

Has Success Managing Red Sox for 13 Years

As manager, he led Boston to seven first division finishes during the period and finished second to the powerful Yankees four times. But, it was not until his playing days were over that he gained the much sought-after American League flag, beating out the Detroit Tigers by the wide margin of 12 games in 1946. Boston lost to the St. Louis Cardinals in the hard-fought World Series four games to three. After managing the Sox to a third place finish in 1947, he was elevated to general manager, and Billy Southworth was appointed manager. Later in 1959, he became president of the American League and served in that capacity through 1973. Cronin died September 7, 1984 in Osterville, Massachusetts.

All-Time Team
Outfield

Edgar Charles Rice
(Sam)

BL TR 5' 9" 150 lbs.
B. Feb. 20, 1890, Morocco, IN.
D. Oct. 13, 1974, Rossmor, MD.
Hall of Fame 1963

	Y	G	AB	R	H	2B	3B	HR	RBI	BB	SO	SB	BA	SA
Was.	19	2307	8934	1466	2889	479	183	33	1045	680	266	346	.323	.429
Life	20	2404	9269	1514	2987	498	184	34	1078	708	275	351	.322	.427

Outfielder Sam Rice posing for a photo in his home uniform.

Sam Rice finished his 20-year big league career only 12 hits shy of 3000, more hits than Babe Ruth, Rogers Hornsby, George Sisler and Lou Gehrig recorded. At the time of his retirement, the only American Leaguers to achieve the 3000 mark were Ty Cobb, Tris Speaker and Eddie Collins. At only 5' 9" and with his playing weight sometimes as low as 144 lbs., Rice did not hit for power but his smooth, compact swing and extraordinary batting eye made him one of the most feared line-drive hitters in the game. Spraying hits to all fields, he was the top singles hitter in the first 79 years of baseball, recording a staggering 182 in 1925. He seldom swung at pitches out of the strike zone, often taking two strikes before offering at a pitch to his liking. He was difficult to strike out, averaging only one strikeout in 34 at bats. He was called "Man O' War" because of his foot speed and only Ty Cobb and Clyde Milan among his peers were better at base stealing. Rice led the league in 1920 with 63 thefts. He was a fine defensive outfielder covering a lot of territory because of his speed.

Wife and 2 Children Killed in Tornado Tragedy

Like Babe Ruth and Goose Goslin, Rice began his professional career as a pitcher. He travelled to Galesville, Illinois for a tryout in April 1912, while his wife and two children went to visit Sam's parents in Morroco, Indiana. A tornado struck his parent's home on April 21, killing all occupants and demolishing the home. Sam had to live with this personal tragedy during his career, keeping the pain within and refusing to discuss the matter with anyone. For a while, he took to wandering, picking up jobs bottling whiskey, working in wheat fields and as a railroad section hand. He enlisted in the navy in 1913 and went ashore at Vera Cruz, Mexico as 19 of his shipmates were killed or wounded when the United States intervened to put down the Mexican revolt. While stationed at Guantanamo Bay in Cuba, he took up baseball again and later while on leave in the States in 1914, he won five straight games for a Virginia minor league team. The team paid for his discharge from the navy and he finished the year at 9-2. In July 1915, the league folded and the owner sent Rice to Clark Griffith in payment of a debt. In announcing Rice's signing to the press, Griff could not remember his first name and called him "Sam." The nickname stuck.

Rice's pitching career was short lived, while appearing in only four games, he posted a 1-0 record with a 2.0 earned run average. In 1916, he was 0-1 with an ERA of 2.95, not bad. But, in his last pitching performance a notoriously weak-hitting pitcher lashed a two-base hit and when Rice returned to the dugout he demanded a knife and an outfielder's glove, cut the toe plate off his pitching shoe and the Senators had right field covered for almost two decades. He finished the season playing the outfield for 46 games and hitting .299.

He was the opening day right fielder in 1917, batting fourth, and Sam was the only .300 hitter on the team, stole 35 bases and played in 155 games, leading the league in that category. The army interrupted his career in 1918 and he served with distinction. He was able to play in seven games while on furlough, though, posting a .348 average.

Became Senators' Best Hitter in 1919

When he returned to the club, he established himself as the Senators' best hitter. He led the club in 1919-21 with averages of .321, .328 and .330. He led the league in games played (141) in 1919. The next year, 1920, he led the league in putouts with 454. Although he dropped off to .295 in 1922, he led the league with 633 trips to the plate and 387 putouts. He led the league in triples (18) in 1923 and tied catcher Muddy Ruel for best average on the team with .316. He achieved a baseball rarity while playing right field in the sixth inning of a game against Cleveland when he turned in an unassisted double play. His run-in with manager Donnie Bush cost the manager his job at the end of the season. Rice and second baseman Bucky Harris had failed to communicate on a pop fly to short right field and the ball fell in for a single. Bush was furious and when Sam entered the dugout, the manager severely reprimanded him in front of the team. The usually mild-mannered Rice shot back at him to everyone's amazement. Bush suspended

Sam but on their return to Washington, Griffith lifted the suspension and later fired Donnie.

In 1924, he finished second to Goose Goslin with a .324 average and he played a major role in the Senators' drive to edge the New York Yankees for the American League flag. In the first game of a crucial August series with the Yanks, he drove in five runs in an 11-6 victory and in the fourth game he kept the Nats in first place with a two run double in the 10th to ice the game. He led the league again with 646 at bats and cracked out 216 hits to lead the league in that department. During the year he hit safely in 31 straight games. But, Sam was not a major factor in the World Championship Series with the New York Giants that year, hitting only .207 in the seven games.

Makes Disputed "Catch" in 1925 World Series

Sam made up for his poor Series performance the following regular season with a sparkling .350 average, leading the team into the 1925 World Series against the Pittsburgh Pirates. Rice played a prominent role in keeping the Series close but the Senators lost to the Pirates four games to three. He batted an eye-opening .364 in the Series and sewed up the first game for the Nats with a two run single, driving in the winning runs. But his most noteworthy contribution was a sensational "catch," which became the most controversial "out" in World Series history. With his team leading four to three in the bottom of the eighth, Rice raced to the temporary center field bleachers in Griffith Stadium for Earl Smith's drive, snagging the ball as he fell over the railing and disappeared among the spectators. After a period of time, which seemed like an eternity, he emerged holding his glove high with the ball nestled in it. When National League umpire Cy Rigler called the batter out, the Pirates stormed the field to argue the call to no avail. They maintained that a Senators fan had retrieved the ball and stuck it in Sam's glove.

Rice refused to answer questions about the "catch" other than to say that the umpire said that he made the catch. Fans who claimed to be in the bleacher seats that day (1,600 of them) submitted affidavits as to whether or not the ball had been caught. The fans were about evenly divided on the subject. Rice enjoyed playing games with the press on the matter and finally decided to put the matter to rest by providing a sealed written statement to the Hall of Fame, which would be opened after his death. Fifty years after the "catch" Sam revealed that "At no time did I lose possession of the ball."

In 1926, he was second to Goslin with a .337 average, leading the league in the number of at bats (641), hits (216) and in assists (25). After slumping to .297 in 1927, he either led the team in hitting or was second from 1928-32, posting averages of .328, .323, .349, .310 and .323. In 1932, the 42-year-old was gradually relegated to a utility role, appearing in only 69 games in the outfield. His last season with the Senators was in '33, when he hit .294 while playing in 73 games and helping the Nats capture the American League pennant. Rice, Goslin and Bluege were the only players on all three-pennant winners. Sam was only sent to the plate once during the World Series, as a pinch-hitter, and he responded with a single. Trailing 4-3 in the bottom of the tenth in the fifth game of the Series, manager Joe Cronin has been criticized for sending reserve catcher Cliff Bolton to the plate as a pinch-hitter with the tying run on first base and only one out. The slow-footed Bolton promptly hit into a double play, ending the Series. Things might have been different, if the veteran Rice had been the pinch-hitter.

Finishes Career with Cleveland Indians

Given his unconditional release by the Senators after the Series, the 43-year-old was picked up by the Cleveland Indians. The aging Rice still was able to bat .293 in 97 games that season. Hampered by a muscle pull, Sam decided to retire before season's end over the objections of the Cleveland management. At his farm in Ashton, Maryland, he raised racing pigeons and later was involved in a prosperous real estate business.

The late Shirley Povich illustrated Sam's remarkable bat control with the following first-hand observation. Dusted off by a Cleveland pitcher after two previous singles, Sam hit the next pitch and leveled the pitcher with a sharp ground ball to his shins. When the next pitcher threw at his head, Rice responded with a low liner off his knee.

At the plate almost 10,000 times and hitting .300 or more in 14 of his 20 seasons, Sam's highest salary was only $18,000 a year. Rice finally received his much-deserved recognition when voted into the Hall of Fame in 1963. He died on October 13, 1974 in Rossmor, Maryland at the age of 84.

All-Time Team
Outfield

Leon Allen Goslin

(Goose)

BL TR 5' 11" 185 lbs.
B. Oct. 16, 1900, Salem, NJ.
D. May 15, 1971, Bridgeton, NJ.
Hall of Fame 1968

	Y	G	AB	R	H	2B	3B	HR	RBI	BB	SO	SB	BA	SA
Was.	12	1361	5139	854	1656	289	125	127	931	487	337	116	.322	.501
Life	18	2287	8656	1483	2735	500	173	248	1609	949	585	175	.316	.500

Goose Goslin taking one of his vicious swings during a game at Griffith Stadium.

Possibly the most popular player, other than Walter Johnson, to ever wear the Washington uniform was the colorful "Wild Goose of the Potomac," Goose Goslin. The Goose earned the nickname not only because of his last name, but also because of his Jimmy Durante-sized nose and his duck-like waddle while chasing fly balls with palms down. The fearless Goslin crowded the plate with a pronounced closed stance and once said that if he could have seen the pitches with both eyes he could have hit .500. Not even the great Walter Johnson could generate the electricity felt by the fans as the Goose strode to the plate and threatened to knock the ball down the throat of the opposing pitcher. In many ways he was Washington's answer to Babe Ruth, providing more power than any other Senator of that era and his training habits were much like Ruth's, requiring disciplinary actions by his managers.

Hits .300 and Drives in 100–plus Runs 11 Times

But first and foremost, Goslin was a fierce competitor and line-drive clutch hitter, who inflicted damage on opposing hurlers for 18 years. He was inducted into the Hall of Fame in 1968. At the time of his induction, Goslin had more hits than Lou Gehrig or Joe DiMaggio, more doubles than Jimmie Foxx or Mel Ott and more RBIs than Tris Speaker or Rogers Hornsby. He hit over .300 and drove in 100 runs or more for 11 seasons and he scored 100 runs or more in seven seasons.

Umpire Bill McGowan discovered Goslin playing sandlot ball in New Jersey and helped him secure a minor league contract with Columbia, South Carolina of the Sally League. After topping .300 twice, he was scouted personally by Clark Griffith who signed him to a Washington contract for $6,000 in 1921. Goslin failed to report on September 15 as scheduled but showed up a few days later for his first major league game and promptly smashed two triples off Hall of Famer Red Faber of the Chicago White Sox. In 1922, he was a sensation in spring training with his bat but he was woefully weak chasing fly balls. After improving his defensive ability with practice, he was installed as the regular left fielder and hit .324 in 101 games. The next year (1923) he led the American League in triples with 18 and batted .300 in 150 games.

Smashes 3 Homers in '24 Series

Goslin played a major role in winning Washington's first American League pennant and one and only World Series Championship in 1924. He hit .344 and took the RBI title from Babe Ruth by knocking in 129 runs. In a crucial series with the New York Yankees late in the season, Goslin helped win the first two games, with a home run, triple and single in the first game and a home run and single in the second game. But, Goose showed even more during the World Series when he crashed three homers and earned respect around the majors as a "money ballplayer." Game Four turned out to be "Goose Goslin Day" as the Senators' top batter had a homer, three singles and four RBI in the Nats' 7-4 victory. He also made a record six consecutive hits as the Nats took the Series four games to three over John McGraw's Giants.

In '25, Goose had another splendid year, hitting .334 and leading the league in triples with 20 and in assists with 24. Washington repeated as American League Champions and faced the Pittsburgh Pirates in the World Series. Again, Goslin rapped three home runs, setting a record six homers in consecutive World Series. In the fourth game of the Series, Goslin's three-run home run secured a 4-0 win and a 3-1 Series lead. Unfortunately, they dropped this Series to the Pirates four games to three.

Wins American League Batting Championship in 1928

On opening day 1926, Goslin drove in the winning run in Walter Johnson's 1-0 victory over the Philadelphia A's in 15 grueling innings. Goslin continued his torrid hitting that year with a .354 average and repeated as assists leader with 25. In 1927, he chalked up an average of .334. But, in 1928, he recorded his best season, leading the league with a .379 batting average. He and Heinie

Manush of the St. Louis Browns were locked up in a tight battle for the batting crown and it came down to Goose's last at bat. The Senators and Manush's Browns faced each other on the last day of the season in a doubleheader, and Goslin would win the title if he didn't take his last turn at bat. Manager Bucky Harris left the decision up to Goose, who at first was inclined to give way to a pinch hitter. But reminded that the Browns would call him a coward, he decided to go to the plate. After the pitcher got two quick strikes on him, he did everything possible to make the umpire throw him out of the game, to no avail. He then proceeded to rap out a base hit and secure the crown.

Earlier in the year, Goslin, who had one of the strongest arms in the league, had injured his right arm badly. There are three versions of how he was hurt, the most popular one is that Goose observed someone putting the shot and decided to throw it himself. Another version is that he injured it during horseplay in a Pullman car. Sam Rice's version is that Goslin and another Nat were trying to throw balls over a fence in St. Louis from farther and farther away. Nonetheless, Griffith said that the injury cost the Senators 12 games that year, as shortstop Bobby Reeves had to race out to left field to get Goose's weak relays as runners took advantage of his arm. He was in the lineup only because of his bat.

Goose's average in 1929 dipped to .288 and his feud with new manager Walter Johnson was common knowledge. Griff was forced to get rid of one of them, so in 1930, after 47 games when he was hitting only .271, Goslin was traded to the Browns during the season for outfielder Heinie Manush and pitcher Alvin Crowder. Goslin hit .326 while with the Browns, and finished the season with a .308 average. Not having to deal with Washington's high right field wall while at home in St. Louis, Goslin clouted 37 home runs, by far his best output. He followed this with a .328 batting average and 24 homers in 1931 and .299 and 17 homers in 1932, leading the league again with 16 assists. On June 23, 1932, Goslin hit three home runs in a game for the third time. In each of three years with the Browns he batted in more than 100 runs.

When Joe Cronin was appointed the new Senators manager in 1933, one of his first requests was to acquire Goose. Griff brought him back to Washington from the Browns along with pitcher Lefty Stewart and outfielder Fred Schulte in exchange for outfielders Sam West and Carl Reynolds and pitcher Lloyd Brown. Goose helped the Senators win their third and last American League Championship. He, Sam Rice and Ossie Bluege were the only players on all three pennant winners. In a crucial series with the Yanks, Goslin came through, faking a catch he retrieved the ball and fired toward the plate, enabling catcher Luke Sewell to tag out both Babe Ruth and Lou Gehrig in quick succession at the plate. The Nats were defeated by the New York Giants in the World Series four games to one. Losing the first game 4-2, Goslin's ninth inning bid to win the game was a long shot over the right field fence, which was foul by inches. In the second game, his home run blast gave Washington a temporary 1-0 lead before they fell 6-1.

Drives in Winning Run to Win '35 World Series for Tigers

Griffith expected Goose to slow down after the '33 season, so he was traded to the Detroit Tigers in time for Goslin to appear in two more World Series in '34 and '35. It's ironic that Goose's greatest triumph occurred in a Tiger uniform. His single in the bottom of the ninth inning in 1935 drove in Mickey Cochrane with the winning run and gave the Tigers their first World Series Championship. His hit touched off a wild celebration in Detroit and Goose became a special Tiger hero. The Tigers also won the pennant the previous year as Goslin hit .305 and drove in 100 runs. But, Detroit lost the World Series to the St. Louis Cardinals in seven games as the Dean brothers, Dizzy and Daffy, were credited with all four wins. Goslin however did his part by driving in the winning run in the Tigers' victory in Game Two. Goose's batting average for all five World Series was .287.

In 1936, he drove in 125 runs with 24 homers and hit for a .315 average, one of his best seasons. This was his last season as a regular and in 1937 his average plummeted to .238 in 79 games but he came through with nine pinch hits, leading the league in that category.

In the off season, Goslin contacted Clark Griffith and asked to return to Washington for one more season and the old gentleman complied. He appeared in just 38 games because of a bad back, hitting only .158. He did, however, hit his fifth career pinch homer on April 24, establishing a new American League record. In his last plate appearance, he aggravated his back injury and the great Goose Goslin had to end his career with a pinch hitter finishing his turn at bat! He was given his unconditional release at the end of the '38 season, but caught on as player/manager of the minor league Trenton, New Jersey team. He held the post for three years, 1939-41. Even approaching 40 years old, he was one of the team's best players. His managerial skills, however, were somewhat lacking. Although he helped the hitters tremendously, he did not know how to handle pitchers well and did not have a good rapport with the players.

After his wife died, Goose retired to a solitary life as a fisherman in South Jersey. His biggest thrill was his enshrinement in Cooperstown, New York. At the ceremonies honoring the 1968 inductees, Goslin was overcome with emotion and said that he would remember the day for the rest of his life. The "good old country boy" who loved the game of baseball, once proclaimed that he would play in the majors for free!

All-Time Team
Outfield

Frank Howard

(Hondo, The Capital Punisher)

BR TR 6' 7" 255 lbs.

B. August 8, 1936, Columbus, OH.

	Y	G	AB	R	H	2B	3B	HR	RBI	BB	SO	SB	BA	SA
Was.	7	1077	3833	516	1071	146	20	237	670	533	854	4	.279	.472
Life	16	1895	6488	864	1774	245	35	382	1119	782	1460	8	.273	.499

Frank Howard autographs his photo for the author and includes a nice comment.

Frank (Hondo) Howard was one of the most popular of all Senators and certainly the best loved member of the expansion franchise. This gentle giant loved Washington fans as much as they loved him. He was openly critical of owner Bob Short's move to Texas, which left the Capital City without baseball. By his own admission, the highlight of his career was his dramatic sixth inning home run in Washington's final game of the '71 season. With the local fans pleading for just one more homer from the big guy, Howard blasted the Yankees' Mike Keckich's fast ball deep into the left field seats igniting the last joyous celebration of Senators baseball fans. Responding to the demands of the fans, Frank took two "curtain calls" throwing his hat and kisses to the fans as he said his last goodbyes.

Hits Ball Harder and Farther than Anyone— Ted Williams

No less an authority than Ted Williams claims that big Frank hit the ball harder and farther than any man that ever played the game. Yankee ace, Whitey Ford, acknowledges that the only batter he was ever afraid to face was Howard. Many other pitchers as well as infielders were fearful of the line drives that rocketed off Hondo's bat. Many of his homers were gargantuan clouts and many seats in the upper deck of RFK Stadium were painted white to show where his home runs had come to roost.

In his only World Series appearance with the Dodgers in 1963, Howard hit two memorable drives off Ford. The first went for only a double, as he laced a low liner (no more than 10-12 feet off the ground) to straightaway centerfield in Yankee Stadium where it caromed off a loud speaker 457 feet away. The other came in the Dodgers clinching fourth game when Frank belted the first homer ever hit into the upper deck of Dodger Stadium, helping Los Angeles win 2-1. Probably his longest homer never made the record books. No one had ever hit one out of old Yankee Stadium, but big Frank cleared the roof down the left field line only to have the umpire rule it foul. Pitcher Bobby Shantz and third baseman Clete Boyer claim that the ball was fair.

Howard constantly had to battle a weight problem and at times it was reported he was nearly 300 pounds. However, during the season no one worked harder to stay in shape and teammates marveled at his boundless energy. A team player, he was well liked by both the players and management. He led the American League in home runs in '68 with 44 and again in '70 with the same number. Also, he was tops that year in RBIs with 126 and drawing bases on balls with 132. He also was first in total bases in 1968 with 330, and 340 in '69. He was voted as an All-Star game starter by the fans in '68, '69 and '70. Although the National League won all three games, Howard provided the one bright spot for hometown Washingtonians in the '69 game, when he smashed a homer off National League starter Steve Carlton.

For most of his career, Howard was used in the outfield and considered to be a liability defensively, especially after injuring his throwing arm early in his career. He also was a notorious bad ball hitter, drawing relatively few walks until manager Ted Williams arrived on the scene in the late 'sixties and converted him into a more disciplined hitter. Frank was a free swinger, thereby chalking up numerous strikeouts including a league leading 155 in 1967. In 1965, he struck out seven times in a twin bill as Washington split with the Red Sox to tie the major league record.

Clouts 10 Homers in One Week

A graduate of Ohio State University, where he starred in basketball as well as baseball, Howard never spent a day playing in the minors. Drafted by the Los Angeles Dodgers in 1958, Frank saw only very limited action the first two years but he appeared in 117 games in 1960 (considered his rookie year) and was voted "National League Rookie of the Year." As a regular with Los Angeles for the period '60-'64, he averaged over 120 games a year. His best year with Los Angeles was '62 when he hit .296 and smashed 31 homers. When his average plummeted to .226 in '64, he was traded to the Senators, where he enjoyed the best years of his career. Hondo was often a streak hitter and he set the all-time record for home runs in one week, when he clouted 10. He also was the league leader in total bases in '68 (330) and '69 (340) and slugging percentage with .552 in '68.

Playing seven years in Washington, Howard established numerous expansion club season records including: most games (161), most runs (111), most hits (175), most homers (48), most extra base hits (75), most RBI (126) and most strikeouts (155). He was a durable regular, appearing in over 150 games a year on the average.

Things went sour for him when the team arrived in Texas, however. Management was committed to a youth movement and Frank was used, usually against left-handed pitching only. Before the end of the season, he was acquired by the Detroit Tigers to help them in their successful stretch drive for a play-off berth. Unfortunately, he was not on the eligible list for post-season play. He wound up his big league career with the Tigers the following year ('73), appearing in 85 games, hitting .256 and belting 12 homers.

Knee Injury Ends Playing Career

In '74, Frank signed to play with the Taiheiyo Lions in Japan. He was well on the way to becoming the team's biggest attraction, when a severe knee injury forced him to retire from active playing. Because of his love for the game, Howard has been associated with the game in various capacities for most of his "retired" years. He has served as manager, coach and batting instructor for a variety of teams, both in the majors and minors, including the Padres, Brewers, Braves, Devil Rays and the Yankees.

Frank Howard waving goodbye to Senators fans after smashing the last home run hit by a Nats' player. It was the last Washington game before the franchise went off to Texas.

The lovable giant will not soon be forgotten by loyal, baseball-starved Washington fans.

All-Time Team
Designated Hitter

Harmon Clayton Killebrew

(Killer)

BR TR 5'11" 213 lbs.

B. June 29, 1936, Payette, ID.

	Y	G	AB	R	H	2B	3B	HR	RBI	BB	SO	SB	BA	SA
Was.	7	390	1242	211	311	45	3	84	215	184	315	4	.250	.494
Life	22	2435	8147	1283	2086	290	24	573	1584	1559	1699	19	.256	.509

A young Harmon Killebrew kneeling on the Griffith Stadium turf, bat in hand.

Harmon Killebrew hit more career home runs than Mickey Mantle, Jimmie Foxx and Ted Williams. Playing for the Senators for all or part of seven seasons, "the Killer" could not be left off the all-time team, so he was welcomed as the team's designated hitter. Most of Harmon's successes were achieved after he left Washington for Minnesota in 1961, but in his two previous seasons with the Nats, he began to live up to the expectations of Washington management.

Washington's Most Expensive "Bonus Baby"

Killebrew was a "bonus baby," Washington's first. As a 17-year-old, on the recommendation of U.S. Senator Herman Welker of Idaho, Washington scout Ossie Bluege signed the youngster in 1954 for $30,000. At the time, he was playing in the Idaho-Oregon League and with Bluege watching, he went 12 for 12 with four homers, including a mammoth drive that cleared the fence at the 430-foot sign. Under the bonus rule at that time, Harmon had to remain with the parent club for two years before he could be "farmed out" to the minor leagues. Although he had considerable power, he had much to learn about the art of hitting and fielding and his progress was considerably delayed because he could not learn in the minors.

While Senator Welker and others wanted to press Killebrew into service immediately, manager Bucky Harris and other knowledgeable baseball men knew that it would be a minimum of four years before the youngster would be ready. In 1954, he was in only nine games with 13 times at bat. He played little more the following year, seeing service in 38 games and connecting for four home runs in 80 at bats. He spent most of his time in the minors with Charlotte and Chattanooga in '56 and '57, although he appeared in 44 games with the Nats in 1956, belting five homers in 99 trips to the plate. In 1957, he was with the Senators for only nine games, getting two home runs in 31 plate appearances.

Harmon hit rock bottom in 1958 and the youngster had serious doubts about his ability to succeed. He had shown that he could hit Double A minor league pitching the previous year, so he was optioned to Indianapolis of the American Association to see if he could succeed in Triple A ball. Indianapolis returned him after he was unsuccessful in 38 games and he was optioned to Double A Chattanooga to finish the season. Killebrew nearly quit at the time but he was raising a family and decided to give it another try.

Led League in Homers in '59

Everything came together for him in 1959, as the strong boy from Idaho finally fulfilled the raw promise he had shown on the diamonds of Idaho. He played in 153 games for Washington, leading the league with 42 home runs and driving in 105 runs. He played 150 games at third base that year but because of his fielding deficiencies, he never found a position he could call "home." During his career, he was used 969 times at first base, 792 times at third base, 470 times in the outfield, and a dozen or so times at second base.

His final season in a Senators uniform was in 1960 and while he did not do as well as the previous season, he still had 31 round trippers. One of them was a prodigious blast by the muscular Killebrew in Detroit. Although both Mantle and Williams had cleared the right field roof at revamped Briggs Stadium, no right-handed batter had ever cleared the roof. But, Harmon delivered the longest blast by any right-hander when his towering home run banged against the roof facing of the second deck. It missed landing atop the roof by inches, Killebrew thus achieved what Hank Greenberg, Jimmie Foxx, Joe DiMaggio and others failed to do. Harmon lashed another memorable homer at Griffith Stadium, estimated to have travelled 480 feet, a reminder of Mickey Mantle's record setting homer over the left field bleachers. Killebrew's major problem was that he struck out over 100 times in each of the two years.

Has Terrific Slugging Average with Twins in 1961

Calvin Griffith moved the club to Minnesota for the 1961 season and the quiet, modest and happy Killebrew became the favorite of the Twins' fans. He responded with a personal high 46 homers, his highest batting average (.288) and a fantastic slugging percentage of .606.

In 1962, Killebrew again led the American League with 48 home runs, 126 runs batted in, and registered a .545 slugging average. On the down side, for the only time in his career, Harmon led the league in strikeouts with 142. But that season he established the fact that he was a "clutch" hitter when five of his homers were game winners, three others tied games and 13 more put the Twins ahead.

In 1963, Killebrew repeated as league leader in home runs with 45 and led in slugging average with .555. After the season, he had surgery on his right knee but that didn't stop him from playing in 158 games in 1964 and smashing home runs at a faster pace than any player but Babe Ruth. He went on to establish a career high 49 homers which led the league in that department for the third consecutive year.

Killebrew's home run output in 1965 was only about half the previous year (25) and he failed to lead the league in any category. The next year, 1966, was somewhat better as he led the American League with 103 walks and had a .281 batting average with 39 homers. He tied Carl Yastrzemski for the league lead in homers (44) in 1967 and once again led in walks with 131. No longer a wild swinger, he had become one of the finest hitters in the game.

American League MVP in '69

But, the following year ('68) because of injuries, he was only able to play in 100 games and his average dipped to its lowest ever .210 and his home run output was only 17. Harmon made up for it in 1969, when he earned the American League's "Most Valuable Player" honor. He swatted 49 homers, drove in 140 runs and drew 145 walks and led the league in games played (162) and on-base percentage with .427. He was an awesome power hitter as attested by his '69 statistics, which showed that 47 percent of his hits were for extra bases and 30 percent of his hits were home runs. He finally got the national recognition he so richly deserved.

While hitting .270 in 1970, he homered 41 times in 527 at bats giving him a league leading home run percentage of 7.8. The following year ('71), he drove in 119 runs and drew 114 walks, both league leading marks. From 1972 through 1974, his career with the Twins was in decline. Hitting .231, .242, and .222 with a greatly diminished home run output, he was given his unconditional release by Minnesota at the end of the '74 season.

The Kansas City Royals signed him for 1975 in what proved to be his final major league season. He appeared in 106 games, batting only .199 and producing 14 homers.

Selected as A. L. All Star 11 Times

Bucky Harris predicted that Killebrew would be one of the greatest sluggers of all time after watching him for the first time. Harmon's lifetime statistics verify that Harris made an accurate prophecy. Willingly playing wherever the manager wanted him to play, he was an All-Star game selection eleven times at three different positions: first base, third base, and the outfield. While he remains high on the list of many lifetime achievements, his most noteworthy accomplishment at the time of his retirement is finishing third in home run percentage.

After retirement, Killebrew became a Twins broadcaster. He was elected to the Hall of Fame in 1984.

CHAPTER TWO

Nineteenth Century, 1871-1899

Introduction

Washington teams in the nineteenth century were by far the worst of any era, and the laughingstock of the nation. These teams and the pre-Clark Griffith teams of the early 1900s gave rise to the oft-quoted phrase associated with Washington baseball, "First in war, first in peace and last in the American League." In fact, they finished last or next to last over half of the time and were in the basement six times during the nineteenth century.

Club owners were more interested in gaining profits than fielding good teams, so there was considerable turnover of personnel as the better players were frequently sold to other teams.

While the first amateur baseball was played in 1859 on the Ellipse opposite the White House, it was not until 1871 that the first professional team, the "Washington Olympics," played in the National Association. Ironically, it was the only one of nineteen teams that century to have a winning record and finish in the first division. Teams in that era played in a little over 2,000 games, but were only able to win about 700, playing at a lowly .349 clip.

Before joining the National league in 1886, Washington teams were members of three different leagues and were known variously as the "Olympics," "Nationals" and "Statesmen." They adopted the name, "Senators" in 1887 while continuing in the National

League through the end of the century, except for 1890 when Washington did not field a team and in '91 when they were a franchise in the American Association.

Due to the frequent roster changes and the instability of the leagues, it was difficult to find players who could be classified as "belonging to the Senators." Far and away the most popular player was Win Mercer, a pitcher, who labored for the Senators for seven of his nine professional years. It may surprise you to learn that the "Grand Old Man of Baseball," Connie Mack began his professional career in 1886 with Washington and played four of his eleven seasons locally.

There were clear choices for two-thirds of the All-Star positions but it was difficult selecting the shortstop and two of the outfielders. I tended to give more weight to length of time and performance while with Washington rather than to career statistics. The team follows:

Nineteenth Century, 1871-1899 All-Star Team

Right-Handed Pitcher:	Win Mercer
Left-Handed Pitcher:	Frank Killen
Reliever:	Al Maul
Catcher:	Deacon McGuire
First Base:	Jumbo Cartwright
Second Base:	Gene DeMontreville
Third Base:	Bill Joyce
Shortstop:	George Shoch
Outfield:	Kip Selbach
Outfield:	Dummy Hoy
Outfield:	Paul Hines

It should be noted that some of the statistics for several of the nineteenth-century players are incomplete. These are denoted with an asterisk.

Selected All-Stars Dummy Hoy and George Shoch are among those pictured in this team photo of the 1888 Washington Senators.

A summary of team performance during the period follows:

Nineteenth Century, 1871-1899

Year	League	Nickname	Finish	#League Teams	#Games	Won	Lost	Pct.
1871	NA	Olympics	4	9	30	15	15	.500
1872	"	Olympics	8	10	9	2	7	.222
1873	"	Nationals	7	9	39	8	31	.205
1874	No Team							
1875	NA	Nationals	9	13	28	5	23	.179
1876	No Team							
1877	"							
1878	"							
1879	"							
1880	"							
1881	"							
1882	"							
1883	"							

Year	League	Nickname	Finish	#League Teams	#Games	Won	Lost	Pct.
1884	AA	Nationals	13	13	63	12	51	.190
1884	UA	Senators	7	12	112	47	65	.420
1885	No Team							
1886	NL	Statesmen	8	8	120	28	92	.233
1887	"	Senators	7	8	122	46	76	.377
1888	"	"	8	8	134	48	86	.358
1889	"	"	8	8	124	41	83	.331
1890	No Team							
1891	AA	Nationals	8	8	135	44	91	.326
1892	NL	Senators	10	12	151	58	93	.384
1893	"	"	12	12	129	40	89	.310
1894	"	"	11	12	132	45	87	.341
1895	"	"	10	12	128	43	85	.336
1896	"	"	10	12	131	58	73	.443
1897	"	"	7	12	132	61	71	.462
1898	"	"	11	12	152	51	101	.336
1899	"	"	11	12	152	54	98	.355
Totals - 18 Years, 19 Teams					2023	706	1317	
Averages -			9	10	106	37	69	.349

Key - NA= National Association AA= American Association
UA= Union Association NL= National League

Nineteenth Century, 1871-1899
Right-Handed Pitcher

George Barclay Mercer
(Win)

BR TR 5' 7" 140 lbs.
B. Jun. 20, 1874, Chester, WV.
D. Jan. 12, 1903, San Francisco, CA.

	Y	W	L	PCT	ERA	G	GS	CG	IP	H	BB	SO	SHO
Was.	7	103	129	.444	4.15	263	236	216	1946	2485	616	449	6
Life	9	131	164	.444	3.99	333	298	251	2470.1	3070	754	528	11

The handsome Win Mercer was a favorite of local fans.

Win Mercer was the darling of Washington fans because of his stellar performances with the Washington National League team before the turn of the century. In addition, he pitched one year for the fledgling American League Senators in 1901. A talented, all-around ballplayer, Mercer was not only a great pitcher but he could hit, run bases and play excellent defense in any position of the infield or outfield. He had the misfortune of being connected with tail-end teams for most of his career.

Win learned to play ball as a youngster in East Liverpool, Ohio, and he made his professional debut in 1893 with the Dover, New Hampshire team in the New England League. Gus Schmelz, manager of the Washington team saw Mercer pitch and signed him for the 1894 season. Schmelz was patient with Win as he lost his first 10 starts despite going the distance six times. The manager's patience paid off on May 29 when Win defeated Louisville 12-2 for his first major league victory. For the season, he posted a 17-23 record with a 3.76 ERA, third lowest in the league, earning the respect of everyone.

For six years, Mercer toiled for the dismal National League Washington teams. During the period, there was constant upheaval as Win played for four different managers and players were shuttled in and out. None of the original pitchers of 1894 were with the club in 1899 with the exception of Win. He was the team's single stabilizing force and the fans grew to love him and admire his exploits.

Mercer did not do well his second season, dropping off to a record of 13-23 while his ERA rose to 4.46. The 17 home runs allowed by Win were most in the league and his 23 losses were second highest. However, in 1896 and 1897 he had two 20 win seasons. He was 25-18 in '96 and 20-20 in '97, with earned run averages of 4.13 and a low 3.25. His 38 complete games in 1896 were third highest in the league. The latter year, Washington made one of its better records of the century when they finished in a sixth place tie with Brooklyn. Win was largely responsible for the feat, pitching in 46 games, hurling three shutouts and registering three saves, all tops in the league.

In "Beanball" Battle with Pittsburgh Hurler

On May 9, 1896, Mercer engaged in a beanball battle with notorious Pittsburgh Pirate pitcher Hank Hawley who had hit three consecutive Washington batters in an 11-run seventh inning, thus tying the mark he had set on July 4, 1894. In only nine seasons, Hawley set the still standing National League record of plunking 195 batters. Win retaliated by hitting three Pirate batsmen during the game. On August 31, Mercer shut out the Chicago White Sox Stockings 1-0 in 11 innings for the first Senators shutout since September 17, 1893, a period of almost three years.

Although he experienced losing seasons his final two years with Washington's National League teams, he became a workhorse for the team, appearing in 80 games in 1898 and an unbelievable 108 games in 1899, playing mostly in other positions. Over his career, Mercer recorded a nice .285 batting average in 561 games and 1761 at bats.

While with Washington, Mercer watched three noted ballplayers make their major league debuts. Roger Bresnahan, who later starred as a catcher, was brought up as a pitcher by Washington in August of 1897. He was 4-0 that year but strangely was sent to Toledo the following year. "Wild Bill" Donovan and future umpire Bill Dineen were also failures in their major league debuts with Washington.

Had 21 Victories for N.Y. Giants

Win's last year with Washington's National League team was 1899. In 1900, the club was squeezed out as the National League reduced the number of its teams to eight, so Win joined the New York Giants along with a rookie named Christy Matthewson. He appeared in 72 games and won 21 while losing 26 for the Giants.

In 1901, he returned to Washington with their new American League club, which had replaced the Kansas City franchise. His record was a disappointing 9-13 with an ERA of 4.56. When Mercer shut out the Chicago White Stockings 8-0 on August 21,

Chicago's shortstop Frank Shugart was so frustrated that he attacked the umpire with his fists and threw a ball at him. He was later banished from the league for the act.

Win left the club for the Detroit Tigers in 1902 with the prospect of managing the Tigers in 1903. In 1902, Mercer had one of his best years, posting his lowest ERA of 3.04 despite going 15-18. True to their promise, the Tigers appointed Mercer player/ manager for the 1903 season.

Unfortunately this was not to be. During the winter, he was a member of an American League team barnstorming in California and he served as its treasurer. The noted pitcher was a great lover of horse racing and he lost a considerable amount of money on the races while in Los Angeles. He became despondent and committed suicide in a San Francisco hotel by inhaling poison gas on January 12, 1903. He left a suicide note warning of the evils of women and gambling. He was later buried near his home in East Liverpool, Ohio.

Nineteenth Century, 1871-1899
Left-Handed Pitcher

Frank Bissell Killen

(Lefty)

BL TL 6' 1" 200 lbs.

B. Nov. 30, 1870, Pittsburgh, PA.

D. Dec. 3, 1939, Pittsburgh, PA.

	Y	W	L	PCT	ERA	G	GS	CG	IP	H	BB	SO	SHO
Was.	3	35	37	.486	3.49	79	70	62	600	615	215	193	2
Life	10	164	131	.556	3.78	321	300	253	2511.1	2730	822	725	13

Lefty Frank Killen poses for a profile shot in his Pittsburgh uniform.

Frank Killen was undoubtedly the best left-handed pitcher Washington had in the nineteenth century. Unfortunately, he only appeared in a Washington uniform for three seasons. He really belonged to the Pittsburgh Pirates, for whom he toiled for six seasons. A native of Pittsburgh, he got his first professional job with Manatee, Michigan of the Michigan State League. In his very first start, he whiffed 17 batters and facing the same team a few days later he pitched a shutout and struck out 15 men. He was quickly promoted to Grand Rapids, Michigan and then to Montreal of the International League. When that league folded, Minneapolis of the Western Association snapped him up. While there, he pitched a no-hitter against Sioux City.

Wins 29 Games for Nats in 1892

He began the 1891 season with them but in mid-season he made it to the big leagues with Milwaukee of the American Association. He posted a 7-4 won-lost record with two shutouts and his career best ERA of 1.68. When the American Association merged with the National League in 1892, Frank became a Washington Senator. This proved to be his best year with the Nats as he appeared in 60 games, winning 29 and losing 26 with an ERA of 3.31. He was a workhorse for them, pitching 459 and two-thirds innings and completing 46 games. He dominated the Senators' pitching staff and was the only pitcher to win more than eight games. After this fine season, Washington offered him only $1,800 for the following year. When Frank held out through spring training, he was traded to the Pittsburgh Pirates for Charley Farrell who was also a holdout.

Pitching for his hometown, Killen posted his best season in the majors in 1893 winning a league leading 36 games, while losing only 14. While other pitchers had a hard time adjusting to the new pitching distance (60 feet, six inches), Frank apparently had no problem. He had one of the best fastballs of the day and hitters had to be wary of his frequent "brush back" pitches. Killen appeared in only 28 games in 1894, winning 14 and losing 11.

His season was ended on July 26 when his arm was broken by a line drive off the bat of Cleveland's Patsy Tebeau.

He was slowly regaining his form in 1895, when he was spiked, covering home plate by New York's Parke Wilson on June 8. Thinking it was done intentionally, Frank punched Wilson and was thrown out of the game. Blood poisoning from the spike wound set in a few days later and he became seriously ill and was finished for that season, too. He had pitched in only 13 games with a 5-5 record. Pittsburgh fans called for his scalp but manager Connie Mack had faith in Frank's ability to stage a comeback, claiming that the Pirates lost the pennant in '95 because of Frank's injuries.

Snaps Keeler's 44–Game Hitting Streak

The left-hander did bounce back in 1896, leading the league in games (52), innings pitched (432 and one-third), complete games (44), shutouts (5) and wins (30). This record was attained despite losing his last five starts. On July 31, 1896, Frank disputed a call with umpire Daniel Lally and punched him in the face. He was arrested and charged with disorderly conduct. Obviously, Killen had a violent temper. He won his first five games in 1897; however, he finished the season with his first losing record at 17-23. He did lead the league, though, in the number of complete games (38). On May 17 Frank allowed only two hits as the Pirates defeated Amos Rusie and the New York Giants 3-2. A month later on June 19 Killen snapped Wee Willie Keeler's consecutive-game hitting streak at 44, while allowing Baltimore only five hits.

After playing in only 23 games in 1898, the Pirates released him outright on August 1, apparently to reduce their payroll, for Frank had just lost a heartbreaker a few weeks before on July 22nd to Amos Rusie and New York in 13 innings. Washington quickly picked up Killen where he finished the season winning six and losing nine in 17 games. In April 1899, Washington released Frank after appearing in only two games, losing both of them.

Boston signed him in May and although he posted a winning record (7-5 in 12 games), he was released in July. The following year (1900), Killen received a six-game trial with the Chicago Colts, five of the games pitching against his old team, the Pittsburgh Pirates. He was dropped in June and was unsuccessful in a one game trial with the Chicago White Sox the same year.

Umpire Killen Assaulted by St. Paul Fan

The next seasons were spent in the minors with Wheeling, Indianapolis and Atlanta. After that he had a brief fling as a minor league umpire. While umpiring a game in St. Paul, Minnesota, Killen made a decision which cost St. Paul the game. When he returned there to umpire another game, he was assaulted after the game and punched in the face several times. He retaliated with his spikes and cut his assailant badly. The league president ruled that he could not umpire in St. Paul again.

Killen is generally recognized as one of the best left-handers of the nineteenth century. If the Senators had been a little more liberal in their salary offer for 1893, it appears that they, instead of the Pirates, would have had the benefit of Killen's fine performances.

After leaving the game, Killen operated a saloon in Pittsburgh and invested in real estate. He died of an apparent heart attack in 1939 at the age of 69.

Nineteenth Century, 1871-1899
Relief Pitcher

Albert Joseph Maul

(Smiling Al)

BR TR 6' 175 lbs.

B. Oct. 9, 1865, Philadelphia, PA.

D. May 3, 1958, Philadelphia, PA.

	Y	W	L	PCT	ERA	G	GS	CG	IP	H	BB	SO	SHO	SV
Was.	5	38	44	.463	4.54	91	85	71	699.1	845	275	158	1	0
Life	15	84	80	.512	4.43	188	168	143	1434.2	1662	518	346	4	1

"Smiling Al" Maul gripping a baseball while with the Pittsburgh Pirates.

It may be a stretch to pick Al Maul as the nineteenth-century relief pitcher since he only served in relief about 10% of the time; however, he was the only other decent pitcher besides Win Mercer and Frank Killen who labored on the mound for the hapless nineteenth-century Senators. His winning percentage was .512 and he stuck around the majors for 15 years and was one of the outstanding hurlers of the era.

The right-hander debuted in the big leagues in 1884 at 18 years of age, appearing in only one game for the Philadelphia Keystones of the Union Association. Although he lost the game, he hurled a complete game and struck out seven while walking only one.

He was back in the minors in 1885 with Binghamton of the New York State League. He was promoted to Rochester of the International League during the '86 season and the following year (1887) he played for Nashville of the Southern Association, but during the season he was brought up by the Philadelphia Phillies of the National League. His pitching prowess had first come to the attention of major league officials when he was with Nashville and he was eventually bought by the Phillies for $2,500, thought to be the highest price ever paid for a minor leaguer up to that time. In seven games, he won four and lost two and showed some promise at the plate when he hit for a .304 average.

Maul caught on with the Pittsburgh Pirates in 1888 but was used sparingly in only three games, as he was unable to produce a win while losing two. The following year (1889) was more of the same when he appeared in only six games but he did notch one victory while suffering four defeats.

Completes 26 of 30 Games for Pittsburgh

Al jumped to the Pittsburgh club of the Players League in 1890 and had one of his finest seasons. He pitched in 30 games winning 16 and losing 12, completing 26 of them and posting two shutouts. He only had four of them in his entire career. Back with the Pirates again in 1891, he was used only sparingly in eight games despite an ERA of 2.31 but his record was just 1-2. He was sent back to the minors the next year (1892) with Buffalo of the Eastern League.

Washington plucked him from the minors in 1893 and Al's fortunes took a turn for the better. In his first year with the Senators, he pitched in more innings (297) and more games (37) than at any time during his career. With the last place team he managed to win 12 games while losing 21. He was a workhorse again in 1894, pitching in over 200 innings and posting an 11-15 record with a team that finished next to last.

Has Best Year for Nats in '95

The following year (1895) proved to be his best with the Nats. He led the league with an ERA of 2.45 while winning 10 and losing five in 16 games. He was not used much in 1896 but he again chalked up a winning percentage (.714) while notching a 5-2 record. He played in only one game (which he lost) in 1897 before being sent to Baltimore of the National League. While with the Orioles the remainder of the season, he had no record in two appearances.

Wins 20 Games for Orioles

Al wasn't through yet, however. In 1898 Baltimore used him liberally and he had one of his best seasons, winning 20 games while losing only seven, registering the second best won-lost percentage in the league (.741). He pitched in 28 games and completed 26 of them; in the 239 and two-thirds innings that he hurled, he recorded a nifty 2.10 ERA, also second lowest in the league.

Unfortunately that proved to be his last significant stint in the majors. With Brooklyn in 1899, he was 2-0 in four games and when he returned to the Phillies in 1900, he was 2-3 in five games. His final year was spent with the New York Giants in 1901 and when he failed to win a game in three tries, he returned to his hometown, Philadelphia and scouted for the Philadelphia Athletics and worked in the ticket department of both Philadelphia teams. He died on May 3, 1958 at the age of 92.

Nineteenth Century, 1871-1899
Catcher

James Thomas McGuire

(Deacon)

BR TR 6' 1" 185 lbs.
B. Nov. 18, 1863, Youngstown, OH.
D. Oct. 31, 1936, Duck Lake, MI.

	Y	G	AB	R	H	2B	3B	HR	RBI	BB	SO	SB	BA	SA
Was.	9	901	3327	481	990	161	45	32	502	294	145	81	.298	.402
Life	26	1781	6290	770	1748	300	79	45	840*	515	214*	117	.278	.372

Durable catcher Deacon McGuire pictured with a mustache and slicked down hair.

They said that Deacon McGuire could "catch anything" and he had the gnarled and broken fingers to prove it. Every finger on each hand was broken at least once. When he broke into professional ball in 1884, catchers stood about six feet behind the batters, in order to catch foul tips or short pops on the fly or on one hop. The rules then considered these to be "outs." Small, fingered gloves were used instead of the mitts of today, making it awfully difficult on the hands. McGuire claimed that pitcher Hank O'Day had the most difficult fastball to handle, so he began using beef steaks in his glove for padding whenever he was called upon to catch O'Day.

Catches Every Senator Game in 1895

Deacon established several records for catchers before retiring at the close of the 1912 season. He was the only ballplayer to play in the majors for 26 seasons until Nolan Ryan duplicated the feat 80 years later upon retiring in 1991. But the unbelievable record, never to be broken, was established when he caught every game for the Washington Senators in 1895, a total of 132 games. Deacon was behind the plate for more games (1611) than any catcher in major league history.

McGuire's family moved to Albion, Michigan while he was a teenager and he built a considerable reputation as a young catcher with powerful hands. He became a professional with the Terre Haute Indians minor league team in 1883 and hit the majors a year later (1884) with Toledo of the American Association, batting a pitiful .185 in 45 games. This was not indicative of the lifetime mark of .278 he would compile over 26 seasons. McGuire acquired his nickname by virtue of the fact that he did not smoke, drink, cuss or chew, unlike many of his day. He was loath to question an umpire's call and was never fined or ejected from a game.

The following year he was acquired by Detroit of the National League and, in limited duty he did not hit well, only .190. While there, "Wild Bill" Donovan uncorked a wild pitch that caught Deacon on the tip of a finger on his bare hand and stripped the flesh from the bone. The umpire took one look at it and fainted dead away. Before the end of the week, he was back in action behind the plate again.

Tops .300 Four Straight Years

Sold to the Philadelphia Phillies of the National League for the 1886 season, McGuire hit only .198 in 50 games. On August 28 he returned to action after suffering a broken finger and committed eight passed balls. With the Phillies again in 1887, he finally found his batting eye and hit .307.

He played for three teams during the 1888 season: Cleveland, Detroit, and Philadelphia, catching in 41 games in all and hitting .259. Back to the minors in 1889 with Toronto and then Rochester of the American Association acquired him in 1890, where he hit .299 in 87 games. This set the stage for his acquisition by the Washington Nationals in 1891 and he played with them through his peak years, a total of eight.

In '91, he led all catchers with 130 assists. He topped the .300 mark four consecutive seasons (1894-1897) while with the Nats but never was able to attain that goal again for a full season. From 1894-1898, he batted an overall .314 with 677 hits, 108 doubles, 27 triples, 23 home runs and 355 RBI, with 58 stolen bases. McGuire led catchers in putouts (408) and assists (179) in 1895, and repeated as leader in putouts (349) in '96. In a game against St. Louis on July 13, 1896, Deacon collected five hits in the Nats' 14-1 victory.

He took over the Senators as player-manager on June 24, 1898 but was replaced by Arthur Irwin the same year after compiling a 21-47 record. Two other managerial opportunities ended in failure. He was below .500 with Boston of the American League in 1907 and '08 before being fired. In 1909, he succeeded Napoleon Lajoie at Cleveland but he was replaced early in the 1911 season because of a losing record. The 1910 season with the Indians was his only complete season as a manager and he never managed a winning season, compiling a 208-289 record and a winning percentage of .419.

Picked Off 3 Base Runners on 3 Straight Pitches

After playing in 59 games in 1899, he was sent to Brooklyn where he caught 46 games. Deacon remained with Brooklyn in 1900 and 1901 posting nice averages of .286 and .296 in a total of 156 games. In 1900, he picked off three base runners on three consecutive pitches. The Dodgers were playing the Pirates when he accomplished the feat. With none out, he picked the great Pirate hurler, Rube Waddell, off second base. On the next pitch, McGuire caught the runner off third. Then, the runner on first base attempted to steal second and was thrown out.

He jumped to Detroit for the 1902 season and when Brooklyn sued for his return a federal judge ruled that Brooklyn had no claim on him. He spent two seasons with the Tigers ('02 and '03), appearing in 145 games with his batting averages dropping sharply to .227 and .250. His last significant years were spent with New York of the American League from 1904-1907.

In 1905, McGuire and his New York teammates found themselves in a tight race for the American League championship. In a virtual tie with one game remaining, Jack Chesbro, one of the first great spitballers, was on the mound for New York with Deacon behind the plate. Late in the game the score was tied with two down and a Boston runner on third. Suddenly Chesbro uncorked a wild pitch, so wild that it hit way up on the grandstand and McGuire had no chance of stopping it. The championship went down the drain with that pitch.

While managing Boston and Cleveland, Deacon made a few plate appearances in 1907, 1908 and 1910 as a pinch hitter. At a time when pinch hitters were rarely used, he was a good one with a career 14 for 41.

Garners Last Big-League Hit at Age 49

McGuire played his last big league game in 1912, six years after he quit playing regularly. When Ty Cobb of Detroit was thrown out of a game in Philadelphia for fighting with a fan, the Tigers refused to play the next day because they believed that Cobb had been "baited." Faced with a $5,000 fine for not fielding a team, club owner Frank Navin was forced to sign some local amateurs. As a coach under manager Hughie Jennings, McGuire was pressed into service also to protect the Tiger franchise. The team lost 24-2 but Deacon was able to garner a hit at nearly age 50.

He scouted for the Tigers for the next few years and uncovered Burleigh Grimes, Bobby Veach and George Burns among others. He then moved to a quiet farm in Michigan overlooking Duck Lake and raised chickens and did a lot of fishing. He came out of retirement briefly in 1926 to coach the Albion College baseball team.

McGuire was in ill health the last five years of his life, succumbing to a stroke and pneumonia at his farm on October 31, 1936, a few days short of his 73rd birthday. Although the Baseball Encyclopedia lists the place of his death as Albion, Michigan, he died at nearby Duck Lake.

Nineteenth Century, 1871-1899
First Base

Edward Charles Cartwright
(Jumbo)

BR TR 5' 10" 220 lbs.
B. Oct. 6, 1859, Johnstown, PA.
D. Sept. 3, 1933, St. Petersburg, FL.

	Y	G	AB	R	H	2B	3B	HR	RBI	BB	SO	SB	BA	SA
Was.	4	420	1620	278	472	88	40	16	273	173	128*	118	.291	.425
Life	5	495	1902	348	562	100	44	24	33	202	128*	144	.295	.432

Washington's Jumbo Cartwright was one of 12 National League team captains in 1895.

Although Ed Cartwright's eight brothers had attended Pennsylvania State College, he decided on Mount Union College in Ohio. After two years, he began playing professional baseball with the Youngstown, Ohio club of the newly formed American Association in 1882. He continued playing for them in '83 and '84 and then headed south.

He was picked up by the Mobile, Alabama club in 1886 and then went under contract to New Orleans in 1887. Jumbo, a nickname acquired because of his portly frame, broke in as a catcher. He was one of the first catchers to step up under the batter to make the catch without the ball bouncing. Before reaching the major leagues, he was switched to first base.

Terrific Long Ball Hitter

Ed was a terrific long ball hitter. It is said that, while in the minors, he twice hit four home runs in a game. A newspaper article claimed that he once hit a ball 590 feet on a fly while playing with New Orleans.

Cartwright drifted to Missouri in 1888 and 1889 and played for, first, the Kansas City Blues and then for the St. Joseph club. From there, he went to Canada and was signed by the Hamilton, Ontario team of the International League in 1890. During the season the league folded and both Rochester and St. Louis of the major league American Association rushed to sign him. The ensuing argument as to who had the rights to Cartwright, escalated to the president of the league before it was settled.

Rochester claimed that they had bought Cartwright's release from Hamilton for $400. Ed claimed that when he was told that Rochester was interested in him, he wired their management with his terms. Jumbo then received a telegram from them, indicating they could not accept his terms. When the Hamilton club failed to pay Ed $132 in back salary, he became a free agent and signed with St. Louis. The president of the league affirmed his position.

He joined the St. Louis team on July 7, 1890 and immediately became a hit with the fans. In 75 games for the remainder of the season, he batted an even .300, drove in 60 runs and slugged eight homers, second in the league despite playing only a half season. Although he had aroused the flagging spirits of St. Louis fans, the city lost his services in 1891 as Jumbo was dropped from the big leagues.

Amazing Speed for Big Man

The Washington Nationals signed him for the 1894 season and Jumbo picked up where he had left off. He hit .294 in a league leading 132 games and drove in 106 runs. The next season (1895) was his best ever as he raised his average to .331 in 122 games and he showed amazing speed for a big man by stealing 50 bases. Jumbo led all first basemen in the league with 95 assists.

Ed led the league again in 1896 by playing in 133 games, a career high. But his hitting began to decline some when his average dropped to .277. His final year in the major leagues was 1897, when he played in only 33 games and hit a lowly .234 with no triples or home runs in 124 at bats. I suppose that age was the major factor in ending his big league career after only five seasons. He was almost 38 years of age when he left the game.

Jumbo died in St. Petersburg, Florida at the age of 73. He was buried in the Cartwright family plot in Youngstown, Ohio.

Nineteenth Century, 1871-1899
Second Base

Eugene Napoleon DeMontreville

(Gene)

BR TR 5' 8" 165 lbs.

B. Mar. 26, 1874, St. Paul, MN.

D. Feb. 18, 1935, Memphis, TN.

	Y	G	AB	R	H	2B	3B	HR	RBI	BB	SO	SB	BA	SA
Was.	4	290	1189	193	398	54	16	11	182	53	31*	63	.335	.435
Life	11	922	3615	537	1096	130	35	17	497	174	35*	228	.303	.373

Infielder Gene DeMontreville's portrait was taken while he was with the Baltimore club in 1899.

Although his name conjures up thoughts of French royalty, Gene DeMontreville was a professional baseball player and a good one. He had great speed and stole 228 bases during his 11 years in the majors. He was particularly adept at executing the delayed steal. In box scores he was generally known as Gene Demont because of space limitations of the typesetters.

Grew Up in Washington

Although a native of St. Paul, Minnesota, DeMontreville moved to Washington, D.C., while young. He began his long professional career with Binghamton of the Eastern League in 1894. He also played for Buffalo of the same league during 1894 and broke into the majors at the end of the season with the Pittsburgh Pirates of the National League. He went 2 for 8 in two games played there.

It was back to the Eastern League the next year with Toronto where he hit .315 and caught the eye of the Washington Nationals management. They bought his contract and brought him up for 12 games near the end of the 1895 season. His .217 batting average was not indicative of what was to come.

Good Hitter but Had Difficulty in the Field

The second baseman/shortstop began his career mainly at shortstop but before his career ended he had played more at the keystone sack. In his first two seasons with Washington, Gene proved to be an accomplished hitter, batting .343 in 1896 and .341 in 1897 and they proved to be the best averages of his career. Unfortunately, Gene had a rough time in the field in the early years, leading the league in 1896 with 97 errors. He did, however, lead the league in number of games played at short (133) and in number of assists (479). Playing in the same number of games in '97, he led the league again with a somewhat reduced number of errors (78), but he also led the league with 566 at bats.

The following year he was traded to the Baltimore Orioles of the National League along with pitcher Jim McJames and first baseman Dan McMann for catcher Jack Doyle, second baseman Heinie Reitz and pitcher Doc Amole. He was shifted to second base where he seemed to be much more comfortable and where he was averaging two errors every three games at shortstop, at the new position he was able to cut his error rate in half. Gene had another fine season with the Orioles in '98, batting .328 in 151 games. He was to pass the .300 mark only one more time in his career. He also had a career high 49 stolen bases that year, third in the league.

Despite his outstanding season, DeMontreville was traded in '99 to the Chicago Cubs for Bill Dahlen. Recognizing their mistake, the Birds reacquired him before the end of the season. Playing in 82 games for the Cubs and 60 for Baltimore, Gene hit .280 for the season. The Orioles were in serious financial trouble so their ballplayers were transferred to the Brooklyn Dodgers at the end of the season. Gene was in 69 games for the Dodgers in 1900 and was used at five different positions. His batting took a severe downturn and he ended with a .244 average.

Best Season with Boston, NL in 1901

Next, he was sent to Boston of the National League for the 1901 season and there he regained his batting stroke and had probably his best season. Playing in 140 games (120 at second base and 20 at third) Gene batted .300 with 72 RBI. He put together a 23-game hitting streak, and committed only 43 errors to lead the league in fielding percentage at .954. In 140 games in 1902, his average dropped to .260 and this proved to be his last season as a regular.

He was brought back to Washington in 1903 to play for their American League team but he played in only 12 games. His last year in the majors was spent with the St. Louis Browns in 1904 and after just nine plate appearances in four games he was given his release and sent to the minors with Atlanta.

From 1905 through 1910, he continued playing and managing in the minors with Toledo, Birmingham and New Orleans. He hung up his spikes at the age of 36. His lifetime major league marks are impressive, hitting .306 in 922 games with 130 doubles, 35 triples and 17 home runs. His playing days were shortened because of ill health.

On February 18, 1935, while running to investigate a minor fire at the fairgrounds in Memphis, Tennessee, where he was the concession manager, he collapsed and died of an apparent heart attack at age 61.

Nineteenth Century, 1871-1899
Third Base

William Michael Joyce

(Scrappy Bill)

BL TR 5' 11" 185 lbs.

B. Sept. 21, 1865, St. Louis, MO.

D. May 8, 1941, St. Louis, MO.

	Y	G	AB	R	H	2B	3B	HR	RBI	BB	SO	SB	BA	SA
Was.	3	306	1139	298	371	66	37	42	235	250	109	82	.326	.559
Life	8	904	3304	820	970	152	106	70	607	718	282*	264	.294	.461

Bill Joyce, despite the fact he posed in his "Sunday best," certainly looks like the intimidator he was purported to be.

In the era of nineteenth-century baseball, the name of the game was to intimidate opponents and one of the prominent "intimidators" was Scrappy Bill Joyce. With his blue-tipped bat and ready fists, most pitchers were wary of "dusting him off." A native of St. Louis, Joyce played with the "Standards," a semi-pro team in the town in 1885 and 1886.

He entered organized ball with Leavenworth of the Western League in 1887. Then signed by Kansas City in 1888, he finished the season with Fort Worth and New Orleans of the Texas League. With Houston in 1889, he was sold in mid-season to Toledo. Bill hit a total of 23 home runs for the two teams (twice slugging three in a game), an unprecedented feat. He then entered the big leagues when he was sold to Brooklyn of the Players League in 1890 where he hit only .252 in 133 games (the most games for a third baseman) but led the league with 123 bases on balls, 43 stolen bases and 121 runs scored.

Breaks Leg in 2 Consecutive Seasons

The third baseman was with the pennant-winning Boston team of the American Association in 1891 but he broke a leg on July 2 and was finished for the season. At the time, he was hitting .309. When the American Association returned to the National League in 1892, Joyce joined the Brooklyn team of the National League. As luck would have it, he broke his leg again almost a year to the day (July 3) and he suffered his worst year in the majors, hitting .245 in 97 games. After the 1892 season, he was traded to Washington who wanted to cut his salary from $2,800 to $1,800 in accordance with league-wide reductions of player salaries. So Joyce decided to sit out the entire season.

Hits .355 for Washington in '94

He did join Washington in 1894 and put together the best year of his career. In 99 games he hit .355 with 14 doubles, 17 triples, 17 home runs and a fabulous slugging average of .648, third in the league. His 17 homers were only one shy of the league lead. He slammed three of them in a single game on August 20, 1894.

Joyce followed with another fine year in '95, averaging .312, falling one shy of the league lead again with 17 home runs and leading the league by drawing 96 walks. On the minus side, however, he did lead the league in number of errors by third basemen with 77.

During the 1896 season, Washington traded Joyce to the New York Giants where he became their playing/manager on August 8 when then manager Arthur Irwin was given a "vacation" by New York. In 87 games with the Nationals and 49 with the Giants, he combined to lead the league with 13 homers and hit .333. On May 30, 1896, he hit for the cycle, garnering a single, double, triple and a home run. He led the league again in number of errors (43).

Record–Tying Four Triples in One Game

The Giants finished strong under Joyce, winning 26 out of 40 games. Bill almost piloted New York to the pennant in 1897, but the team faltered in the last week of the season, finishing third with an 83-48 record. Joyce helped his cause: batting .306, scoring 110 runs in 110 games. On May 18, 1897, Joyce had a record tying four triples in one game. It is the last time that the feat has been accomplished.

Bill continued as manager through mid-1898 when he was replaced by Cap Anson, who lasted only 22 games until Joyce returned to the job for the remainder of the season. Anson had been criticized for being unable "to handle men in the up-to-date style." Joyce's average dipped to .258 and his playing and managing days were over. He did, however, manage to slug 10 home runs, score and drive in 91 runs and steal 34 bases in his final year.

Nearly Precipitated a Riot

In Joyce's first game with Washington back in 1894, he had a run-in with umpire Tim Hurst and after two called strikes, Bill threw his bat at the umpire on the next pitch. The umpire threw it right back at Joyce and hit him in the shins. Bill was fined $35 the next day. Also, in a Washington-Baltimore game, big Dan Brouthers smashed a triple and when he reached third base Joyce pushed him off the bag and tagged him out. A near riot ensued.

On May 30, 1894, Scrappy Bill made a triple and a home run in the same inning, and on August 20 of the same year, he smashed three homers and a single in the same game.

Joyce played only eight years in the majors but he left an indelible mark on the game. He was aggressive, fearless and a prolific batsman. His fielding was not polished but he got the job done. He found ways to reach home plate as attested by the fact that he scored almost as many runs (820) as hits (970).

Joyce is credited with helping to coin the term "Texas Leaguer." Bill and another player, Arthur Sunday, reported to Toledo from the Houston team of the Texas League. The fans anticipated some long ball swatting from the two, but when each garnered bloop singles they were dubbed "Texas Leaguers."

After retiring from active play, Joyce scouted for many years for the St. Louis Browns. He died in St. Louis at the age of 75.

Nineteenth Century, 1871-1899
Shortstop

George Quintas Shoch

BR TR 5' 6" 158 lbs.

B. Jan. 6, 1859, Philadelphia, PA.

D. Sept. 30, 1937, Philadelphia, PA.

	Y	G	AB	R	H	2B	3B	HR	RBI	BB	SO	SB	BA	SA
Was.	4	216	785	116	175	19	5	4	71	68	56	63	.223	.275
Life	11	706	2536	414	671	89	28	10	323	298	115*	138	.265	.334

Shortstop George Shoch is ready to field the baseball bare handed.

George Shoch is selected for the nineteenth-century All-Star team by default. Infielders, especially, were very transient members of the Washington organization during that period. Although Shoch played mainly in the outfield while with the Nationals, he did play 60 games at shortstop during the four seasons he was with them. George, however, was used more in the infield than outfield when you consider his entire major league career.

First–Year Captain of Washington Team

Shoch made his first appearance as a professional baseball player with Hartford in 1885 and after completing the season, he was re-signed for 1886. His first major league job was in a Washington uniform in the same year, when he was brought up late in the season on September 10. Although he played in only 26 games and had less than 100 trips to the plate, he was an immediate hit with players and fans alike. He showed that he could handle the bat, hitting .295 and his fielding skills, as well, demonstrated that he had been well coached and was a good all-around player. He was promptly named captain of the team.

In 1887, he played in 70 games, mostly in the outfield, and though his average dropped precipitously to .239, he demonstrated good base-running skills with 29 stolen bases, a career high. The following year (1888) was more of the same when in 90 games his average took a nosedive to .183, but he was able to pilfer 23 bases. This time he was used most of the time at shortstop, where he played in 52 games with 168 assists 84 putouts and made an error about every two games. The infields were not in any way similar to the manicured ones of today, and infielders had to contend with pebbles, rocks and uneven surfaces.

Shoch's last year with Washington was in '89, when he played only 30 games but he was able to bring his average back up to .239. He was out of the major leagues in 1890 but when he returned to the big time in 1891 with Milwaukee of the American Association, better days were ahead for him. In 34 games that year, mainly at shortstop, he achieved his highest batting average thus far, .315 and his highest slugging average, .409.

Has Best Years with Dodgers

George was picked up by Baltimore in '92 and used mostly at shortstop again. His average fell to a decent .276 but he experienced his best year fielding-wise at shortstop, with 95 putouts, 197 assists, and 17 double plays. The Orioles then sent him off to his last major league club, Brooklyn of the National League. With the Dodgers he had his best years. Eighteen ninety-three saw him establish many career highs including most games (94), most at bats (327), most runs (53) most hits (86), most doubles (17), most RBI (54) and most walks (48). He followed that up the next year (1894) with his best batting average, a nice .322 in 64 games.

Shoch's average dropped to .259 in 61 games in 1895 but he did hit a career high seven triples. He regained his batting eye the next year (1896) and hit .292 in 76 games. His final year (1897), he played in 85 games and batted .278.

In George's 11 years in the big time, he proved to be a valuable utility man, especially in later years. He ended up playing in 298 games in the outfield, 179 at short, 157 at second base and 73 at third. He even pitched in one game for Washington in 1888, going three innings and allowing no runs, just two hits and one walk. One wonders why he was not given another chance on the mound.

He lived to the age of 78.

Nineteenth Century, 1871-1899
Outfield

Albert Karl Selbach
(Kip)

BR TR 5' 7" 190 lbs.
B. Mar. 24, 1872, Columbus, OH.
D. Feb. 17, 1956, Columbus, OH.

	Y	G	AB	R	H	2B	3B	HR	RBI	BB	SO	SB	BA	SA
Was.	7	797	3087	568	919	143	95	29	408	405	76*	201	.298	.434
Life	13	1610	6158	1064	1803	299	149	44	779	783	76*	334	.293	.411

Outfielder Al Selbach is pictured while with the Washington American League club at the beginning of the twentieth century.

Kip Selbach began playing ball as a catcher with the Defiance and Columbus Reds teams on the sandlots of Columbus. He began his professional career, catching for the Chattanooga Lookouts club in 1893. When manager Gus Schmelz was named manager of the Washington Nationals for 1894, he took Kip along. The Nats had Deacon McGuire and other good catchers, so Selbach converted to the outfield. Despite his stout build, he covered a lot of ground, often among the leaders in putouts by outfielders. He was an excellent batter and gave Washington five .300 seasons. He usually was leadoff man or batted second in the lineup.

Leads League in Triples

In 1894, his average was .306 for 97 games. He followed that the next year with .322, leading the league with 22 triples and making 21 assists from the outfield in 129 games. He had a very strong arm. Batting .304 in 127 games in 1896, he had a career high 100 runs batted in and in '97 he drew 80 walks and hit .313. On May 20 Selbach stole five bases against the Chicago Colts. In 1898, his final year with Washington, his average was .303 and he made 24 outfield assists.

Another lowly team, Cincinnati, purchased Selbach for $5,000 for the 1899 season. He dropped below .300 for the first time but still was close with a .296 batting average and he made a career high 29 outfield assists. On June 11, in a game against Cleveland, pitcher Frank Bates walked Selbach five times in succession. The Cincinnati owner was also part owner of the New York Giants and he transferred many players, including Kip, to New York for the 1900 season. According to Kip, this was his finest season, hitting .337 and finishing eighth in the race for the batting title. He also had career highs in hits (176), doubles (29), on-base percentage (.425) and slugging average (.461). He led the league in the number of games played (141) and in double plays participated in by outfielders.

He fell off the next year (1901) to .289 but in a game against his former team, Cincinnati, Kip collected six hits in seven trips to the plate. In 1902, John McGraw gave Selbach a $4,000 contract to jump to Baltimore of the new American League. When McGraw left for the New York Giants during the season and took many of his players with him, Kip refused to go. He hit .320 but Baltimore finished last and the franchise folded so Selbach was assigned to Washington for the 1903 season.

Running Catch Clinches Flag for Boston

At the age of 31 his hitting was on the decline and he never reached the .300 level again, batting .251 in 140 games that year. Kip finally got the opportunity to play with a good team when he was traded to Boston at season's end. Although his hitting had fallen off, Selbach was still able to help his team to the 1904 American League pennant. He later said that the highlight of his career was a knee-high catch of a sinking line drive for the last out, as Boston clinched the American League flag with that victory. Unfortunately, the New York Giants refused to play the Boston Pilgrims that year, so Selbach lost his chance to appear in World Series play.

In 1905, Selbach played in 121 games and hit .246. Boston dropped to last place in 1906 and Kip sustained an injury, which shortened his major league career. Playing against Cleveland, Selbach attempted to steal second and the throw from the catcher was high, causing Napoleon Lajoie who was covering the base to leap very high. Coming down, his heel spike made a nine-inch rip in Kip's groin. After he recovered from the injury, he found that his legs had lost their "zip." He appeared in only 60 games and hit .211.

Selbach played and managed in the minor leagues with Providence and Harrisburg from 1906-1910 after his big-league career was over.

Professional Bowler

For years Selbach toured in the off season as captain of a bowling team and in 1903 he and another member won the national ABC doubles title with a three game score of 1227. In 1908, his Columbus team won the national team championship. In later years, he found that the bowling underhand motion had an adverse effect on his shoulder muscles and may have accelerated the decline in his hitting. He warned other players about the dangers of bowling.

In 1911, he returned to Columbus and operated a bowling alley. Several years before his death, he sold it and relaxed to enjoy his diamond memories. He died at the age of 83.

Suspended by League President

At one time, early in the twentieth century, he was voted an outfield position in an all-time Washington selection. Selbach usually hit around .300, stole 20 bases or more nine times (with a career total of 334) and was solid defensively. Nevertheless he was sometimes the target of critics who blamed him for his teams' shortcomings. When he made three errors in one inning during a 1904 game, American League President Ban Johnson suspended him for a time "for indifferent play."

Nineteenth Century, 1871-1899
Outfield

William Ellsworth Hoy
(Dummy)

BL TR 5' 6" 160 lbs.

B. May 23, 1862, Houckstown, OH.

D. Dec. 15, 1961, Cincinnati, OH.

	Y	G	AB	R	H	2B	3B	HR	RBI	BB	SO	SB	BA	SA
Was.	4	545	2167	389	581	52	28	5	188	296	110	225	.268	.325
Life	14	1796	7112	1426	2044	248	121	40	726	1004	210*	594	.287	.373

In his rookie 1888 season with Washington, Dummy Hoy poses with bat in hand.

Dummy Hoy was the first of only a few deaf-mutes to break into the big leagues. In early childhood, he was stricken with either spinal meningitis or scarlet fever to cause the disability. He had the greatest career of any seriously handicapped player in the majors. Hoy was one of 29 players to play in four major leagues.

"Dummy" seems like a cruel name to have, but people at that time with the handicap were often tagged with it. Hoy, for some reason liked it and told the press to use it. Hoy was very bright and it seems that he completed his elementary and high school studies at the Ohio School for the Deaf in just six years and graduated as class valedictorian.

Keen Eye at the Plate

He ran a cobbler shop in his hometown after graduation but had time in the summer to play a lot of baseball. He was a smart player, very fast, played a shallow centerfield, and possessed a strong arm. Of course, he had some difficulty playing the outfield because he couldn't hear the other players calling for the ball; however, they learned to give way on fly balls when they heard Hoy making a "squeaking sound." Although he made 394 errors in his major league career, he had 3,958 putouts and 273 assists. The fans showed their appreciation for Hoy's skills in the field, at the plate, or on the bases by standing and waving their arms vigorously.

Hoy played for seven major league teams during his 14-year career and compiled a lifetime batting average of .287 (three times he hit over .300), accumulated over 2,000 base hits, scored 1,400 runs, hit 40 homers (mostly inside the park) and made almost 250 doubles. The statistic that jumps out is his over 1,000 bases on balls. His keen eye enabled him to register four seasons with an on-base average exceeding .400.

Leads League in Stolen Bases

Hoy is credited with 594 stolen bases. This figure is somewhat inflated, since runners were credited before 1898 with a stolen base whenever they took an extra base, for example going from first base to third on a single. Nevertheless, Dummy was a speedy and clever base runner, stealing 30 or more bases in his first 12 major league seasons.

Hoy gained his first pro contract with Oshkosh in 1886 after the Milwaukee Brewers failed to sign him with a ridiculously low offer. The first year he did not do well, and hit only .219 when pitchers "quick pitched" him while he turned to the umpire to see what the previous call was. The following year, he had his third base coach flash the calls to him and he hit .367 and led the team to the league championship.

His first big league club was Washington in the National League for the 1888 and '89 seasons. He was ridiculed at first by teammates because of his handicap, but they soon grew to respect him because of his playing ability. He hit .274 each year and in '88 led the league in stolen bases with 82 and set National League rookie records for games, at bats, hits, singles and walks as well. On June 19, 1889, he experienced one of the highlights of his career when he threw out three base runners at the plate during the game. All tried to score from second on a single. Only two other ballplayers have equalled the feat.

Hoy and Connie Mack left Washington in 1890, when the team lost their National League franchise, and moved to Buffalo of the new Players League. Dummy hit .298 there but the new league disintegrated after just one year so it was on to St. Louis of the American Association in 1891. He led the league with 119 walks and led all outfielders in games played at 141. When the National League was expanded in 1892, Dummy returned to Washington for two seasons, first hitting .280 and then slumping to .245 in 1893.

In his home state with Cincinnati from 1894-1897, Hoy enjoyed his finest years, averaging .292 for the period. In 1897, he led the league in putouts and total chances per game. He transferred to a weak Louisville team in 1898 and 1899, where he put together his only two .300 seasons, hitting .304 in '98 and .306 in '99. When the National League reduced the number of teams in 1900 and Louisville lost its franchise, Dummy signed on to play for the Chicago White Sox who would be awarded a franchise in 1901 in the newly formed American League.

Hit First Ever American League Grand Slam

In 1900, he played in the minors with the White Sox and won the Triple Crown in fielding with a .977 percentage, 337 putouts and 45 assists in 137 games. With Clark Griffith managing the new American League entry in 1901, Hoy hit .294, led the league in drawing bases on balls (86) and hit the first ever American League grand slam on May 1, 1901.

Hoy wound up his big league career back home in Cincinnati in 1902 but the year was not a pleasant one. It was a turbulent year for the franchise and three managers were used. Hoy still batted .290 and on May 26, 1902 two deaf-mutes opposed each other. On the mound for the New York Giants was Luther "Dummy" Taylor who had a nine-year major league career. As Hoy walked to the plate to bat for the first time, he signed to Taylor "Glad to see you." He later rapped out two hits and scored a run in a losing cause. Dummy wound up his major league career at the end of the 1902 season, but it is not clear whether Cincinnati released him or whether he just quit.

That was not the end of his professional career, however, since he signed on with Los Angeles of the Pacific Coast League and put up some impressive numbers for a 42-year-old. In 211 games in 1903, he hit .261, collected 210 hits, stole 46 bases and played a major role in their drive to the championship. All players were promised a genuine "Panama hat" by the owner if they could win 15 straight games. They put together a string of 16 victories and Dummy proudly wore his hat often in retirement.

May Have Been Responsible for Unique Hand Signals

Hoy's career has stirred two controversies, which still are active today. First, umpire Bill Klem is credited by baseball authorities for creating, in 1905, the hand signals for designating "out" and "safe" used by umpires today. There seems to be ample evidence that the signals were in wide use considerably earlier in association with Dummy Hoy's play and many purists are trying to see that he gets official credit.

Second, there are repeated protests at Hall of Fame induction ceremonies in Cooperstown concerning the absence of Hoy from the hall. Many of the protesters are deaf-mutes and they argue that special consideration should be given for the breakthrough Hoy made for the handicapped, just as Jackie Robinson received special recognition for his breaking of the color barrier.

It is true that Hoy's statistics are very good and compare favorably with several who have gained admittance to the hall, but it is also true that others have been left out whose stats exceed Dummy's. But, pressure will continue to be placed by many until the door is opened for Hoy.

Dummy lived to the ripe old age of 99, stayed in good physical shape throughout his lifetime and at 99 he threw out the first pitch for the third game of the 1961 World Series in Cincinnati. More remarkable is the fact that his mind was active and his memory acute right up to the end. When he passed away, he had lived longer than any other major leaguer before him.

Nineteenth Century, 1871-1899
Outfield

Paul A. Hines

BR TR 5' 9.5" 173 lbs.
B. Mar. 1, 1852, Washington, D.C.
D. July 10, 1935, Hyattsville, MD.

	Y	G	AB	R	H	2B	3B	HR	RBI	BB	SO	SB	BA	SA
Was.	5	348	1401	230	429	81	21	20	193	105	62	73	.306	.439
Life	20	1659	7062	1217	2134	399	93	57	855	366	304	163*	.302	.409

While with Indianapolis in 1887, center fielder Paul Hines is about to make the catch.

One of the best ballplayers to don a Washington uniform in the nineteenth century was slick-fielding and hard-hitting center fielder Paul Hines, a native Washingtonian. One nineteenth-century writer states: "as an outfielder, Paul Hines has few if any equals, and the wonderful and brilliant running catches made by him are too numerous to mention." He specialized in running, barehanded catches of low line drives. Hines could hit, too, for he compiled a lifetime batting average of .302 over 20 seasons, above .300 in 11 of them. He was the National League's first Triple Crown winner in 1878.

Paul played "on the island" in Washington (probably Haines Point) with the Rosedale team in 1870. In 1871, when professional baseball was born in Washington, he shifted to the Junior Nationals club. His first professional job was in the National Association in 1872, when the Nationals of Washington signed him. He played first base in just 11 games (the team lost all of them) and hit .245. Hines was used the next year by the Washington club as an outfielder and he demonstrated what was to come by hitting .331 in 39 games.

Sparked White Stockings to First N. L. Pennant

Hines then joined the Chicago White Stockings in 1874 with whom he played through 1877. After hitting .295 and .328 in '74 and '75, Paul sparked the White Stockings to the first Championship of the fledgling National League in 1876. He hit .331 and led the league with 21 doubles and fielding percentage (.923). The following year (1877) his average dropped to .280 and he was sent in 1878 to the Providence Grays where he achieved his greatest fame. He was the only player to play all eight seasons in the club's brief history (1878-1885). His first year there, he had, perhaps, his finest season, when he won the Triple Crown, batting .358, smashing four homers and driving in 50 runs in 62 games. These numbers are not bad when you consider the small number of games played and the "dead" ball used. The feat puts him in with an elite group of Triple Crown winners: Foxx, Williams and Mantle among others. He also led the league in slugging percentage (.486).

Involved in Controversial Triple Play

It was on May 8, 1878 that Hines claimed he made baseball's first unassisted triple play. This achievement set off one of the most hotly disputed controversies among baseball researchers. The play in question occurred while the Grays were playing the Boston Red Caps. Boston had runners on second and third with none out when the batter hit a short fly ball over the shortstop's head. The two runners streaked around the bases but Hines came racing in from the outfield at top speed and made a shoe top catch and continued on to tag third base and then threw to the second baseman who tagged second.

Hines claimed that both runners had passed third base before he touched the bag and therefore both had not returned in time and that both were out according to the rules. Some of his teammates, however, disputed the claim and said that the runner from second base had not reached third at all and that after Hines chased him back toward second and couldn't catch him, he threw to the second baseman for the third out. The official records now record it as only a triple play, not an unassisted one. In any case, it was a marvelous play that excited the spectators and players alike.

Won "MVP" Award in 1879

In 1879, he led the way in Providence's drive to the National League pennant, when he drove in the winning run in the deciding game. He led the league again with a .357 batting average and won the "McKay Gold Medal Award" for most hits (146). The award is somewhat akin to today's MVP award. Over the next four years (1880-1883), Hines continued his steady play, averaging an even .300 over the period. In 1880, he led the league's outfielders in fielding percentage with a .927 and in 1881 he had a league leading 27 doubles. He compiled batting averages of .309 in 1882 and .299 in 1883.

In 1884, Paul helped Providence to their second National League flag by making a running catch in the tenth inning against Troy to end the game and clinch the flag. Playing in 114 games, going to the plate almost 500 times and hitting .302, he continued to play at an outstanding level at age 32. In the first World Series, Hines hit only .250 as Providence swept the New York Mets of the American Association 3-0.

Beaning in 1885 Causes Deafness

Paul claimed he sometimes had prophetic powers and near the close of his tenure with Providence, he went over to the official scorer during a game and grabbed the scorebook and wrote in a "home run" for his next at bat. Sure enough, he called the shot, a la Babe Ruth, and swatted a homer. Hines' average dropped to .270 in 1885 as a result of a tragedy during the season. He was severely beaned by "Grasshopper" Jim Whitney of Kansas City and became instantly deaf as a result of the blow. Some umpires used hand signals afterwards to make him aware of their decisions. When deaf-mute Dummy Hoy arrived on the scene later, the practice became more widespread. When the Providence club folded after the season, Hines signed with Washington again.

In September of 1886, Connie Mack made his major league debut as a catcher for Washington and it was Hines who tied the score that day with a sacrifice fly in the eighth inning, enabling Mack to later win his first big league game. Paul hit .312 that year and he gave the Nationals another fine year in 1887 with a .308 average in 123 games.

While with Washington, Hines was involved in a publicity stunt during the off season. He was to catch a baseball dropped from the recently completed Washington Monument. A New York paper wrote that he could be killed if the ball, which would accumulate much weight in its travels, hit him in the head. Wisely, he changed his mind and allowed someone else to catch it and break two knuckles in the process.

He was with Indianapolis in 1888 and 1889 and while his hitting was still good (.308 and .281) he had a lot of difficulty playing the outfield in '88, so he was shifted to first base in 1889. Not used to the position, he committed 43 errors that year. He split 1890 with Pittsburgh and Boston, hitting only .239 in 100 games.

In his final year (1891), Hines was back in his hometown where he belonged. This gave Paul a shot in the arm and he raised his average to .282 in 54 games. Washington was a member of the American Association that year and unfortunately they finished last and the league folded after the season, driving Hines to retire from the major league scene.

For the next several years, Paul was a player/manager in the minor leagues with Nashville, Burlington, and Mobile.

Friend of President William McKinley

When with Washington in '86 and'87, Paul became friendly with then Congressman William McKinley who often attended the ballgames. When McKinley became president, he appointed Hines "postmaster" of the agriculture department.

More than anything else, Hines was remembered by his peers for conducting himself in a gentlemanly manner that was a credit to baseball. One sportswriter wrote: "A cleaner, more upright player never set foot on the bag." Hines died July 10, 1935 at the Sacred Heart Home in Hyattsville, Maryland, at the age of 83.

CHAPTER THREE

Dead Ball Era, 1901-1919

Introduction

Washington had no team in 1900 but with the emergence of the American League in 1901, the city had franchises in that league through 1971. From 1901 through 1911, the locals continued to play miserably. They never managed to rise above sixth place in the eight-team league and they finished last or next-to-last nine of the eleven seasons, playing at a slightly improved clip of .377.

There were two new individuals who came upon the scene, however, to drastically improve the team's fortunes. One was arguably the greatest pitcher who ever lived, Walter Johnson, who brought his blazing fastball to the Nats in 1907. Another was the new part-owner and manager, former pitcher Clark Griffith, who arrived in 1912. Griffith made sweeping changes to the roster and his teams finished in the first division five of eight years, finishing second twice while playing at a .518 pace through 1919. With this drastic improvement, the "dead ball" teams provided Washington fans the second best baseball of the five eras, as their winning percentage was .440.

Griffith procured four new starters for his everyday lineup to meld with the few solid ballplayers he inherited. They were second baseman Ray Morgan, third baseman Eddie Foster and outfielders Howard Shanks and Danny Moeller. The continuity, thus gained, enabled the teams to play respectable ball for the rest of the period. Of course, Johnson is synonymous with Washington baseball, and as the mainstay of the team, he was the idol of the fans that turned out in droves when he was scheduled to pitch. Other key players from the period were speedy Clyde Milan, who spent his entire career with the Senators and later coached for them for many years, and slick-fielding George McBride. Griffith brought in Nick Altrock, the perennial coach of the Nationals in 1912 and the comedian served with the team well into his eighties. He was a fine pitcher but he was more famous for his comedy act with Al Schacht.

It was relatively easy to select the All-Star team for this period; the only difficult choices were for first base and the pitchers. So here goes:

Dead Ball Era, 1901-1919 All-Star Team

Right-Handed Pitcher:	Long Tom Hughes
Left-Handed Pitcher:	Nick Altrock
Relief Pitcher:	Doc Ayers
Catcher:	Eddie Ainsmith
First Base:	Germany Schaefer
Second Base:	Ray Morgan
Third Base:	Eddie Foster
Shortstop:	George McBride
Outfield:	Clyde Milan
Outfield:	Howard Shanks
Outfield:	Danny Moeller

Nick Altrock, Walter Johnson, Long Tom Hughes, George McBride, Clyde Milan and Germany Schaefer were all members of the 1909 Washington team pictured here.

A summary of team performance during the period follows:

Dead Ball Era, 1901-1919

American League
8 Teams

Year	Nickname	Finish	# Games	Won	Lost	Pct.
1900	No Team					
1901	Senators	6	134	61	73	.455
1902	"	6	136	61	75	.449
1903	"	8	137	43	94	.314
1904	"	8	151	38	113	.252
1905	Nationals	7	151	64	87	.424
1906	"	7	150	55	95	.367
1907	"	8	151	49	102	.325
1908	"	7	152	67	85	.441
1909	"	8	152	42	110	.276
1910	"	7	151	66	85	.437
1911	"	7	154	64	90	.416
1912	"	2	152	91	61	.599
1913	"	2	154	90	64	.584
1914	"	3	154	81	73	.526
1915	"	4	153	85	68	.556
1916	"	7	153	76	77	.497
1917	"	5	153	74	79	.484
1918	"	3	128	72	56	.563
1919	"	7	140	56	84	.400
Totals - 19 Years, 19 Teams			2806	1235	1571	
Averages -		6	147	65	82	.440

Dead Ball Era, 1901-1919
Right-Handed Pitcher

Thomas J. Hughes

(Long Tom)

BR TR 6' 1" 175 lbs.
B. Nov. 29, 1878, Chicago, IL.
D. Feb. 8, 1956, Chicago, IL.

	Y	W	L	PCT	ERA	G	GS	CG	IP	H	BB	SO	SHO
Was.	9	83	125	.399	3.01	285	205	139	1776	1726	567	884	17
Life	13	131	175	.428	3.09	399	313	227	2644	2610	853	1368	25

Washington pitcher Long Tom Hughes poses in 1909 with the stands of National Park II in the background.

The "original" Tom Hughes hurled for Washington from 1904-1914 with the exception of a year in the minors in 1910. He was often confused with a Colorado-born Tom Hughes who also pitched in the American League for several years during the same period. The Senators' tall right-hander was known as "Long Tom Hughes" because of his height (6' 1") and he was, perhaps, the Nats' best pitcher from the turn of the century until Walter Johnson appeared on the scene.

Long Tom first played professional baseball with Ft. Wayne, Indiana, in 1897, but he did not play regularly again until he joined the Omaha, Nebraska team in 1900. From there, late in the season, he began his big league career in the National League, playing for Chicago. He appeared in only three games with a win and a loss and an ERA of 5.14. Still considered a rookie in '01, he worked 37 games, completing 32, while winning 10 and losing 23 with an improved ERA of 3.24. The 115 walks allowed were second high in the league but his 225 strikeouts rank as the third-best National League rookie total ever.

Important Factor in Red Sox A. L. Win

The following year (1902) he jumped to Baltimore of the American League, posting a 7-5 record before switching to the Boston Red Sox during the season. With the Sox his record was 3-3 and his season ERA was 3.71. In 1903, Hughes was a major factor in Boston's drive for the American League pennant. He had a 20-7 record and a low ERA total of 2.57 as the Sox's third starter. His winning percentage of .741 was runner up in that league category. Hughes was the only other Red Sox pitcher besides Cy Young and Bill Dineen to appear in the World Series when he started and lost Game Three. He was not able to complete three innings after giving up three runs. He was replaced by Young as the Red Sox won an exciting seven-game series.

He began the 1904 season with the New York Yankees, recording a 7-11 record and an ERA of 3.70, but Hughes and pitcher Barney Wolfe were traded to Washington for outfielder/

pitcher Al Orth on July 13, the day after Orth, playing centerfield, made a nice running catch on a drive over his head. Hunter Hill, St. Louis Brown's third baseman was on second base at the time. Unfortunately for Orth, he continued to grandstand the catch and jogged to the fence while Hill easily scored from second. The Washington management, obviously, was extremely unhappy with Orth. Long Tom appeared in 16 games for the Nats, winning only two while dropping 13, with an ERA of 3.47. His total of 24 losses was second highest in the league that year.

Best of Senators' Staff

In 1905, he was the best of the Senators' twirlers despite his 17-20 record, posting a nice ERA of 2.35. He fell to 7-17 in 1906, with his ERA rising to 3.62. His performance in spring training, earned Hughes the opening day pitching assignment against Clark Griffith's New York Highlanders in 1907, but he lost a tough one 3-2. He finished the year at 7-14 with an improved ERA of 3.11 and although he was mainly a starter, he led the American League with four saves.

The big right-hander had his best year in 1908 when he posted a record of 18-15 with his best ERA of 2.21, leading the Washington pitchers including Walter Johnson. In 1909, he appeared in only 22 games despite an ERA of only 2.70 and he was released to Minneapolis of the American Association for the 1910 season. He made a great comeback as the leading pitcher of the American Association with a 31-12 record for the fourth place team. The Senators purchased his contract and brought him back for the 1911 season, but he won only 10 games while losing 17 and his ERA rose to 3.47.

Hughes' Loss Snaps 17–Game Win Streak

In 1912, new manager Clark Griffith planned to build his team around Walter Johnson, Bob Groom and Hughes. They became the workhorses of the team that season. During an unbeaten western swing, the Nats won a record 17 straight games with Long Tom posting five of the victories. He started the string by beating the St. Louis Browns, 8-3, but the streak was broken at home with Hughes on the mound. He deserved a better fate and had a 1-0 lead with two out in the ninth when catcher John Henry muffed Home Run Baker's foul pop up. Given new life, Baker homered to tie the game. Eddie Collins' "Texas Leaguer" dropped in and won the game for the Philadelphia A's in the eleventh inning. The Nats put together another winning streak of 10 games in July and Hughes was the loser again, this time to the Cleveland Indians, 9-3. He finished the season 13-10 and his ERA was a nice 2.94.

His last season in the majors was 1913 as Hughes' record fell to 4-12 and his ERA soared to 4.30, highest since his first year and he was sent to Los Angeles of the Pacific Coast League for 1914. He was released to Salt Lake City of the same league in 1915 and he wound up his professional pitching career there in 1916. He secured a position with the Salt Lake City Police Department in 1917 and later returned to his native Chicago where he died on February 8, 1956.

Dead Ball Era, 1901-1919
Left-Handed Pitcher

Nicholas Altrock
(Nick)

SW TL 5' 10" 197 lbs.
B. Sept. 15, 1876, Cincinnati, OH.
D. Jan. 20, 1965, Washington, D.C.

	Y	W	L	PCT	ERA	G	GS	CG	IP	H	BB	SO	SHO
Was.	8	2	6	.250	4.73	23	8	3	78	105	18	18	0
Life	16	83	75	.525	2.67	218	161	128	1514	1455	272	425	16

Left-hander Nick Altrock, left, clowning with his famous partner Al Schacht.

Nick Altrock was a fixture on the Washington scene for more than a half century! He was most certainly the best left-handed pitcher on the Senators' rosters through 1919, although he registered only two victories for them. His lifetime winning percentage of .525 and ERA of 2.67 was second only to the great Walter Johnson in the early days of Washington baseball. He played for the Senators for 11 different years from 1905-1933 as a pitcher and pinch hitter, and served as a coach the remainder of the time until he retired in 1957.

Altrock and Schacht—Famous Clown Duo

It was not as an effective and respected pitcher that Altrock gained national fame, but as a clown. Teamed with Al Schacht, they not only entertained and won the hearts of Washington fans but they were in demand for appearances in cities throughout the country. Their crazy antics kept Washington fans laughing and in good humor and eased their anguish oftentimes when Senators teams did not fare well. They entertained at All-Star and World Series games.

One of their best acts was performed spontaneously during a rain delay of the seventh and deciding game of the 1925 World Series between the Nats and Pittsburgh Pirates. In his book, *My Own Particular Screwball,* Schacht described it as follows: "The infield had been covered with the canvas tarpaulin, and I noticed a pool of water forming around the pitcher's mound. I got hold of a broom and broke off the sweeping part, leaving the long stick. Then, taking two bats and a bottle filled with water, Altrock and I ran out into the downpour to the mound. There we sat down facing each other, me 'rowing' with the bats and Altrock 'fishing' with the broomstick. The crowd roared.

"Suddenly Altrock got up as though he'd hooked a big one, lost his balance and started rocking the boat, with me yelling to sit down. He fell overboard, right into the small lake surrounding the mound. Having sneaked a mouthful of water from the bottle, I dove in to save him. Then grabbing Nick like a lifeguard, I 'swam' for shore (toward the third base line), spouting water out of my mouth. The crowd loved it."

Nick began his career in Kentucky, playing for Covington in 1896 and Nicholas in 1897. He made his professional debut with

Grand Rapids in 1898 against New Castle and had to settle for a 10 inning 3-3 tie. Later in the season, Louisville of the National League purchased his contract. He appeared in 12 games and posted only a 3-4 record and as a result he was sent back to the minor leagues for the 1899 through 1901 seasons. He returned to the big leagues with the Boston Red Sox in the fall of 1902 appearing in only three games. He was sick at the start of the 1903 season and did not do well so the Chicago White Sox picked him up.

Meets "Three Fingered" Brown in World Series Opener

It was with the White Sox that he blossomed into a fine pitcher. During the next three years (1904-06), Altrock won 62 and lost 39 games for the Sox. He was 19-14 in '04, with an ERA of 2.96, won 23 and lost 12 games in '05, and 20-13 with an ERA of 2.06 in '06. That year the "Hitless Wonders" won the American League pennant and played a "subway" series with the Chicago Cubs. Much to the surprise of experts, Altrock started the first game of the series against Hall of Famer Mordecai "Three Fingered" Brown and bested him 2-1, permitting only four hits and the lone run allowed was as a result of a wild pitch. Later in the series he lost a heartbreaker to Brown, 1-0. The only run he allowed was in the seventh inning on a single, two sacrifice outs and a shot past third by Johnny Evers scoring Frank Chance.

In 1907, he won only seven games while losing 13 (ERA 2.57) and in 1908 he won five while losing seven with an ERA of 2.71. After losing his only start for the White Sox in 1909, he was traded to Washington where he won one and lost three before being sent back to the minors in July. He had already begun his career as a comedian, and a local writer wrote: "Altrock has been shipped to Minneapolis and his vaudeville stunts will be missed by the populace for many moons."

Altrock Defeats Yankees Despite Booing of Home Fans

He returned to the Senators in 1912 and was used only sparingly through 1915 when he seemingly completed his active career. He did, however, substitute for the sore-armed Walter Johnson during the period. The fans, disappointed because Johnson was the advertised pitcher, booed Nick at first and then threw cushions on the field. But, Altrock responded with a brilliant effort, pitching a seven-hitter to defeat the New York Yankees, 9-3.

World War I caused manager Clark Griffith to make Altrock one of his starting pitchers for part of 1918. He won one and lost two in June, pitched an inning in August and two against the Philadelphia A's in September. In his last at bat, he hit a phantom home run to the crowd's delight, skipping second and third and being carried to the plate. He made another appearance on the mound in 1919, facing only four batters, each hitting safely. On the mound for the last time in 1924, he gave up four hits and no runs in two innings.

Leads A.L. with 1.000 Batting Average

Altrock wound up his active career with three late season appearances as a pinch hitter in 1929, 1931 and 1933. He led the American League with a 1.000 average in '29, as a result of a pop fly which was allowed to drop so the fans could laugh at his antics on the bases. Needless to say, these games had no bearing on the league standings.

Because of his ability to make people laugh, it is generally forgotten that Altrock was a crafty pitcher with a good curve, change of pace and wonderful control. He was known as a great money pitcher and he was an excellent fielder as well. At one time, he was tied for the league record for the number of chances (13) accepted in a nine-inning game by a pitcher. Besting Hall of Famer Chief Bender on August 6, 1904, Nick recorded three putouts and ten assists against the Philadelphia A's. He finished the year with 49 putouts, an American League record for pitchers.

Nick held the record as a five-decade player until Minnie Minoso tied it on September 11, 1976. Washington was privileged to have a fine pitcher and one of the best known comedians in the game as a part of the local scene for so many years!

Dead Ball Era, 1901-1919
Relief Pitcher

Yancy Wyatt Ayers
(Doc)

BR TR 6' 1" 185 lbs.
B. May 20, 1890, Fancy Gap, VA.
D. May 26, 1968, Pulaski, VA.

	Y	W	L	PCT	ERA	G	GS	CG	IP	H	BB	SO	SHO	SV
Was.	7	53	62	.461	2.64	227	111	47	1123	1043	287	487	13	14
Life	9	65	79	.451	2.84	299	140	58	1428.2	1357	382	622	17	15

Doc Ayers demonstrates his pitching motion while with the Detroit Tigers near the end of his nine-year career.

After graduating from Woodlawn High School in Carroll County, Virginia, Yancy Ayers attended the medical college of Virginia studying dentistry. His education was interrupted when he signed a professional contract with the Richmond, Virginia baseball team. He acquired the nickname "Doc" because of his dental pursuits and the name stuck with him throughout his career.

The Senators obtained him from Richmond in 1913 and brought him to their training camp in Charlottesville, Virginia. He saw limited action that year, appearing in four games and posting a 1-1 won-lost record. With his 1.53 ERA, one wonders why he was not used more.

In spring training camp the following year (1914), Ayers was one of two pitchers who stood out. In an exhibition game against Brooklyn, Doc struck out eight Dodgers in a row. He was brought back to Washington again but this time he was used frequently, mainly as a starting pitcher. In fact, he pitched more innings (265.1) that season than at any other time during his career as he helped the Nats to a first division finish with a record of 12 and 15 and a nice earned run average of 2.54. He was second in the league in game appearances with 49.

Switched to Reliever—Has Best Year

Doc enjoyed his finest year in the major leagues in 1915 when he won 14 games, while losing only nine. That year, he assumed the role of a reliever and for the rest of his career, except for 1918, he continued in that capacity. He reduced his ERA by .33 to a low 2.21. But, in 1916, Yancy had his worst year with Washington when he went 5-9 and his ERA rose above 3.00 for the first and only time with the Nats at 3.78. It was in 1916 also, that Doc began a three-year off-season job with the Intelligence Department of the United States. Ayers did not serve in the military during World War I, but this was his way of making an important contribution to his country's war effort.

He pitched over 200 innings in 1917 and rebounded with a winning record of 11-10 and an ERA of 2.17. And, in 1918, used primarily as a starter again, he was just under .500 with a 10-12 record in 219 and two-thirds innings. His ERA rose to a still respectable 2.83.

When Doc went 0-6 in 11 games during the first part of 1919, he was traded to the Detroit Tigers of the American League for a big Swedish pitcher, Eric Erickson, who stuck with the Senators through the 1922 season despite a 30-49 record. The trade put new life in Doc and with Detroit he was 5-3 with an ERA of 2.69.

When the spitball was banned after the 1919 season, Doc was given permission to continue to use it. He was second in the league again in the number of games played (46) while with the Tigers in 1920, pitching a total of 208 and two-thirds innings but his ERA (3.88) was the highest of his career and he suffered his worst losing season at 7-14, despite the use of his favorite pitch.

Ayers was put on waivers by Detroit early in the 1921 season and when no one claimed him he completed his professional career in the minors with Toledo and Minneapolis. Doc returned to his home in Draper, Virginia and was employed at a nearby automobile agency as a salesman.

Dissatisfied with Baseball Career

Doc was not the typical ballplayer of the time; one of the sportswriters described him at retirement thus: "the game loses one of its finest characters, a gentleman with manners and character." At the age of 71, Ayers demonstrated that difference when he filled out a questionnaire which had been sent to him by the Hall of Fame. They asked: "If he would play professional baseball again, if he had it to do all over again." Unlike practically all other ballplayers his answer was "no."

Ayers died in Pulaski, Virginia at the age of 78.

Dead Ball Era, 1901-1919
Catcher

Edward Wilbur Ainsmith

(Eddie, Dorf)

BR TR 5' 11" 180 lbs.
B. Feb. 4, 1892, Cambridge, MA.
D. Sept. 6, 1981, Ft. Lauderdale, FL.

	Y	G	AB	R	H	2B	3B	HR	RBI	BB	SO	SB	BA	SA
Was.	9	620	1681	159	348	56	26	2	154	138	193*	66	.207	.275
Life	15	1078	3048	299	707	108	54	22	317	263	315*	86	.232	.324

Eddie Ainsmith in a New York Yankee uniform displaying his catching form.

Eddie Ainsmith was purchased from the Lawrence, Massachusetts club of the New England League during the 1910 season and he played in 33 games for the Senators that year. During his 15-year major league career, he twice batted .290 or better and was over .270 four times. However, he was primarily known as a brilliant fielding catcher, ranking with the leaders in his profession. His main claim to fame was that he replaced Gabby Street as Walter Johnson's regular catcher in 1911. Johnson recognized that handling his fastball was extremely difficult if it was high or low and he was quoted as saying, "Ainsmith does the best job."

On April 15 of that year with Ainsmith catching, Johnson struck out four men in one inning yet was scored on. After fanning two batters, Ainsmith was charged with a passed ball on the second batter, enabling the runner to reach first base. Johnson struck out the next batter but Hall of Famer Tris Speaker doubled to drive in a run. Duffy Lewis then became the fourth strikeout victim.

In 1912, the Senators were battling for second place in the American League near the end of the season and Johnson was brought in to relieve in the seventh inning of a tie game. He pitched shutout ball for 10 innings but in the seventeenth inning, Ainsmith broke his finger and had to be replaced by third string catcher Rippy Williams. According to umpire Billy Evans, Walter was still throwing "cannonballs" and Williams was having a horrible time catching them. When a passed ball nicked the umpires ear, he immediately called the game because of darkness, although there appeared to be sufficient light to continue.

Often Was Only One to Catch Johnson

As a rule, until 1917, Ainsmith seldom caught anyone but Johnson because he claimed that his catching hand was so beat up that he needed as much rest as Johnson did between turns. Eddie had pretty good speed for a catcher, stealing 17 bases in 1913 and 16 in 1917. Three of the stolen bases in 1913 were recorded on June 26 against the Philadelphia Athletics' pitcher Chief Bender who had a big lead in the ninth inning and completely ignored

Ainsmith as he stole second, third and home. When the Senators stole eight times in the first inning against the Detroit Tigers and catcher Steve O'Neill in 1915, Eddie stole both second base and home plate.

Suspended for Punching Umpire

In 1914 when umpire Sheridan lost his head and punched Washington second baseman Ray Morgan for throwing dirt on him, Ainsmith came to Morgan's rescue. Coaching at first base, he left the coaches' box and knocked Sheridan down. It took nearly the entire team to overpower the muscular Ainsmith and prevent him from seriously injuring the arbiter. Needless to say, Ainsmith was ejected from the game and later fined and suspended. Normally a likable fellow, Ainsmith had a nasty temper and he narrowly escaped a jail term in 1915 after severely beating a streetcar motorman.

Eddie averaged playing in only 57 games a year and averaged less than 150 at bats from 1910 through 1916. In 1917, however, he played in 125 games, batted 350 times but hit only .191. In his last season with the Nats (1918), he appeared in almost 100 games but again did not hit well at .212. It was that year that he applied for a deferment from the draft but the secretary of war ruled that baseball was a non-essential occupation and that all players of draft age were subject to the "work-in-essential-industries-or-fight" rule. The secretary did exempt players from the rule until September 1 and both leagues voted to end the season early on Labor Day, September 2 as a result.

After serving for nine years as Johnson's favorite battery mate, Eddie was traded in 1919 to the Detroit Tigers via the Boston Red Sox because of a salary dispute. Unfortunately for the Nats, Ainsmith did much better with the bat after he left Washington. All four of his .270 or better years were with other teams. He became manager Ty Cobb's regular catcher, but when his performance slacked off, he was traded to the St. Louis Cardinals of the National League in mid-season of 1921. While with the Cardinals, Ainsmith proved to be a thorn in the side of the world champion New York Giants beating them twice with late inning homers, and another time, breaking a 16-inning tie with some daring base running. Against the Giants, he was the Cardinals' leading hitter. The Giants solved the problem by signing Eddie for the 1924 season; however, he appeared in only 10 games and ended his career there.

Takes Babe Ruth to Brewery

Ainsmith was friendly with Babe Ruth off the field. While with Detroit, he and Harry Heilmann decided to entertain the Babe and center fielder Bob Meusel. They took them to a nearby brewery and kept them out late in hopes that the Babe would not be in good playing condition for the next day's game. Ruth called and wanted to go back at 7 A.M., so they did. It didn't seem to affect him adversely, since he socked two booming home runs later in the day.

Later, Eddie was an American League umpire for a while. He lived in Brooklyn, New York, for many years, retiring to Ft. Lauderdale, Florida where he died on September 6, 1981.

Dead Ball Era, 1901-1919
First Base

Herman A. Schaefer
(Germany)

BR TR 5' 9" 175 lbs.
B. Feb. 4, 1877, Chicago, IL.
D. May 16, 1919, Saranac Lake, NY.

	Y	G	AB	R	H	2B	3B	HR	RBI	BB	SO	SB	BA	SA
Was.	6	380	1092	158	321	34	17	1	91	129	17*	62	.294	.359
Life	15	1150	3784	497	972	117	48	9	308	333	28*	201	.257	.320

Germany Schaefer (left) shaking hands with teammate Merito Acosta.

Germany Schaefer was one of the most colorful ballplayers of his era. He began his career with the Sioux Falls, South Dakota team in 1899 as a third baseman. He did so well that the Kansas City Blues drafted him for 1900 and the next year he was in the majors as an infielder with the Chicago Club of the National League. When the famous infield double play combination of Tinkers to Evers to Chance made their debut in 1902, Schaefer was at third base. After two years in the majors, he was back in the minor leagues in 1903 and 1904 with St. Paul and Milwaukee. He returned to the big leagues in 1905 with the Detroit Tigers of the American League after hitting .356 in 131 games the previous season.

Schaefer was a powerless hitter who occasionally hit for a good average but it was his versatility in the field that kept him in the big leagues for 13 years. In his first two years with the Tigers (1905-06), he was their regular second baseman, leading the league in putouts in 1905 and in total chances per game in 1906. He had only one other season in which he played 100 games in a single position.

Spoils Burns' No–Hitter

His best season offensively was probably 1908, when he reached career highs with 96 runs (third in the league), 40 steals (also third in the league) and 20 doubles to help the Tigers win the American League flag for the second year in a row. Washington left-hander, "Sleepy" Bill Burns, lost a no-hitter with two outs in the ninth inning on May 21, 1908 when Schaefer singled in the winning run for Detroit's 1-0 victory. His pitiful performance at the plate in World Series play (.143 in '07 and .125 in '08) matched the Tiger's fruitless effort against the National League Chicago Cubs as they won only one game in the two Series.

One of the Earliest "Clown" Coaches

The good-natured Dutchman performed well with Detroit until his legs began giving him problems. Traded to Washington during the 1909 season, he remained with the club for six seasons, first as a versatile utility player and later as a clown coach on the baseline. He was the forerunner of similar clowns, notably Nick Altrock and Al Schacht, who amused fans around the entire league. Germany's most popular antic was an imaginary "high wire" act. An earlier vaudeville act with former teammate Charley O'Leary was the inspiration for the MGM musical *Take Me out to the Ball Game*, starring Gene Kelly and Frank Sinatra.

"Stole" First Base

Schaefer had an over-developed sense of humor but he never intended to harm anyone, although his favorite sport was umpire baiting. On one occasion an umpire was reluctant to call a game, even though it was pouring rain, until Germany went out to his position, wearing rubber boots and carrying an umbrella. Another time, with Schaefer on first and the speedy Davy Jones on third, a double steal was attempted but catcher Nig Clarke refused to throw to second base. On the next pitch, Schaefer created an uproar with the umpires and the other team by "stealing" first base. On the next pitch, Schaefer broke for second and the rattled Clarke threw the ball to second too late, enabling Jones to score the winning run with a steal of home. At the time there was no rule against stealing first base but a new rule was passed a few months later.

In early July 1914, Washington was forced to forfeit a game with the Philadelphia A's when the umpire became confused over the rules. For his part in the squabble, Germany was fined $25 for "unfit language toward the umpire." In his defense, Schaefer claimed he was directing his remarks to "a guy in the stands."

Washington Senators manager Jimmy McAleer announced his resignation at the close of the 1911 season, and fans and the press endorsed the popular Schaefer as his replacement. Germany approved, and appeared in public with a boisterous Kelly Green necktie as a promotional gag. This prompted a local songwriter to pen the following tune:

Has Anybody Seen Kelly? (A Parody)

Has anybody here seen Schaefer?
Schaefer with the green necktie?
Has anybody here seen Schaefer?
Have you seen him passing by?
His hair is dark, and his eyes are blue,
And we hope he's manager next year, too.
Has anybody here seen Schaefer?
Schaefer with the green necktie.

Fortunately for Washington baseball, Clark Griffith was named manager instead.

Despite his ailing legs, Germany had his best year with Washington in 1911, leading the team with a batting average of .334. He hit over .300 two years later with a mark of .320. Despite his clownish behavior, Germany was a distinct asset to his team with his intricate knowledge of the game and his versatility. During his career, he played every position but catcher even appearing on the mound for two games in 1912 and 1913, for a total of one inning, compiling an ERA of 18.00! While with Washington, he played more games at first base than at any other position.

Clark Griffith used Germany more and more in the coach's box as the ailing Schaefer's performance tailed off. Griff recognized the value of humorous coaching; first it kept the team in good spirits and second it sometimes distracted opposing players. Sometimes teaming with Nick Altrock on the baselines, there was plenty of clowning; however, when it was necessary to treat the game with seriousness and acumen, Germany was equal to the task.

In 1915, Schaefer switched to Newark of the new Federal League, appearing in 59 games but batting only .214. So the following year, he resumed his clowning and coaching duties with the Senators only to contract tuberculosis and be forced to resign. Still he was able to play one game for the New York Yankees later in the year and one for the Cleveland Indians in 1918 before succumbing to the disease on May 16, 1919 in Saranac Lake, New York.

Dead Ball Era, 1901-1919
Second Base

Raymond Caryll Morgan

(Ray)

BR TR 5' 8" 155 lbs.

B. June 14, 1889, Baltimore, MD.

D. February 15, 1940, Baltimore, MD.

	Y	G	AB	R	H	2B	3B	HR	RBI	BB	SO	SB	BA	SA
Life	8	741	2480	278	630	90	33	4	254	320	184*	87	.254	.322

Second baseman Ray Morgan, with bat in hand, awaits the pitch.

Ray Morgan spent his entire major league career with the Washington Senators. The former Baltimore sandlotter began his professional career with Frederick of the Blue Ridge League in 1910 and, during the year, also played with Goldsboro of the East Carolina League and Danville of the Virginia League. He was purchased from Danville in the Virginia League in the summer of 1911 while hitting .331 and converted from a shortstop to a second baseman by the Senators. He made his debut August 25 of that year, lashing out a triple and two singles and he added a stolen base. The next day he went four for five and made a lasting impression on Washington management.

In 1912, he became a valued member of new manager Clark Griffith's "little team," along with newcomers, Eddie Foster, Danny Moeller and Howard Shanks. The Nats put together a string of 17 consecutive victories that year, rising from the cellar to finish the season in second place. By the end of June that year, Ray had become a regular with the fourth highest batting average in the American League. On July 8, 1912, Morgan singled in the tenth inning along with Moeller and Foster and scored the winning run for Walter Johnson to extend his consecutive game-winning streak to 16 games. But, he was injured in July and had to be replaced.

Punched by Umpire

He was in the opening day lineup in 1913 and had his most productive year, batting .272 in 137 games. He led the league that year and in 1914 for second baseman participating in double plays. The latter year, he had career highs in putouts (290) and assists (379). He also played in a career high 147 games in 1914, hitting .257. On July 30, 1914, Ray was ejected for throwing dust on umpire Sheridan, who landed a "haymaker" on Morgan's cheek. Coach Eddie Ainsmith rushed to Morgan's defense, flattening Sheridan. The Nats reaped some solace when they won the game 9-7.

Griffith believed that Morgan never lived up to his potential as a ballplayer because he let outside interests interfere. Often, he reported to spring training camp out of shape, and he frequently motored to Baltimore during the season to have a good time with his friends while breaking training rules. Things were brought to a head in July 1915 when he had an automobile accident while in transit between Washington and Baltimore. He was suspended for a time and later forced to serve in a utility role; he played in only 62 games and his average fell to .233. The former "playboy" settled down in 1916, regaining his starting job, and he had one of his best years, hitting .267 in 99 games.

Last Good Year Was 1917

He had his last good year in 1917 when he batted .266 in 101 games. On June 3, 1917, with Babe Ruth pitching for the Boston Red Sox, Ray drew a leadoff walk. Ruth argued with umpire Brick Owens about the calls and was thrown out of the game. The Babe punched Owen and later was suspended for 10 days and fined $100. Ernie Shore relieved Ruth and pitched a perfect game after Morgan was caught stealing by catcher Sam Agnew.

Although he was in the opening day lineup at second base in 1918, he was later relegated to a utility role and his batting average fell to .233. By the spring of 1919, he was put on waivers and claimed by the Philadelphia Phillies of the National League. He refused to report and was sold to the Baltimore Orioles in the minors, but a dispute with management caused him to quit in mid-season. Upon being sent to Akron in 1920, he retired from the game.

After retirement he operated a café in Baltimore until he died of a heart attack and pneumonia on February 15, 1940.

Dead Ball Era, 1901-1919
Third Base

Edward Cunningham Foster

(Eddie, Kid)

BR TR 5' 6" 145 lbs.

B. Feb. 13, 1887, Chicago, IL.

D. Jan. 15, 1937, Washington, D.C.

	Y	G	AB	R	H	2B	3B	HR	RBI	BB	SO	SB	BA	SA
Was.	8	1121	4418	579	1177	145	59	6	355	385	198*	166	.266	.330
Life	13	1500	5652	732	1490	191	71	6	451	528	255*	195	.264	.326

Third Baseman Eddie "Kid" Foster demonstrating his vertical leap.

Eddie "Kid" Foster was the smallest of Clark Griffith's "little team." When he was obtained by the Senators in 1912, Griffith rated Foster above "hit 'em where they ain't" Willie Keeler, who played for Griffith earlier on the New York Highlander's team. This brought a sharp rebuttal from manager Bill Dahlen of the Brooklyn Dodgers, who acknowledged that Foster was a great place hitter but said "none could hit them around the lot like Willie did." In any event, Eddie was so effective at getting his bat on the ball that he was given a "blank check" to swing whenever a runner was on base, and the base runner was always instructed to run unless the instruction was cancelled by a sign from Foster himself. From this evolved Griffith's famous "run and hit play." To take advantage of this skill, Foster batted second in the lineup for most of his career.

Foster began his major league career with the New York Yankees in 1910, playing in 30 games but hitting only .133. In the minors in 1911, Eddie and outfielder Danny Moeller were drafted from Rochester of the International League after the season, and like Ray Morgan, Eddie reported to training camp in 1912 as a shortstop. With George McBride a fixture at shortstop, Eddie was converted to a third baseman and he became a defensive star at the "hot corner" for many years. On August 23, 1912, Foster made a key hit in the ninth inning to drive in the winning run and enable Walter Johnson to chalk up his record setting 16th straight victory that year. He played in all 154 games for the Nats, had his best year at the plate with a .285 average, led the league in at bats with 618 and led American League third basemen with 348 assists.

Contracts Typhoid Fever in '13

Although Foster was a durable athlete who led the league four times in at bats, he contracted typhoid fever during the 1913 season and was confined to Georgetown University Hospital and out of action for a long period. Two years later he married one of the nurses who cared for him there. Upon his return to action in '13, he had shaved his head so he took a merciless ribbing from jokesters Nick Altrock and Germany Schaefer. In the abbreviated season his average dropped to .247 in 106 games.

In 1914 and 1915, he made a nice comeback, hitting .282 and .275 respectively and leading the league both years in number of at bats with over 600 each year. In '14, he led American league third baseman in fielding with 25 double plays. In '15, he split his time between second base and third base. At the beginning of the 1916 season, he was shifted to second base and replaced at third by Joe Leonard. It was not a permanent shift since he was back at third for most of the year.

Spoils Eddie Plank's Bid for No-hitter

In 1917, he continued to split time between second and third and the movement seemed to affect his batting averages as they dropped to .252 in 1916 and .235 in 1917. Foster's clutch hitting deprived Hall of Famer Eddie Plank of his last bid for a no-hitter in 1917. In his final year with the St. Louis Browns, the 42-year-old pitcher had two outs in the ninth when Foster's double drove in a batter who had walked.

Back as a fixture at third base for the 1918 season, he regained his batting eye and produced another fine season, hitting .283 and leading the league in the number of at bats for the last time with 519. The season was shortened because of World War I. His playing time was reduced in 1919 but he continued to contribute to the team with a batting average of .264. This proved to be his last season with Washington and he was traded to the Boston Red Sox for the 1920 season. He was installed as the Sox's regular third baseman that year and he continued in that capacity in 1921. He gave Boston two pretty good years hitting .259 and .284. In 1922 he was relegated to a utility role and eventually traded to the St. Louis Browns during the season to assume the same role. Although he hit .300 while with the Browns, his average for the entire season was .265. He wound up his career with the Browns in 1923, seeing action in only 27 games and hitting only .180.

He returned to coach for the Senators and when the Black Sox scandal broke he was put in charge of the team while president/manager Clark Griffith attended league meetings. He died an accidental death in 1937 when struck by an automobile near Chicago.

Dead Ball Era, 1901-1919
Shortstop

George Florian McBride

(Pinch)

BR TR 5' 11" 170 lbs.

B. Nov. 20, 1880, Milwaukee, WI.

D. July 2, 1973, Milwaukee, WI.

	Y	G	AB	R	H	2B	3B	HR	RBI	BB	SO	SB	BA	SA
Was.	13	1458	4833	461	1068	127	43	5	393	381	271*	116	.221	.268
Life	16	1659	5526	516	1203	140	47	7	447	419	271*	133	.218	.264

Fancy fielding shortstop George McBride showing his throwing technique.

George McBride is recognized as one of the greatest fielding shortstops of all time and the premier defensive shortstop of his day. His sensational fielding was responsible for keeping him in the major leagues for 16 seasons. His lifetime batting average was a pitiful .218 and his best batting average was only .253 when he was with the St. Louis Cardinals of the National League. While he didn't hit for a high average, he acquired the nickname "Pinch" for coming through in the clutch.

George began his professional career with Sioux Falls, South Dakota, in 1901 and he appeared in his first big league game the same year by fortuitous circumstance. After completing the minor league year, he returned home to Milwaukee, Wisconsin to attend a major league game among other things. The Milwaukee Brewers were in the American League at the time and their regular shortstop sprained his ankle just before the game; McBride was called out of the stands and pressed into service. He responded with one hit in four trips to the plate and handled a number of chances in the field flawlessly.

He spent the next three seasons in the minors, first with Kansas City and Milwaukee of the American Association in 1902 and then with the Peoria club in 1903 and 1904. The Pittsburgh Pirates purchased his contract early in the 1905 season and installed him at third base. After only 27 games with the Pirates, he was traded to the St. Louis Cardinals and became their regular shortstop. After appearing in 90 games for the Cards in 1906 but hitting only .169, he was sent back down to the minors to Kansas City again for the 1907 season.

Given a "George McBride Day"

Washington purchased his contract in 1908 and he remained in the capital city as a player through the 1920 season. His sparkling plays thrilled Washington fans for over a decade and earned him acclaim as one of their favorite ballplayers. In 1912, the *Spaulding Baseball Guide* wrote "a tower of strength at short is George McBride, who has been playing steadily and consistently at that position for several seasons without being given one-tenth the credit his work merited." The fans and Washington management, however, recognized his considerable skills and on September 29, 1913 the Washington Club held a "George McBride Day," and the popular player was given a diamond-studded watch by the fans and the presentation was made by the Vice President of the United States Marshall. Walter Johnson did his part in making the day enjoyable for McBride by notching his 36th win of the season in shutting out the Philadelphia Athletics 1-0.

On August 2, 1915 in a game between the Nats and the Detroit Tigers, the Senators scored a run in the second inning with no official time at bat in the inning. After two walks and a sacrifice bunt, George hit a sacrifice fly to drive in the runner on third who scored before the runner on second was doubled up.

One of Best Fielding Shortstops

McBride possessed a keen baseball mind and he served as field captain of the team for six years. While with Washington, he led the American League four times in the number of games played, five times in fielding percentage, three times in the number of putouts by a shortstop, once in the number of assists, and six times in participating in double plays. These stats seem to reinforce the assertion that he was one of the best fielding shortstops of all time. His range at short compares favorably with Hall of Famers Pee Wee Reese and Phil Rizzuto, as George handled 5.47 chances per game during his career as opposed to Reese's 4.93 and Rizzuto's 4.79.

In 1916, the aging McBride was designated as a player/coach and that was the last year that he appeared in over 100 games as a player, and from 1917-20 he did more coaching than playing. At the end of the 1920 season, George retired as an active player.

Installed as Manager in 1921

In 1921, Griffith stepped down as manager of the Nats and McBride was named to replace him. That same year, McBride the longtime bachelor, married the lovely Anne C. Monday. His marital career lasted a lifetime but his managerial career ended before the year was out. Unfortunately, George was hit in the face by a throw during infield practice, which paralyzed one side of his face. This developed into a painful and troubling injury and led to a nervous breakdown. Although the Senators finished fourth, Griffith was not satisfied, so he named Clyde Milan as a replacement for McBride. This seemed somewhat unfair, since Griffith still called most of the shots while George was field manager.

George remained in professional baseball until 1929, coaching for the Detroit Tigers and the Newark Bears of the International League. McBride never needed to wear glasses and at the age of 92 he still drove an auto, played golf and bowled! He died July 2, 1973 in Milwaukee, Wisconsin, a few months short of his 93rd birthday.

Dead Ball Era, 1901-1919
Outfield

Howard Samuel Shanks

(Howie, Hank)

BR TR 5' 11" 170 lbs.
B. July 21, 1890, Chicago, IL.
D. July 30, 1941, Monaca, PA.

	Y	G	AB	R	H	2B	3B	HR	RBI	BB	SO	SB	BA	SA
Was.	11	1396	4887	529	1232	173	87	21	520	355	379*	177	.252	.336
Life	14	1665	5699	604	1440	211	96	25	620	415	443*	185	.253	.337

Outfielder Howard Shanks chokes up on the bat.

Although born in Chicago, Shanks moved to Monaca, Pennsylvania at an early age and his play with the local semi-pro clubs earned him his first professional contract with East Liverpool of the old Ohio and Pennsylvania League in 1909.

At the end of his second minor league season with them (1910), at the age of 20, Howie Shanks was given only three months to live by a doctor who examined him for the Pittsburgh Pirates of the National League. Instead, recovering from tuberculosis in 1911, he returned to the minors 50 pounds heavier and had his best year in the minor leagues. Drafted by Washington at the end of the year from the Youngstown Ohio team, he reported to the Senators in the spring of 1912. He made his debut as a major leaguer on May 9 and by May 25 he was inserted in the lineup as a regular and hit safely in his first 11 games.

Executed Rare Double Play

A few weeks later he was the talk of the league when he executed a rare double play in Chicago. Playing in left field, he registered a putout at second base and threw out a runner at the plate, completing the double play. It occurred in the fifth inning of a game between the Senators and the White Sox. With runners on first and third the White Sox batter grounded to the pitcher who threw to the plate to trap the runner off third. When the catcher's throw went by both the third baseman and shortstop, Shanks, alertly, was near the infield backing up the play, so the base runner returned to third. When the runner on first took too wide a turn around second, Howie chased him down and tagged him out. When the runner on third broke for the plate, Shanks fired a strike to the catcher to complete the double play!

Hank was a truly versatile player, performing at all positions except for pitcher and catcher in his 14-year career. He played the outfield more than any other position and had one of the most feared throwing arms of any of the league's outfielders. He began to shift to the infield in 1915, playing third base part of the season.

In 1916, he played most of the games in the outfield but played in a number of games at third, short and first base. In 1917, he was installed as the regular shortstop and played most of the season there. In 1918, 1919 and 1920, he alternated at various posts and proved equally good at all.

Has Finest Year in 1921

Shanks was not a good hitter until he reached the age of 30. His averages until then were .257 or less and he remained in the big leagues because of his fielding, throwing and versatility. He hit .268 in 1920 and enjoyed his finest year in 1921 at the age of 31. After constantly switching positions for nine years, he was installed at third base where he didn't miss a game (leading the league in that category), achieved the .300 level for the only time in his career, hitting .302 while also leading the league in triples with 18. In addition, he topped all third baseman in fielding percentage (.960), putouts (218), and double play participation (35).

He continued hitting well in 1922 with a .283 average but Howard broke his finger and was out of the lineup for an extended period as a result. After playing in over 100 games each year that he had been with the Senators (a decade), he was able to play in only 84 games. The veteran utility player was then traded to the Boston Red Sox in 1923 in a five-player deal that enabled Washington to acquire valuable catcher Herold "Muddy" Ruel. With the Bosox that year, Shanks' average dropped to .254 in 131 games. He played in only 72 games for them in '24 and his average was about the same at .259. He was sent to the New York Yankees for 1925 where he hit .258 in 66 games and finished his major league career that year when the Yankees gave him his unconditional release on December 16, 1925.

In 1926, he joined the Louisville Colonels of the American Association, playing third base. The Colonels dropped him in late '27 and he signed with Rochester of the International League where he ended his playing career.

Coaches for Cleveland

Following the end of his active career, Shanks joined the Cleveland Indians as a coach in 1928 and he remained with them until the middle of the 1932 season. His last connection with organized baseball was as manager of the Beaver Falls club of the Pennsylvania State Association in 1938 and '39. After the 1939 season he retired from the game and worked for the Real Estate Department of Beaver County, Pennsylvania.

Along with Walter Johnson, Clyde Milan, and George McBride, Shanks was rated among the outstanding players of the Washington teams during the years 1912-1922. While entertaining friends, he suddenly fell dead at his home in Monaca Pennsylvania on July 30, 1941. He was only 51 years old.

Dead Ball Era, 1901-1919
Outfield

Jesse Clyde Milan

(Clyde, Deerfoot)

BL TR 5' 9" 168 lbs.
B. Mar. 25, 1887, Linden, TN.
D. March 3, 1953, Orlando, FL.

	Y	G	AB	R	H	2B	3B	HR	RBI	BB	SO	SB	BA	SA
Life	16	1982	7359	1004	2100	240	105	17	617	685	197*	495	.285	.353

Speedy Clyde "Deerfoot" Milan became a *longtime coach for the Washington Senators.*

The fleet Clyde Milan gained national fame as a prolific base stealer who continually challenged Ty Cobb for the major league base-stealing crown. Clark Griffith and Bucky Harris maintained that Milan was faster than Cobb and that Ty was able to register more steals because he played in considerably more games, was a better hitter and his team did not fall behind as much as the Senators. In those days it was rare to see a stolen base attempt from a team that was on the short end of the score. During his career Milan pilfered 495 bases and he was ranked second to Cobb at the end of his big league career.

Nats' Best Defensive Center fielder

Clyde is recognized as the best defensive center fielder that the Nats ever had. In fact, he was their best outfielder until Sam Rice appeared on the scene. Manager Jimmy McAleer took Milan under his wing and chastened the rookie for making fancy one-handed catches. McAleer, himself a former outfielder impressed upon Milan that he could catch most balls with two hands and if a one-handed catch had to be made, it was because he misjudged it, loafed or made some other mistake. Clyde played a shallow center field, relying on his speed to catch up with long drives.

Milan entered the professional ranks in 1905 with Clarksville in the North Texas League, but shifted to McAllister and Shawnee of the Oklahoma State League before the season was over. He switched to Wichita of the Western Association in 1906 and 1907 and while there Washington catcher Cliff Blankenship, who was idled with a broken finger, discovered him. Cliff had been sent to scout Walter Johnson and he recommended that the Senators sign both ballplayers. They reported late in the season, became fast friends and roommates until Clyde left the team in 1922. They had similar dispositions for both were kind, loyal and easygoing. Clyde proved to be a morale booster with his good humor and tall tales about baseball, hunting and fishing.

In 1908 and 1909, Milan had his worst seasons with the exception of his final year in 1922. Despite his weak hitting, he played in 130 games each year because of his outstanding defensive ability.

He improved his batting skills in 1910 with a .279 average, contributed 44 stolen bases and led the American League outfielders with 30 assists and 10 double plays. Both he and Johnson were holdouts in the spring of 1911 but Milan was signed before the start of the season for $4,000, the sum he asked for. The money proved to be an incentive for Clyde and he registered his first .300 batting average, hitting .315 and leading the league in games played and the number of at bats.

Breaks Cobb's Stolen Base Record

He really came into his own in 1912, breaking Cobb's stolen base record with 88 and hitting .306. On June 14, Milan stole five bases as the Nats won their 15th straight game. The only drawback that year was Milan's 25 errors, which lead the American League. He topped Cobb again in 1913, stealing 75 bases to Ty's 52 and he finished just under .300 with a .299. Bob Ganley, an American League outfielder, had nicknamed Milan "Zeb." However, Chief Bender of the Philadelphia A's gave him a more appropriate nickname "Deerfoot." He was also married that year on November 19 to Margaret Bowers.

The wily Milan was very durable and didn't miss a game for three seasons, 1911-13. Unfortunately, in 1914 he collided with right fielder Danny Moeller while chasing a fly ball in Cleveland and suffered a broken jaw, restricting his play to 115 games. But, the "iron man" bounced back playing in 150 games or more in each of the following three seasons, 1915-17. He had another fine defensive year in 1916 when he led the league outfielders in putouts (372) and assists (27). In one game during the period, Johnson lost to the New York Yankees 1-0 when an outfield hit rolled between Clyde's legs. The mild-mannered Johnson said, "Goodness gracious, Clyde doesn't do that very often."

Replaces McBride as Manager in '21

He continued to hit, play a fine defensive game and be among the leaders in stolen bases until his final year in 1922. In fact, he had his best hitting year in 1920 when he posted a .322 average. In

'21, he was called upon to replace George McBride as manager towards the end of the season when the team finished in fourth place. He was at the helm in 1922 as player/manager for what proved to be his final season in the big leagues. His team finished a disappointing sixth and he was replaced as manager for the 1923 season because Griffith believed he was too easy going. He was also given his unconditional release to play in the minors for Minneapolis of the American Association. At age 36, he played in 101 games for them and batted .296.

Clyde managed New Haven in 1924, Memphis in 1925 and 1926, returned to Washington as a coach for two years and then piloted Birmingham for six years. He managed the Nats' Chattanooga farm club in 1935, 1936 and part of 1937 when ill health forced him to resign and perform scouting duties. He came back to Washington to coach in 1938 and remained in that capacity until 1953.

Trained Case and Coan in Running and Hitting

Milan was dedicated to his job as coach and he patiently helped many a ballplayer improve his game. According to Fred Baxter, the former Senators clubhouse custodian, Clyde was the first man to come to the stadium, coming oftentimes at three o'clock for a night game. The speedy George Case learned the finer points of taking a lead and of base running from Milan, and gives him considerable credit for helping him achieve the American League stolen base crown six times. Gil Coan gives Clyde credit for his two .300 seasons, achieved because he used a crouch recommended by Clyde.

Milan died the way he wanted to: while in uniform during spring training on March 3, 1953. The 65-year-old was hitting grounders to the infielders when he began experiencing chest pains. He was rushed to an Orlando, Florida hospital, where he succumbed to a second heart attack.

The small town hunter and fisherman, like Johnson, had made a lasting impression on Washington fans with his baseball skills. Clark Griffith was impressed, too, for he named him to his all-time Washington Senators team as its center fielder.

Dead Ball Era, 1901-1919
Outfield

Daniel Edward Moeller

(Danny)

SW TR 5' 11" 165 lbs.
B. Mar. 23, 1885, DeWitt, IA.
D. Apr. 14, 1951, Florence, AL.

	Y	G	AB	R	H	2B	3B	HR	RBI	BB	SO	SB	BA	SA
Was.	5	632	2357	356	583	79	41	5	179	284	290*	163	.247	.335
Life	7	704	2538	379	618	83	43	15	192	302	296*	171	.243	.328

Outfielder Danny Moeller ready to make the catch.

Danny Moeller began his professional career with Burlington of the Iowa State League in 1905. He played for Troy of the New York State League in 1906 and 1907. He was acquired by the Pittsburgh Pirates late in the latter year and played in 11 games and hit .286. When his average fell to .193 in 36 games in 1908, he was back in the minors in 1909 with Jersey City of the International League. He switched to Rochester of the same league for the 1910-11 seasons.

The switch-hitting Danny Moeller was Washington's regular right fielder for four years, 1912-15. Clark Griffith had drafted Danny and Eddie Foster from Rochester of the International League at the end of the 1911 season. He opened the 1912 season batting in third position but was moved to leadoff on June 1 to take advantage of his speed, and by the end of June, Moeller was leading the team with a .391 batting average.

President Taft Offers Moeller Assistance

In July, he was one of those who delivered a key base hit to keep a rally alive in the tenth inning to enable Walter Johnson to register his 16th straight win. Sometimes called the "Rochester Rambler," Danny sprained his ankle sliding into second base shortly thereafter and was forced to the sidelines for a few weeks. He also damaged his left shoulder, which was easily dislocated from time to time for the remainder of his career. President William Howard Taft, an avid Senators fan, was so concerned about Danny's shoulder that he offered the services of his personal U.S. Army surgeon. The shoulder was never repaired,, however, and he was never able to regain his batting form afterwards and by the end of the year his average had dropped to .276. At that, he enjoyed his best season ever.

Although Moeller did not hit for average, he was a valuable leadoff man who did not swing at pitches out of the strike zone, thereby drawing a considerable number of walks. For his career, his on-base average was a respectable .324. Danny drew a career-high 72 bases-on-balls in 1913, sixth in the league. Using his speed to good advantage that year, Danny finished second in the

American League in stolen bases to teammate Clyde Milan when he pilfered 62 bases. The great Ty Cobb stole only 42 bases that year to finish fourth. On the down side, though, he led the league with 103 strikeouts that year and hit just .236.

Collides with Milan in Outfield

The following year (1914), Moeller collided with center fielder Clyde Milan while chasing a fly ball and he broke Milan's jaw, putting Clyde out of action for 30 days. Moeller, however, was able to play in all but three games, raising his average to .250 and finishing sixth again in the league with 71 walks.

When Danny and outfielder Merio Acosta were both injured at the same time in 1915, pitcher Walter Johnson was installed in right field for two weeks. Danny was still able to play in 118 games but when his batting average fell to .226 this proved to be his last season as a Senators regular. In each of his four seasons as a Nat regular, Moeller connected for exactly 10 triples and he averaged 38 stolen bases per year during the period. That same year on July 19th, the Senators stole catcher Steve O'Neill of the Cleveland Indians blind by stealing eight times in the first inning. Moeller led the way by stealing second base, third base, and home plate.

In 1916, he appeared in 78 games, hitting .246 for the Nats, before being sent to the Cleveland Indians for the remainder of the season. He ended his major league career there, appearing in only nine games and batting .067 for them.

Had Strong Throwing Arm

Danny was an excellent fielder with a strong throwing arm, registering 25 and 27 assists in 1912 and 1913 respectively. He always gave his team his best efforts and this made quite an impression on manager Clark Griffith who leaned toward those who were always trying. One writer of the time wrote "Moeller, hitting an even .300, would be next to Cobb and Speaker in value among American League outfielders."

Moeller returned to his home state, Iowa, and caught on with the Des Moines club of the Western League for the 1917 season. Out of baseball in 1918 and 1919, he returned to the same club for two more seasons, 1920-21. At 37 years of age in '21, Danny played in 144 games, hit .284 and still demonstrated his remarkable speed by stealing 28 bases.

Moeller died in Florence, Alabama at the age of 66.

CHAPTER FOUR

Post-World War I Era, 1920-1945

Introduction

The glory days of Washington baseball occurred during this period! One World Championship and three American League pennants were among this team's trophies. They finished in the first division over half of the time and played over .500 ball for the period. The teams were remarkable through 1936; thereafter there was a decidedly downward spin, except for two years during World War II when they finished second. In the 26-year period, they finished in the basement only once.

The Senators defeated the National League Champion New York Giants in the 1924 World Series four games to three. Clark Griffith had named the "Boy Wonder," Bucky Harris as the team's manager that year. The aging Walter Johnson finally got the opportunity to pitch in a World Series, but it was not until the final game that he notched his first victory and that in a relief role.

After capturing the flag again in 1925, the Nationals gained a lead of three games to one, only to lose the Series to the Pittsburgh Pirates four games to three, on a cold, rainy, and windy day in Pittsburgh. Walter Johnson suffered the disappointing seventh game loss. Their last American League Championship was gained about 70 years ago in 1933, but the Nats fell quickly to the New York Giants in the World Series, four games to one.

Six Hall of Famers played the majority of their careers for the Senators during this period. Bucky Harris, Sam Rice, Goose Goslin, Joe Cronin Rick Ferrell and Heinie Manush all donned the Senators uniform. They gave loyal Washington fans plenty to cheer about. This was an era of high batting averages and many sluggers wore Washington uniforms. While they had no one to match the "Big Train" hurling for them, a number of capable pitchers performed for them, too.

The 1933 Washington Senators' American League championship team.

Again, it was not too difficult selecting the players for this team, except for the relief pitcher and one outfield position. Alex Carrasquel pitched well in relief for Washington and Sammy West was an excellent outfielder but they were not selected. My selections are:

Post-World War I Era, 1920-1945 All-Star Team

Right-Handed Pitcher:	Dutch Leonard
Left-Handed Pitcher :	George Mogridge
Relief Pitcher:	Jack Russell
Catcher:	Muddy Ruel
First Base:	Joe Judge
Second Base:	Bucky Harris
Third Base:	Buddy Lewis
Shortstop:	Cecil Travis
Outfield:	Heinie Manush
Outfield:	George Case
Outfield:	Johnny Stone

A summary of team performance during the period follows:

Post-World War I Era, 1920-1945

Washington Nationals
American League
8-Team League

Year	Finish	# Games	Won	Lost	Pct.
1920	6	152	68	84	.447
1921	4	153	80	73	.523
1922	6	154	69	85	.448
1923	4	153	75	78	.490
1924	1	154	92	62	.597
1925	1	151	96	55	.636
1926	4	150	81	69	.540
1927	3	154	85	69	.552
1928	4	154	75	79	.487
1929	5	152	71	81	.467
1930	2	154	94	60	.610
1931	3	154	92	62	.597
1932	3	154	93	61	.604
1933	1	152	99	63	.651
1934	7	152	66	86	.434
1935	6	153	67	86	.438
1936	4	153	82	71	.536
1937	6	153	73	80	.477
1938	5	151	75	76	.497
1939	6	152	65	87	.428
1940	7	154	64	90	.416
1941	6 (Tie)	154	70	84	.455
1942	7	154	62	89	.411
1943	2	151	84	69	.549
1944	8	153	64	90	.416
1945	2	154	87	67	.565
Totals - 26 Years, 26 Teams		3975	2029	1946	
Averages	4	153	78	75	.510

Post-World War I Era, 1920-1945
Right-Handed Pitcher

Emil John Leonard

(Dutch)

BR TR 6' 175 lbs.

B. Mar. 25, 1909, Auburn, IL.

D. Apr. 17, 1983, Springfield, IL.

	Y	W	L	PCT	ERA	G	GS	CG	IP	H	BB	SO	SHO
Was.	9	118	101	.539	3.27	262	251	130	1899	1951	403	657	23
Life	20	191	181	.513	3.25	374	375	192	32181	3304	737	1170	30

Emil "Dutch" Leonard probably delivering his famous knuckleball.

Emil "Dutch" Leonard's 118 victories in a Washington uniform are more than any other Senators pitcher, except the great Walter Johnson. His amazing control of his best pitch, the knuckleball, enabled him to stick around the majors for 20 years, nine of which were with the Senators. Emil is sometimes confused with the "Dutch" Leonard who was a fine major league pitcher in the early part of the twentieth century. But, Washington's "Dutch" outdid his predecessor by appearing in almost twice the number of games in almost double the number of years.

Emil was raised in a poor coal-mining town and after three days with his father in the mines, he escaped to Chicago where he began his long baseball career. While playing semi-pro ball in the area one of his teammates helped him get a contract with Mobile, Alabama of the Southern Association in 1930. He was shuffled around to five other minor league teams until the Decatur team of the Three-I League folded in 1932 because of the depression. After a brief time hauling coal, the York minor league club signed Leonard in 1933, where he posted a 12-15 won-lost record and then was sold to the Brooklyn Dodgers, his first major league club.

Develops Knuckleball in Minors

Dutch appeared in 10 games in '33, winning two and losing three. In 1934, he pitched in 44 games with a winning record of 14-11 and in '35 he was in 43 games with a disappointing 2-9 record although he led the league with eight saves. After only 16 games in 1936, with no record, he was sold to the minor league Atlanta club where he worked on a knuckleball in sheer desperation to return to the majors. Because the pitch darts and wobbles unpredictably on its way to the plate, catchers are reluctant to call for it. Atlanta's catcher was Paul Richards (later a very successful big league manager) and he was not afraid to call for the pitch. Richards even called for the knuckler in spots where Leonard hesitated to use it. Dutch, with Richard's help, was able to gain exceptional control of the pitch. He averaged only 2.06 walks per game for his career.

The new pitch enabled him to catch on with the Washington Senators in 1938 and become the ace of the pitching staff for most of the next nine years. Following a 12-15 won-lost record in '38, Dutch was a 20-game winner in 1939 while only losing eight games with a 3.54 ERA. Used mainly as a starter from the outset, he pitched in almost 300 innings in 1940 but his record dropped to 14-19 although his earned run average was slightly better at 3.49. His 124 strikeouts that season, however, were tops for his career. On opening day, before President Roosevelt, he lost a tough 1-0 decision to the great Lefty Grove and things seemed to go downhill the rest of the season.

Line Drive Breaks Ankle

Dutch had another banner season in '41 when he finished with an 18-13 record despite an ERA that rose to 4.11. A highlight of the season was Joe Dimaggio's sixth inning single off Leonard, enabling him to tie George Sisler's consecutive-game hitting streak at 41. He missed most of the next season (1942) when he was hit by a line drive, which broke his ankle, so he was able to appear in only six games.

Dutch returned to form in 1943 and 1944, starting more than 60 games and winning a total of 25. He was the starting pitcher for the American League All-Stars in 1943, holding the opposition to just two hits in his three-inning stint and gaining credit for the victory on Bobby Doerr's three run homer in the second inning. He was selected as an American League All-Star four times.

Beats Tigers Despite Bribe Offer

On the final day of the 1944 season, he enabled the St. Louis Browns to win their one and only American League flag by leading the last place Senators over the Detroit Tigers 4-1, despite the fact he had been offered a $20,000 bribe the morning of the game. In November 1944, Dutch was one of a number of players who toured the war theaters for the USO.

Leonard was never able to pitch in a World Series but he came the closest in 1945 when the Detroit Tigers barely edged out the Senators on the last day of the season. In the Nats' last game, Dutch was leading the Philadelphia Athletics 3-0 in the eighth inning, when center fielder Bingo Binks lost a fly ball in the sun, enabling the A's to tie the score and win in extra innings. With a 17-7 record, his .708 winning percentage and 2.13 ERA were career highs as a starter.

Selected for N.L. All–Star Team

Emil's final year with the Nats was 1946 when he broke even at 10 wins and 10 losses in only 26 games. Griff sold Leonard to the Philadelphia Phillies after the season and he finished his major league career in the National League. In two seasons with the Phillies ('47 and '48), Dutch was 29-29, posting back-to-back 17-12 and 12-17 records as a starter. In 1948, his 2.51 earned run average ranked second in the National League.

In 1949, he was traded to the Chicago Cubs along with Monk Dubiel for Eddie Waitkus and Hank Borowy. He was used as a starter that year but had a disappointing 7-16 record in 33 games. For his final four seasons, the Cubs used him in a relief role and he was very effective in that capacity. He won a total of 19 games over the period and notched 28 saves. He was selected for the 1951 National League All-Star team, an honor he achieved in both leagues. His best season in relief was 1952, when he saved 11 games and his earned run average was his second best at 2.16.

One of his highlights as a reliever was against the Brooklyn Dodgers when he was brought in to protect a one run lead. The bases were loaded with none out and he was able to retire Jackie Robinson, Gil Hodges and Roy Campanella without damage.

Dutch was released by the Cubs at the close of the 1953 season and brought back as the pitching coach in '54. He remained in that capacity through 1956 when he retired from the big league scene. He died in Springfield, Illinois on April 17, 1983 at the age of 74.

Post-World War I Era, 1920-1945
Left-Handed Pitcher

George Anthony Mogridge

(George)

BL TL 6'2" 165 lbs.
B. Feb. 18, 1889, Rochester, NY.
D. March 4, 1962, Rochester, NY.

	Y	W	L	PCT	ERA	G	GS	CG	IP	H	BB	SO	SHO
Was.	5	68	55	.552	3.35	145	134	73	1016.2	1102	273	285	12
Life	15	132	131	.502	3.21	398	261	138	2265.2	2352	565	678	20

Lefty George Mogridge poses for a photograph in front of the dugout.

After pitching for Rochester University in 1910, George Mogridge began his professional career with the Galesburg team of the Central League the following season. Upon registering 20 victories, he was sold to the Chicago White Sox. He won three and lost four in the first half of the 1912 season but was optioned to Lincoln of the Western League in July where he won eight and lost five and was recalled late in the season. He was then released to the Minnesota club of the American Association early in the 1913 season, going 13-10 there. He was sent to Des Moines of the Western League the following year, compiling a record of 21-15. With Des Moines most of the 1915 season, he won 24 and lost 11 before being sold to the New York Yankees in August where he was only 2-3, although his ERA was an astonishing 1.76.

Hurls No-Hitter in 1917

Used as a starter his first two full seasons with the Yanks, he was only 6-12 and 9-11 but again his ERAs were a respectable 2.31 and 2.98. On April 17, 1917, he hurled a no-hitter against the Boston Red Sox, although he did give up a run in a 2-1 victory. Until Dave Righetti's no-hitter in 1983, Mogridge was the only Yankee to accomplish the feat.

Shifted to the bullpen in 1918, Mogridge finally came into his own. He led the American League in appearances with 45 and was second in the number of saves with seven. His won-lost record was 16-13 and his ERA 2.77. He had one more good season with the Yankees in 1919, winning 10 and losing seven with an ERA of 2.50, before posting a losing record in 1920 when he went 5-9 with a disappointing ERA of 4.31. This set up his trade to the Washington Senators and this trade proved to be one of the "Old Fox's" best.

Top Man on Pitching Staff

With Washington he became a starter again with much success. The long, lean left-hander was 18-14 in 1921, replacing the aging

Walter Johnson as the top man on the pitching staff. He was second in the league with an ERA of 3.00 and second with four shutouts. The use of resin by pitchers had been banned in 1920 but George found a convenient and effective way of using the illegal substance by working the powder into the underside of the bill of his cap. Its use was never discovered during his playing days.

He was given the opening day assignment before President Harding in 1922. He outlasted "Sad" Sam Jones and the New York Yankees and won 6-5. He proved to be the ace of the staff again that year winning 18 and losing 13.

He was only .500 the next year (1923) but on August 15 he became the only pitcher to steal home in extra innings, scoring an insurance run in the 12th in Washington's 5-1 victory over the Chicago White Sox. In 1924, he reached the zenith of his career and his 16-11 record helped to propel the Senators into the World Series. One example along the way was a masterful shutout of the Cleveland Indians (1-0). He permitted only two hits and faced just 28 batters.

Wins Fourth Game of World Series

He was entrusted by manager Bucky Harris to start the fourth game of the World Series and George responded by allowing just two runs and three hits in seven and two-thirds innings. With relief help from Fred Marberry, he chalked up an important victory, 7-4.

He is best remembered, however, for his part in winning the seventh and deciding game against the New York Giants. Executing manager Bucky Harris' brilliant plan to negate the contribution of left-handed slugger Bill Terry, Mogridge was brought in to pitch after right-handed starter Curly Ogden faced just two batters. George pitched shutout ball and was clinging to a 1-0 lead, giving up just a bunt single and a double over the first five innings, when he ran into trouble in the sixth inning. When he gave up a walk and a single to the first two batters in the sixth, Giant manager John McGraw removed slugger Bill Terry for a pinch hitter as

Washington manager Bucky Harris had hoped. Bucky responded by lifting Mogridge and bringing in right-handed ace reliever Firpo Marberry. Two errors in the inning, however, enabled the Giants to score three runs and take the lead. The Senators bounced back to tie the game and Walter Johnson was on the mound when the Senators eventually won the game in the twelfth inning, gaining their first and only World Championship.

In 1925, George lost the opening game in New York, 5-1, to set the tone for what was to follow that year. He was 4-3 in 10 games with the Nats when he was traded to the St. Louis Browns in June. He saw only limited action with the Browns and was sent to the Boston Braves of the National League at the close of the season.

Closes Career in N.L.

He wound up his career with the Braves in 1926 and 1927, winning 12 and losing 14 over the period. In '27, his final year in the majors, he did lead the National League relief pitchers with six wins in 19 relief appearances.

Mogridge died of a heart attack at his home in Rochester, New York on March 4, 1962 at the age of 73.

Post-World War I Era, 1920-1945
Relief Pitcher

Jack Erwin Russell

(Jack)

BR TR 6' 1.5" 178 lbs.
B. Oct. 24, 1905, Paris, TX.
D. Nov. 3, 1990, Clearwater, FL.

	Y	W	L	PCT	ERA	G	GS	CG	IP	H	BB	SO	SHO	SV
Was.	4	24	27	.471	4.43	165	24	8	457.1	534	150	102	0	26
Life	15	85	141	.376	4.46	557	182	71	2050.2	2454	571	418	3	38

Ace reliever Jack Russell warming up in Griffith Stadium's right field.

Washington's last American League championship was gained about 70 years ago in 1933 when the second "boy wonder," Joe Cronin was their rookie pilot. The squad pulled the trick with considerable help from the bullpen and its ace reliever in particular, Jack Russell. He was one of the last survivors of that pennant-winning team, succumbing to a series of mini-strokes and heart attacks while in his 80s. He was one of the real nice guys in baseball.

Gives Up Otts' Homer in Series Loss

He made the pitch that ended the greatest decade in Washington baseball history. It was a sinker that was a little high in the strike zone. Hall of Famer Mel Ott's drive glanced off center fielder Fred Schulte's glove and fell into the temporary seats in old Griffith Stadium, giving the New York Giants the World Championship four games to one. Jack and Senators fans deserved a better fate, for if those despicable temporary bleachers had not been installed the Nats might have won their second World Series. Still, from 1924 through 1933, the Senators won one World Championship, three American League pennants, and finished in the first division all but once.

Russell was a star outfielder for his high school team in Paris, Texas but the right-hander was converted to a pitcher by Dickie Kerr, a former member of the Chicago Black Sox who was working out with the team. In addition to a good fastball and change of pace, Russell had a natural sinker because of a fractured middle finger on his pitching hand which didn't heal properly. The pitch, his best, broke down and away from left-handed hitters and gave them fits.

He was signed in 1925 to a professional contract with the Paris team of the Class D East Texas League. The Red Sox signed him the same year on the recommendation of scout Steve O'Neill. The lanky Russell stuck with the Sox in 1926 after a fine spring in their New Orleans training camp. The second division Red Sox of that era were a woefully weak-hitting and sloppy-fielding bunch. Jack soon became the ace of the pitching staff and remained so until he was traded in 1932 to the Cleveland Indians. His record for more than six years with Boston included four seasons pitching over 200 innings, twice winning 10 games or more and three times posting an ERA of less than four runs a game.

Makes First Start in Fenway Park in 1926

Used in 36 games in 1926, he made his first start in Fenway Park against the Senators, giving up only five hits in eight innings but losing on Stan Covaleski's shutout 2-0. He was 0-5 that year and did not win his first game until June 16, 1927, an 11-10 victory over Cleveland. Considered one of the best pitchers in the league by the end of the year, he outdueled the great Ted Lyons of the Chicago White Sox 3-0 late in the season. On one occasion in 1928, he was an "extra infielder," handling 11 chances on the mound flawlessly. Later on, he won his own game in the ninth with a single to left field.

During the period 1929-1931, Jack was considerably less effective, losing 18 games twice and a league leading 20 games in 1930. This was not surprising, however, considering the pitiful support provided by his teammates. Over one stretch of six games, the Sox scored a total of one run on his behalf. Jack often drew starting assignments against the league's top hurlers. One of his toughest losses was in 1931 to the Philadelphia A's and the magnificent Lefty Grove. Each team was scoreless through 11 innings but Russell weakened in the 12th, losing 5-0. At times, he tried to help his cause with his bat and had surprising power for his size. In 1930, Jack smashed a 400-plus foot home run into Griffith Stadium's left field bleachers to lead his team to a 7-1 victory over Washington.

Russell pitched the Sox's opening home game in 1932, only to lose to the Senators on Heinie Manush's ninth-inning homer. One week later, he recorded the first Red Sox shutout of the season, but before the end of the season he was traded to the Cleveland Indians for another former Senator, Pete Jablonowski (who later changed his name to Appleton). He was with the Indians .when spacious municipal stadium was opened before a record crowd of 80,284. He remembered that Washington's clown duo of Nick Altrock and Al Schacht performed that day. Russell won his first start in the new stadium 7-4 against the Nationals.

Manager Cronin Urges Griff to Acquire Russell

While with Boston and Cleveland, Russell made a habit of beating the Senators. When Joe Cronin was named the new Washington manager before the 1933 campaign, he reasoned that it would help the Nats' cause if they could acquire Russell, so Clark Griffith made one of his shrewdest winter moves, obtaining him from the Indians. Cronin ordered Jack to add some weight and he reported to camp at a stronger 180 lbs. Unselfish and always a team player, Russell willingly went to the bullpen at his manager's request. This move by Joe was one of the most important factors in Washington's ascension to the American League championship. As the Senators' bullpen ace and "closer," he appeared in 50 games, pitching 124 innings while posting a 2.69 ERA (third best in the league), and winning 12 games (11 as a reliever) and losing six. His 13 saves led the league and he also handled 52 chances on the mound without error. Griffith rated Jack the best fielding pitcher in the league. By July, he was 6-1 and on July 4 he shut out the Yankees from the eighth inning through the tenth in the second game of a doubleheader to ensure Washington's twin victories. These were vital games, for the Senators had to battle the Yankees down to the wire.

Jack Has Remarkable '33 Series

It is unfortunate that Jack is remembered mostly as the pitcher who gave up Ott's home run and the one who took the loss in the final Series game. Russell pitched brilliantly during the Series and Ott's homer was the only run given up in over 10 innings of relief.

He made appearances in three of the five games, scattering eight hits and issuing no walks. His ERA was a remarkable 0.87!

In the first Series game, Russell pitched five innings in relief of Walter Stewart, holding the Giants scoreless and allowing only four hits from the third inning until he was lifted for a pinch hitter in the eighth. After the game, Cronin commented: "Jack Russell did one of the finest bits of relief pitching it has been my pleasure to see." Russell retired all the batters he faced in the fourth game in relief of Monte Weaver. In the final game, relieving "General" Alvin Crowder, he permitted only four hits in almost five innings, with Ott's blow the only damaging safety.

After the Series, Cronin was quoted as saying: "If proof was necessary, the Series certainly has shown what a great relief pitcher Jack Russell is." Although Carl Hubbell was voted MVP of the Series, three Senators received honorable mention: Russell, Goose Goslin and Schulte. Recognized as Washington's best relief pitcher since the fiery, quick-tempered Fred Marberry, Russell was completely opposite in personality. Jack, during his playing days, was quiet, cool and friendly.

Russell continued to hurl for Washington until Joe Cronin was traded to Boston for a record $250,000 in 1936. Joe asked owner Tom Yawkey to trade for Jack and just prior to the June 15 trading deadline, he went to the Red Sox for pitcher Joe Cascarella. Before leaving the Senators, his won-lost record was 5-10 in '34, 4-9 in '35 and 3-2 in '36 before the trade. In 1934, he led the league by appearing in 54 games and notching seven saves and was the first reliever ever to be named to the American League All-Star Team.

With the Red Sox in '36, Jack's won-lost record was a disappointing 0-3, so Boston gave him his unconditional release during the spring of 1937. The Detroit Tigers picked him up and he sparkled in relief during the early part of the season but his performance tailed off later.

Helps Chicago Cubs to Pennant

After being released by the Tigers at the end of the season, Russell had the good fortune of signing with the 1938 National League champion Chicago Cubs. He played a valuable role in their pennant winning season by appearing in 42 games and recording a 6-1 won-lost record and a 3.34 ERA. In the World Series, he appeared in two games for one and two-thirds innings, allowing no runs and giving up only one hit and a walk, but it was to no avail as the Yanks swept the Series in four straight games. He returned to the Cubs in '39 but did not do quite as well, winning four games and losing three in 39 games with a 3.67 ERA. He was given his unconditional release at the end of the season.

The St. Louis Cardinals brought him back in 1940 for what proved to be his final year in the majors. He won three and lost four but posted an ERA of 2.50. With that ERA, one wonders why the Cardinals released him and no other team would sign him for the '41 season.

After retiring from the game, Jack was active in Clearwater, Florida civic affairs, serving as a commissioner for several years. Largely due to his foresight, the Philadelphia Phillies continued to train in Clearwater. A new stadium built in 1956 was named "Jack Russell Stadium."

It is refreshing to find a player like Jack Russell, who loved the game and displayed many admirable character traits. The cordial, humble and genial Russell was still as likable in his eighties as he was during his playing days. He loved recalling his big league experiences and although his top salary was $6,500 per year, it is a safe bet that he wouldn't have traded his memories of baseball's "golden age" for some of the millions thrown around in the game today.

Post-World War I Era, 1920-1945
Catcher

Herold Dominic Ruel
(Muddy)

BR TR 5' 9" 150 lbs.
B. Feb. 20, 1896, St. Louis, MO.
D. Nov. 13, 1963, Palo Alto, CA.

	Y	G	AB	R	H	2B	3B	HR	RBI	BB	SO	SB	BA	SA
Was.	8	903	2875	336	834	116	24	2	371	403	123	44	.290	.349
Life	19	1468	4514	494	1242	187	29	4	534	606	238	61	.275	.332

Herold "Muddy" Ruel, wearing his Washington home uniform, assumes his catching position.

What baseball fan would have guessed that catcher Herold "Muddy" Ruel would become an attorney after his major league baseball career was over and that he practiced before the United States Supreme Court? But, it's true!

It was his brains, not brawn that made him the great catcher that he was. He stood only 5' 9" tall and weighed just 150 pounds. His ability to get his throws away quickly and accurately enabled him to throw many would-be base stealers out. Washington manager Bucky Harris described Muddy as a "wonder." Club owner Clark Griffith considered Ruel to be the best of all Senators backstops.

Hits into Triple Play

At the age of 19, Ruel left the sandlots of his hometown St. Louis to become a catcher for the St. Louis Browns. He made his professional debut with them on May 29, 1915. He saw limited action, appearing in only 10 games and he failed to garner a hit in 14 plate appearances. He was let go by St. Louis and he reappeared in the majors with the New York Yankees in 1917. The Yankees also used him sparingly the first two years and he played in only nine games over the period. In 1919 and 1920, however, he was used quite a bit, appearing in a total of 161 games. On August 14, 1919, the Yankees defeated the Detroit Tigers 5-4 in 15 innings despite Ruel hitting into a triple play. He hit only .240 in '19 and .260 in '20, but etched in his memory the latter year was the awful thud of Carl May's submarine pitch as it struck Ray Chapman in the head and his struggle to regain his feet. Muddy was behind the plate at the time and believed that Mays was blameless because Chapman froze and lost sight of the ball.

Ruel was traded to Boston for the 1921 season and became the Red Sox's regular catcher, playing in 113 games and raising his batting average to .277. Playing in 116 games the following year, his average fell to .255, so the Red Sox sent him on to Washington in February 1923, despite the fact that he led all American League catchers with 17 double plays.

Walter Johnson needed someone special who could handle his fastball. Muddy was the right choice, and he became "The Big Train's" favorite catcher. For the next six seasons, Ruel did the bulk of the catching for the team and in his first year with the Senators he also proved he could handle the bat when he hit .316. During the period, he recorded two more .300 seasons and barely missed another when he hit .299. But, he was even more valuable defensively, leading the league's catchers three times in putouts, assists and double plays and twice in fielding percentage and number of games during his career. Ruel's second year with the Senators vaulted him into the 1924 World Series against the New York Giants. Entering the seventh and deciding game of the Series, Muddy disappointingly was batting zero for 14 times at bat. In the eighth inning, however, with Washington trailing by a score of 3-1, Ruel got his first hit of the series, a single sending Nemo Leibold to third and putting the tying run on base. Bucky Harris eventually drove them in to tie the score.

Scores Winning Run in '24 World Series

In the twelfth inning, with Johnson pitching in relief and looking for his first Series win, Muddy came to bat. Taking a healthy cut, he hit an easy foul pop-up behind the plate. But, Giant catcher Hank Gowdy, after flipping off his mask, got his foot entangled in it, and he dropped the ball. Ruel then doubled to left field. Earl McNeely followed with a bad hop grounder, which bounced over the third baseman's head. Ruel, who was not really fast on the bases, was nevertheless waved home. Muddy became one of the World Series heroes by beating the throw to the plate, thus winning the World Series for the Senators!

When the Senators gained the American League flag again in 1925, Ruel was behind the plate again, this time making a significant contribution during the Series. He hit .310 during the season and improved his woeful '24 Series batting average of .095 to .316. He had fine years at the plate in 1926 and 1927 with batting averages of .299 and .308. In 1928, his batting average dropped to .257 and he was not used as much during his final two years with the Nats ('29 and '30), appearing in 135 games over the period and hitting .245 and .253. He was traded to the Boston Red Sox for the 1931 season.

For the rest of his playing career, he was used in a utility role and used only sparingly. He didn't last the '31 season with the Red Sox, moving over to the Detroit Tigers and then on to the St. Louis Browns and Chicago White Sox. He wound up his career with the White Sox in 1934. Over his last four years ('31-'34), he appeared in only 156 games and was never able to raise his average above .235.

Acquired Nickname as a Boy

The nickname "Muddy" could probably be tagged on most any catcher who was around home plate after a rain. But, that moniker seemed to fit Ruel very well. He acquired his nickname as a boy, improvising a messy game using a mud ball.

Actually, he was meticulous in maintaining a very neat uniform, even during doubleheaders.

Worked in Commissioner's Office

After his playing days were over, he served briefly in the front office of the Cleveland Indians and managed the St. Louis Browns in 1947. For a long period he was farm director, general manager and assistant to the president of the Detroit Tigers. At one time, he was an assistant to baseball Commissioner Happy Chandler.

While on leave of absence from his job with the Tigers, Muddy and his family lived in Italy for several months. He later took up residence in Palo Alto, California. At the age of 67 on November 13, 1963, he died of an apparent heart attack after dining at home with his wife.

Post-World War I Era, 1920-1945
First Base

Joseph Ignatius Judge
(Joe)

BL TL 5' 8" 155 lbs.
B. May 25, 1894, Brooklyn, NY.
D. March 11, 1963, Washington, D.C.

	Y	G	AB	R	H	2B	3B	HR	RBI	BB	SO	SB	BA	SA
Was.	18	2084	7663	1154	2291	421	157	71	1001	943	463	166	.299	.423
Life	20	2171	7898	1184	2352	433	159	71	1034	965	478	213	.298	.420

A portrait of longtime Washington first baseman Joe Judge wearing the Senators' cap.

Joe Judge was recognized as one of the best first basemen to play in the first decades of the twentieth century. He was in a class with the famed Hal Chase and George Sisler. The graceful, sure-handed and near-flawless fielder led the league's first basemen in fielding percentage six times, still an American League record and he compiled a brilliant lifetime fielding average of .993, an American League record that stood for more than 30 years. At the time of his retirement, he also held American League career marks for first basemen for games played, putouts, total chances and double plays. His 131 double plays in the 1922 season also set a league record, since broken.

He was a steady hitter also; his lifetime batting average was just a shade under .300. Judge played 18 of his 20 seasons with Washington and was on Washington's pennant winning teams of 1924 and 1925. Along with second baseman Bucky Harris, shortstop Roger Peckinpaugh and third baseman Ossie Bluege, he was part of what Clark Griffith and others called the "finest fielding infield of all time."

Surprising Power for a Little Man

Joe could hit for extra bases, because he had surprising power for a little man. He could hit left-handed pitching as well as right-handers. Judge wore a small first baseman's glove but was able to make some astonishing catches with his dexterity around the first base bag.

Raised in a hard Brooklyn neighborhood, Judge gave his life to baseball early. He played in grade school at St. Vincent Ferrer and worked his way up to a highly regarded semi-pro team, the Dexter club. He was paid $5 a game. A mailman named John Hannah had recognized the lefty's potential, bought him a glove and encouraged him to play first base.

In 1913, Judge was called by manager John McGraw of the New York Giants and asked to pitch batting practice for a week. One day with another pitcher on the mound, Joe tried to sneak in a few swings during batting practice. When McGraw thundered "drop that bat," Judge did so immediately. McGraw, however, was forced to watch Joe take his swings during the 1924 World Series and wreak havoc on his Giants with a .385 batting average.

Back in 1915, Chick Gandil, later a prime figure in the Black Sox scandal, was the Washington first baseman and Griffith was disenchanted with him because he broke training rules so often. On a mission to Buffalo, New York, to purchase outfielder Charlie Jamieson, he spotted Judge playing first base. The "Old Fox" talked Buffalo into the deal and obtained both for $8,000. Buffalo had wanted $7,500 just for Jamieson.

Replaces Gandil as Regular First Baseman

Judge was brought up by the Senators' near the close of the 1915 season and by the end of the season, Joe had completely usurped Gandil's first base job and he was to be the Nats' regular first baseman for the next 15 years. When he and Jamieson first reported minutes before the start of a game, Griff told him he was leading off. He had no official welcome and no pre-game practice.

For the next four years Judge really struggled although he was pencilled in the lineup for more than 100 games each year. In 1916 he hit .220 with 24 errors. In 1917, he improved with a .285 average and 12 errors, but broke his leg sliding while playing against the Detroit Tigers. In 1918, he hit .261 with 21 errors and in 1919, he fell to .218 with 15 errors.

Saves Johnson's Only No-Hitter

After Babe Ruth and Ernie Shore of the Boston Red Sox's no-hit, the Senators on June 23, 1917, Judge greeted Shore three days later with a leadoff triple en route to a revenge victory for Washington. On July 1, 1920 Walter Johnson pitched the only no-hitter of his career; thanks to Joe Judge. With two out in the ninth inning, Harry Hooper of the Red Sox lashed a hot grounder labelled "base hit" just inside the first base line but Judge made a spectacular backhand stab and flipped the ball to Johnson covering the bag to preserve the "Big Train's" no-hitter.

By 1920, he had matured as a player and he hit a career high .333 and reduced his errors to only 10. In fact, his success that season began an 11-season string with Joe hitting over .300 in all but two and in those he hit over .290.

It was Judge who tipped off Clark Griffith that the 1919 World Series may be fixed. He was told by a star pitcher of another team that gambler Arthur Rothstein had gotten to some of the Black Sox players. The disbelieving Griffith attended the first two games of the Series, then abruptly returned home informing Joe that he was right.

Joe was a .301 hitter in 1921, under .300 in 1922 with .294 and back over the mark with a .314 in 1923. In 1924, Judge did his part in bringing the American League flag to Washington. He hit .324 and lashed out a career high 38 doubles. He proved to be one of the main thorns in Giant manager John McGraw's side during the World Series.

When the Senators repeated as American League champions in 1925, Joe did his part again hitting .314. He got a hot start that year and was leading the league with a .455 average on May 1. He homered in the second game of the Series and his stop of Max Carey's grounder past first base was one of the fielding gems of the Series.

Judge continued to give the Nats a solid performance in the field as well as at the plate from 1926-1929, recording batting averages of .291, .308, .306 and .315. Griff, however, maintained that Judge always seemed to need competition at first base in order for him to put out that "little extra effort" so he repeatedly brought others to training camp to challenge Joe. These included Mule Shirley, George Sisler, Moon Harris and finally the rookie Joe Kuhel.

Judge was 36 when Kuhel was purchased from Kansas City for $65,000 in 1930. At first, not even Kuhel could replace him, as Judge recorded the second highest batting average of his career that year at .326. But in 1931, when new manager Walter Johnson had a falling out with his one-time roommate, Walter told Griffith that he wanted Kuhel at first. Instead, Griff optioned Kuhel to Baltimore of the International League. Four days later Judge was stricken with appendicitis and Kuhel was recalled and took over the job. Although Judge returned to the team in July, he only appeared in 20 more games that season.

Replaced by Joe Kuhel

He was fully recovered from his appendectomy when he reported to spring training in 1932. He won back his job from Kuhel and was the starter at first base on opening day. By July 1, he showed his first signs of slipping when his average dipped to .265. The handwriting was on the wall and a week later it was the beginning of the end when Judge had to leave the game with a charley horse. Kuhel took over the job and kept it for years to come.

At the end of the year, Judge was released unconditionally but he caught on with the Brooklyn Dodgers of the National League in 1933, where he did his lifetime batting average no good by hitting .214 in 42 games. Before the season ended, he was sent over to the Boston Red Sox where he fared better, hitting .296 in 35 games. His final season was with the Red Sox as a player/coach when he played in only 10 games but hit .333.

Joe was a hard-nosed player who like Bucky Harris personified the 1924 World Champions. Joe was a team leader and his managers always listened when he recommended strategy. Griffith bypassed him three times, however, when he filled managerial openings with Harris, Johnson and Joe Cronin.

Georgetown U's Baseball Coach

After his playing days, Judge coached briefly for the Red Sox and Senators and managed the Baltimore Orioles of the International League. Except for two years, however, he was Georgetown University's baseball coach from 1936-1958.

The famed player died of a heart attack on March 11, 1963 after shoveling snow at his home in northwest Washington, D.C. He was 68.

Post-World War I, 1920-1945
Second Base

Stanley Raymond Harris
(Bucky)

BR TR 5' 9" 156 lbs.
B. Nov. 8, 1896, Port Jervis, NY.
D. Nov. 8, 1977, Bethesda, MD.
Hall of Fame 1975

	Y	G	AB	R	H	2B	3B	HR	RBI	BB	SO	SB	BA	SA
Was.	10	1253	4717	718	1295	223	64	9	506	469	307	166	.275	.355
Life	12	1263	4736	722	1297	224	64	9	506	472	310	167	.274	.354

1924 - 1925 Washington Senators

Bucky Harris 2b-Mgr

Second baseman Bucky Harris was one of the best in turning the double play.

Stanley Raymond "Bucky" Harris was the son of Welsh parents. He was raised and worked in a coal-mining district. This undoubtedly contributed to his aggressive play on the ball field and to his feisty disposition. Three years before his purchase by the Senators, Bucky was invited to try out for the Detroit Tigers by manager Hughie Jennings, but with Jennings late reporting to spring training, Harris was quickly dispatched to the minors. While there, he briefly played with Joe Judge on the Baltimore Oriole's minor league team and on his and scout Joe Engel's recommendation, he was scouted by owner Clark Griffith and signed in late 1919, after Harris had gone six for eight in a doubleheader.

Johnson Consoles Harris after Error Loses Game

Right away, Harris was inserted in the lineup for a doubleheader against the New York Yankees. The great Walter Johnson pitched in one of the games and although Bucky drove in two runs, he misjudged a pop-fly and the Senators lost 5-4. The kindly Johnson spent quite a bit of time, trying to console the rookie. Despite a broken finger he played the last two games of the season and went three for eight. His spunkiness endeared Harris to Griffith and it would pay huge dividends for him later. Although he had appeared in only eight games in the fall that year, he was promised a fair trial to win a regular spot in the lineup at second base in 1920.

Indeed, he did win the job in spring training and he was a fixture at second base for the next nine years. Bucky showed the best defensive ability of anyone who ever played second for the Nats. He finished the season with over 500 at bats and recorded a batting average of .300, his only .300 season. He was third on the team in RBI with 68, despite batting in the second slot and lacking power. His ability to produce with runners in scoring position earned him a "clutch hitter" `reputation.

The following year (1921), Harris continued to show amazing fortitude. Hit on the head by one of Johnson's fastballs during batting practice, he took his turn again (after collecting his wits) as if nothing had happened. Playing in all 154 games (second in the league), he hit .289 and led all American League second basemen with 91 double plays, and was second in stolen bases with 29.

In 1922, he again played in all 154 games, hitting .264 and combining with shortstop Roger Peckinpaugh for a league record 116 double plays. He also led all American League second basemen with 992 chances, a figure that puts him high on the all-time list.

Appointed Team Captain

He was appointed captain of the team by Griff for the 1923 season, a precursor of things to come. That year, he hit .282, had 13 triples and was fourth in the league in stolen bases; he led the other league second basemen in putouts and he and "Peck" broke their previous season's record by turning 120 double plays.

Manages Nats to Consecutive A. L. Flags

In 1924, while in Tampa, Florida for a month of golf, Bucky received a letter from Clark Griffith asking him to manage the Senators that year. Elated, Harris tried to phone Griffith immediately, but there was a bad connection. To ensure Griff that he accepted the offer, he sent the same telegram four times in succession. He promised to win the American League Pennant and the "Boy Wonder," only 27 years old and the youngest American League manager with little more than three years major league experience, fulfilled his promise.

Harris' managerial skills were primarily responsible for the Senators' success, but Bucky hit .269, and he and Peckinpaugh again led the league with 100 double plays. His clutch hitting was never more evident than in the 1924 World Series when he hit .333. Trailing the New York Giants three games to two, Harris drove in both runs in the crucial sixth game to lead the Nats to a 2-1 victory. In the seventh and deciding game, Bucky equalled his season output by homering in the fourth inning, then singling in the eighth inning to drive in the tying run, setting the stage for Walter Johnson's twelfth inning victory and his first in a World Series, and Washington's first and only World Championship. Harris' strategy of starting Curly Ogden, a right-hander for just two batters and then bringing in southpaw George Mogridge, forced Giant manager John McGraw to remove dangerous Bill Terry and aided the Senators' cause. The strategy gained him instant fame.

Bucky led Washington to its second consecutive American League Flag in 1925, batting .287 and reeling off, with Roger Peckinpaugh, a league-leading total of 107 double plays. The Senators were not as lucky this time, as the Pittsburgh Pirates won the World Series in seven games, despite the fact that the Nats were ahead three games to one at one time. Harris did establish a World Series record in the fourth game by accepting 13 chances without an error.

Bucky began 1926 on a high note when his hit helped Walter Johnson win the opening game 1-0 in 15 innings; however, the Senators slipped to fourth place in the standings that year despite Harris' .283 average. Roger Peckinpaugh was relegated to part-time duty at shortstop, so Bucky failed to lead the league in double plays for the first time in six seasons. He did lead the league, though, in putouts with 356.

1927—Last Year as Regular Player

Nineteen twenty-seven proved to be Harris' last year as regular second baseman. He appeared in 128 games, hit .267 and led the league in fielding average at .972 and putouts with 316. As manager, he led Washington to another first division finish by ending up in third place.

Nineteen twenty-eight would be the last year for Harris' first tenure as manager of Washington. In the fourth game of the season he tore a ligament in his foot, so he was only able to play in 99 games, hitting a measly .204. His playing days were essentially over and after a World Championship, two American League pennants, and first division finishes each year, Griffith reluctantly fired Bucky and named Walter Johnson as the new manager.

Manages 29 Years for 5 Different Teams

Recognizing Bucky's managerial skills, the Detroit Tigers quickly signed him for the '29 season. He managed the Tigers for five years, playing in only seven games in 1929 and four in 1931. From there he went on to manage the Boston Red Sox, the Senators again, the Philadelphia Phillies, New York Yankees, the Senators (a third stint) and finally the Tigers again. For his job in managing the Yankees to the 1947 American League pennant, he was selected as the *Sporting News*' "Manager of the Year." His major league managerial career covered a span of 29 years and between jobs he managed in the minors in the International and Pacific Coast Leagues.

Later, he served as assistant general manager for the Red Sox and a scout for the White Sox and the expansion Senators.

He was elected to the Hall of Fame in 1975, primarily for his managerial skills. He was popular with his players as confirmed when the Phillies threatened to strike when management fired him. He was patient and, unlike his feisty playing style, was always a gentleman in dealing with his players. He was also recognized as an exceptional fielder who finished high up on the all-time list for second basemen in the average number of putouts per game and the average number of chances per game. He led the league in putouts four times and double plays a record five consecutive years, 1921-1925.

He died in Bethesda, Maryland on November 8, 1977 on his 81st birthday.

Post-World War I Era, 1920-1945
Third Base

John Kelly Lewis
(Buddy)

BL TR 6' 1" 175 lbs.

B. Aug. 10, 1916, Gastonia, NC.

	Y	G	AB	R	H	2B	3B	HR	RBI	BB	SO	SB	BA	SA
Life	11	1349	5261	830	1563	249	93	71	607	573	303	83	.297	.420

Third baseman Buddy Lewis is intently surveying the field.

John Kelly "Buddy" Lewis played American Legion ball in his hometown of Gastonia, North Carolina. He led them to a regional title in the national tournament. He began his professional career with the Washington farm team, Chattanooga, of the Southern Association. Playing third base, he hit .303 in 154 games and was brought up by Washington on September 16, 1935. He appeared in eight games with the Nats, hitting only .107.

Replaces Bluege at Third

Nevertheless, he was invited to the Senators' training camp the next year and impressed manager Bucky Harris so much that he was slated to start at third base on opening day. With President Roosevelt in attendance and the usual capacity opening day crowd, Lewis became too nervous and asked Harris to scratch him from the lineup. He had plenty of other opportunities that year to demonstrate his abilities, playing in 143 games and going to the plate 601 times, scoring 100 runs and finishing with a .291 batting average. By the end of May he had displaced veteran Ossie Bluege as the regular third baseman. He did, however, show that his fielding needed a lot of improvement, leading the league in '36 with 32 errors. Buddy Myer took a special interest in helping the youngster adjust and as a result Lewis was given the nickname, "Buddy."

With Cecil Travis playing shortstop, Lewis joined him as fixtures on the left side of the infield through 1939. The two became fast friends and roomed together when the club was on the road. With the bat, the left side of the Senators' infield was as good as any in baseball. Both had classic swings but Lewis swung harder and had a slightly higher career slugging average than Cecil's.

Selected for A.L. All–Star Team

In 1937, Buddy hit over .300 (.314) for the first of four times in his 11-year career. He led the league by playing in 156 games, banged out 210 hits and topped the club in runs scored (107).

On August 10, however, Buddy made four errors in a game against the Philadelphia A's, tying a record set in 1901. In 1938, Lewis was selected for the American League All-Star Team and almost hit the .300 mark again, finishing with a .298 average and scoring 122 runs, a career high. His fielding improved and he led all third basemen with 329 putouts and 32 double plays in 151 games. Unfortunately, he also led the league in number of errors with 47.

Shifted to Outfield

Buddy hit his peak in 1939 when he hit .319, led the league with 16 triples and posted his highest slugging average of .478. Nineteen forty was a transition year for Buddy. He was shifted to the outfield with fear and trepidation. He had never played the position but Clark Griffith had purchased Jimmy Pofahl for a large sum and he was installed at shortstop. This necessitated Travis' move to third base, hence Lewis to the outfield was designed to keep his bat in the lineup.

Lewis took the move in stride, indicating that he didn't care where he played as long as he was in the lineup. To everyone's delight, Buddy made the adjustment remarkably well, hitting .317 and, in fact, said that he would like to remain there for the rest of his career. Buddy had another fine year in '41, hitting .297 in what proved to be his last season before leaving to do his part in World War II. He had topped .300 three times and scored 100 runs or more four times before entering the service.

Awarded Distinguished Flying Cross

Buddy missed nearly four years of play, years that should have been his prime years. Lewis had gone against Griffith's rules and taken flying lessons in Florida while he was there for spring training and these stood him in good stead as a pilot of C-47 transports in the army air corps. When he received his wings at Bolling Field, he attended a Senators' game with Griffith and had to leave early. Shortly thereafter he flew the giant aircraft over the field and dipped his wings. Unlike many of the other players who had recreational jobs to boost morale of the troops, Lewis flew 351 missions over the Burma hump, many times landing behind Japanese lines. Clark Griffith was pleased to learn that Lewis had dubbed his plane "The Old Fox." Lewis was awarded the Distinguished Flying Cross on December 28, 1944 for precision flying in the Burma War Theater.

Luke Sewell, former Washington catcher and then manager of the Cleveland Indians, made a morale-boosting tour of the area with Lewis as his escort. Luke said that Buddy was recognized as one of the top pilots there and could land the giant airplane on very short airstrips.

Buddy was welcomed back late in 1945 to help in the Nats' last serious drive for an American League pennant. He played in 69 games and hit for his highest average at .333. But, the Senators lost the race to the Detroit Tigers on the last day of the season. It appeared that Lewis' comeback was going smoothly, when he hit .292 the following year (1946) and led the league with 16 assists from the outfield.

In late 1947, however, it became apparent that Lewis' war experiences had taken a heavy toll on his young body. Just 30 years of age, he began the year hitting very well and he was selected for the All-Star team again but over the last part of the season his hitting tailed off dramatically and his average dipped to .261.

Failed Comeback in '49

Lewis sat out the entire 1948 season, claiming that his old back and hip injuries were bothering him. It might have been, though, that he realized that he had lost too much while away from the game. When he returned in 1949, at the prodding of Griffith, he played in 95 games but only hit .245. He recognized that it was time to retire and return to Gastonia and devote more time to running his automobile agency there. He made his retirement request to Griffith on February 25, 1950.

Buddy also kept his hand in the game by coaching the local American Legion team he had played for years before.

Post-World War I, 1920-1945
Shortstop

Cecil Howell Travis

(Cecil)

BL TR 6' 1.5" 185 lbs.

B. Aug. 8, 1913, Riverdale, GA.

	Y	G	AB	R	H	2B	3B	HR	RBI	BB	SO	SB	BA	SA
Life	12	1328	4914	665	1544	265	78	27	657	402	291	23	.314	.416

Infielder Cecil Travis (right) with manager Ossie Bluege upon his return from the army on September 8, 1945.

Cecil Travis, the tall, gangly farm boy from Riverdale, Georgia was a favorite of Washington fans, not only because he was a quiet, kind and modest gentleman both on and off the field but because he was a steady fielder and one of the best hitters ever to wear a Washington uniform. After 12 years in the majors, Cecil retired with a lifetime batting average of .314.

Travis' left-handed batting stroke was natural, smooth and classic. Initially, he was prone to collect many of his hits to the opposite field in the spacious left field expanse of Griffith Stadium. Later, he began hitting with more power to right field, just before World War II interrupted his baseball career.

Began Pro Career at Age 16

As a youngster, Travis attended a baseball camp, run by Kid Elberfield, former major league infielder. Washington scout, Joe Engel had Clark Griffith pay $100 for three of the camp graduates and Travis, at 16 years of age, was sent to Chattanooga of the Southern Association. Engel said that he wasn't much of a ballplayer on defense and that Cecil once spiked himself while awkwardly trying to field a ground ball. Playing in 18 games for the Lookouts, he batted .429 for the Washington farm team that year (1931). Cecil rarely hit for extra bases but he sure banged out plenty of singles. Engel informed Griffith that he would soon be sending the kid north as heir apparent to long time Washington third baseman Ossie Bluege's job.

Raps Out 5 Hits in Debut with Nats

In 1932, Travis played in 152 games for Chattanooga and hit an eye opening .362. During the Senators' pennant year (1933), Ossie Bluege was hurt for awhile and Travis filled in admirably at third base for 18 games, batting .302. In his first big league game against the Cleveland Indians on May 16, 1933, Cecil rapped out five consecutive hits in Griffith Stadium. Travis says that was the highlight of his career with the Nats. When Bluege recovered, he returned to third base but he knew that the position would be Travis' in 1934.

First Three Full Years Hits Over .300

Ossie was right and Cecil became the Nats' regular third baseman, hitting .319 in 109 games. He was a consistent hitter and posted similar numbers the next two years, playing in 138 games each year and batting .318 in '35 and .317 in '36. It was almost impossible to consistently fool him at the plate; with a pronounced crouch and choked-up bat, he was going to get wood on the ball. His fielding improved with regular play at third and, in 1935, he led all American League third basemen by participating in 29 double plays.

In 1937 and 1938, Travis joined the elite American League batters, compiling averages of .344 and .355 respectively. He was a member of the American League All-Star squad in '38. The following year broke a chain of six consecutive .300 seasons when in an off year his average fell to .292. But, he bounced back again in 1940 with a .322 average and again was on the All-Star team.

Runner–up for A.L. Batting Title

Cecil's banner year was 1941 when he finished second to Ted Williams in the American League batting championship race with a robust .359 batting average. He garnered career highs with 218 league leading hits, 39 doubles, 19 triples, seven home runs, 101 runs batted in and a slugging average of .520. In his first nine years (eight hitting over .300) with the Nats, he had put numbers on the board, which made him a surefire bet for the Cooperstown Hall of Fame. For the third time, Travis was picked for the American League All-Star Team in 1941 and the Baseball Writers Association of America named him as the outstanding shortstop of the major leagues.

Misses Four Years for World War II

But, fate would not have it that way, as his U.S. Army duty forced an absence of almost four years from major league baseball, with the exception of his participation in a military relief charity All-Star game. Military All-Stars lost to the American League All-Stars in Cleveland on July 7, 1942, raising $160,000 for the fund. Travis was later sent to the European Theater where he was thrust in the middle of the Battle of the Bulge. In the extremely cold Christmas weather, Cecil suffered severely frozen feet, which prevented him from regaining his previous form upon his return to the big leagues.

The Nats were in a dogfight for the 1945 pennant with the Detroit Tigers when Travis was discharged from the army in September of that year. Out of shape, Cecil tried to help their losing cause by appearing in 15 games but he hit only .245 in 54 trips to the plate. It was obvious the next year that this was not the Travis that played before World War II, when Cecil played in 137 games and batted only .252. Cecil, however, had provided a glimmer of hope earlier in the year, when on May 4, 1946 he collected six straight hits before being stopped by Cleveland's Steve Gromek.

Nineteen forty-seven was Travis' last year in the majors, as he played in only 74 games and hit a weak .216. But, 15,228 Washington fans and league and world leaders did not forget Travis' stellar performances in a Washington uniform as they turned out on August 15, 1947 to pay tribute to a genuine hero. Glowing tributes by General Eisenhower, other military brass, league officials and adoring fans were heard, as well as an unending assortment of gifts for him, his wife and two sons.

After the season, Cecil retired to his farm in Riverdale, Georgia and did a little scouting for the Senators in the region.

As of this writing, Travis may be the last living member of the Senators' last American League championship team of 1933.

Post-World War I Era, 1920-1945
Outfield

Henry Emmett Manush

(Heinie)

Hall of Fame 1964

BL TL 6' 1" 200 lbs.

B. Jul. 20, 1901, Tuscumbia, AL.

D. May 12, 1971, Sarasota, FL.

	Y	G	AB	R	H	2B	3B	HR	RBI	BB	SO	SB	BA	SA
Was.	6	792	3290	576	1078	215	70	47	491	205	131	29	.328	.478
Life	17	2008	7654	1287	2524	491	160	110	1183	506	345	114	.330	.479

Line drive hitter and Hall of Famer Heinie Manush swinging the bat at Griffith Stadium.

When Henry "Heinie" Manush was in the minor leagues, he was something of a home run hitter, a la Babe Ruth. But, under the tutelage of manager Ty Cobb of the Detroit Tigers, he was converted into one of the greatest "line-drive" hitters of all time. With a lifetime batting average of .330 for 17 seasons, he reeled off eleven .300 seasons, seven of them consecutively. He won the American League batting championship in 1926 with an average of .378 and six times finished among the top five hitters in the league. Twice he led the league in the number of hits made and twice he led in doubles.

When he broke in with the Tigers in 1923, he was platooned in the outfield because Detroit was loaded with .300 hitting outfielders. Despite that, he appeared in 109 games and hit for a .334 average. Although his average dropped to .289 in 1924, he played in 120 games and had 422 trips to the plate. He lost his job the next year to Al Wingo, a .270 hitter, and Heinie only had 278 at bats but he pushed his average up to .302.

Wins Batting Title in 1926

Manush regained his starting spot in 1926 with his league leading .378 hitting in almost 500 at bats. Heinie began the last day of the season behind Babe Ruth and two of his teammates, but went six for nine in a doubleheader to win the crown. When Cobb resigned as manager after gambling allegations, umpire George Moriarity replaced him. Heinie did not get along with the new manager and his average fell to .298, although he was second in the league with 18 triples.

Loses Batting Crown on Last Day

After the season ended, Manush got his wish and was traded to the St. Louis Browns along with Lu Blue for Chick Galloway, Elim Vangilder and Harry Rice. Heinie found St. Louis to his liking, playing in every game in 1928 and battling Goose Goslin down to the wire for the batting championship. Although they each hit .378, Goslin won by percentage points by obtaining a hit in his last plate appearance of the season. Manush, however, did lead the league with 241 hits, and he tied for lead with 47 doubles, while also smashing 20 triples and 13 home runs. He lost the Most Valuable Player award to Mickey Cochrane by two points.

Manush led the league in '29 with 45 doubles and ended up third in the race for the batting crown with a .355 average. On June 30, 1930, he and pitcher Alvin "General" Crowder were traded to the Washington Senators for outfielder Goose Goslin. Again, Heinie liked the change and he caught fire with the Nats, hitting .362 in 88 games and finishing the season with a .350 average. His average fell to .291 in 1931, but he regained his batting eye in 1932, finishing with a .342 average.

In 1933, Manush almost captured the batting title again, when he finished second, only three percentage points behind Jimmie Foxx at .336. He hit safely in 33 consecutive games (a Washington record) and topped the league again with 221 hits and 17 triples. He was one of the main factors in Washington's successful quest for the American League flag.

Thrown Out of '33 Series Game

Appearing in his only World Series, Manush caught President Roosevelt's "first pitch" and presented it to Earl Whitehill who won the Nats' only Series victory. Heinie may have been largely responsible for the Nats' loss in five games. Trailing in games two to one in the sixth inning of Game Four, Manush grounded a shot into the hole between first and second but Giants second baseman Hughie Critz stabbed it and threw to first to nab Heinie on a close play. Manush and the Senators were irate at umpire Charlie Moran's call and disputed it vehemently. In the turmoil, Manush grabbed Moran's bow tie and stretched it and let it snap back. Moran immediately threw Manush out of the game. The Senators' objections fell on Judge Landis' deaf ears and Dave Harris was forced to replace him. Down two to one in the bottom of the eleventh inning, the Senators loaded the bases with one out but pinch hitter Cliff Bolton hit into a game ending double play to put the Senators down three games to one. Had Manush not been thrown out of the game, Harris would have likely been used as the pinch hitter and who knows what might have happened.

Closes Career in NL

Manush had an even better year in '34 when he hit .349 and finished third in the batting race behind Lou Gehrig and Charlie Gehringer. Heinie was the starting left fielder in the All-Star game that year, won by the American League, 9-7.

When he finished the 1935 season with his lowest average ever (.273), Washington gave up on him and traded him to the Boston Red Sox for outfielders Roy Johnson and Carl Reynolds. In 82 games in 1936 with the Sox, he raised his average a bit to .291, and was picked up by the Brooklyn Dodgers for the '37 season. Manush regained his batting form and hit .333 in 132 games.

Heinie saw limited action with Brooklyn in 1938 appearing in only 17 games and hitting just .235. Before the end of the season, he was acquired by the Pittsburgh Pirates and with the change of scenery he responded with a .308 average in 15 games. He wound up his major league career in 1939, going 0-12 in 10 games with the Pirates before receiving his unconditional release.

He played and managed in the minors until 1945, then scouted for the Braves and Pirates before replacing Clyde Milan as a coach for the Washington Senators in 1953 and 1954. Later, he scouted in Florida for Washington's expansion franchise through 1962.

Manush was a top golfer and often finished near the top in the annual baseball player's tournament. In 1964, the Veteran's Committee elected him to the Cooperstown Hall of Fame.

He died after a long battle with cancer on May 12, 1971 in Sarasota, Florida at 69 years of age.

Post-World War I Era, 1920-1945
Outfield

George Washington Case

(George)

BR TR 6' 183 lbs.

B. Nov. 11, 1915, Trenton, NJ.

D. Jan. 23, 1989, Trenton, NJ.

	Y	G	AB	R	H	2B	3B	HR	RBI	BB	SO	SB	BA	SA
Was.	10	1108	4532	739	1306	210	39	20	355	392	259	321	.288	.365
Life	11	1226	5016	785	1415	233	43	21	377	426	297	349	.282	.358

Speedster George Case is safe at home on the front end of a double steal when catcher Bill Dickey drops the ball.

George Washington Case's main claim to fame was as a base stealer. He came to the Senators during the waning days of the 1937 season and stayed with them for 10 of the 11 years that he was in the majors. Scout Joe Cambria found the winged-foot schoolboy pitching for Peddie Institute in New Jersey. He then took him to Trenton where he was converted into an outfielder.

Fastest Man in Baseball

From the time he entered the majors in 1937, he was the fastest man in baseball. For six of his eleven seasons in the majors, he led the American League in steals and between 1939 and 1943 he led for five straight seasons, accomplishing his high of 61 in 1943. On September 14 of that year, he broke the record time for circling the bases, which had stood for one-third of a century. Hans Lobert of the New York Giants had done it in 13.8 seconds in 1910. Case did it in 13.5 seconds and was awarded a $100 U.S. War Bond by owner Clark Griffith for the feat.

His grit and determination also matched his great speed. After swiping three bases in the first game of a doubleheader on September 26, 1943 to wrest the league lead from Wally Moses of the Chicago White Sox, George admitted that his leg ached like a toothache. He had pulled a muscle the week before and had been playing with a mass of tape around his leg. However, for that crucial late season game, he had removed the hampering tape. When he doubled in the nightcap, his leg nearly buckled as he beat the throw into second base. When manager Ossie Bluege and coach Clyde Milan rushed to him to ascertain if he could continue, George, who had learned that Moses had since tied him for the lead, said he wanted to stay in the game. He later stole a base, enabling him to regain the lead over Moses.

Milan's Base-Stealing Tips Help

When Case first arrived with Washington, coach Clyde Milan, an accomplished base stealer himself, took George under his wing and taught him how to slide, take a lead, and to get the jump on the pitcher when attempting to steal. Clyde played a major role in George's success in base stealing. Case, however, never was able to match Milan's club record of 88 thefts. Case was once quoted as saying, "You have to have the drive to steal, just like some ballplayers have the drive to hit. Stealing is the same as hitting, except not so many players want to do it."

George's excellent hitting ability contributed to his base-stealing records. If you don't get on base, you can't steal. In the 22 games he played in the first year ('37), he batted .307 and in his second year he appeared in 107 games and hit .305. Hitting over .300 for the third consecutive year in 1939, he was selected for the American League All-Star squad and he also won his first league base-stealing championship with 51 thefts. In 1940, he played in all 154 games but his average dipped below .300 for the first time when he hit .293, and stole 35 bases. Playing center field and leading off, he missed only one game in 1941, led all outfielders with 21 assists, hit .271, and stole 33 bases.

In 1942, he opened the season in left field with Stan Spence in center and had a little difficulty making the adjustment in the outfield when he committed a league-leading 14 errors. It didn't affect his hitting, however, for he had his best career batting average of .320 in 125 games and finished in sixth place among American League batters. His base running wasn't affected either, as he posted a league leading base stealing mark of 44.

Steals Career High 61 Bases

He led the American League with 102 runs scored in 1943, appearing in 125 games and batting .294. His five-year reign as American League base-stealing champion was completed that year when he stole his career high 61 bases. He was the starting right fielder for the American League in the first night All-Star game that year. He played in 119 games in 1944 but his batting average took a severe drop to .250. Although he stole 49 bases that year, he lost his American League crown. Despite this he was selected for the All-Star squad again.

He regained his batting eye with a vengeance in 1945 when he went on a spring hitting spree and raised his average to .556 in May. His early season heroics earned him a spot on the American League All-Star Team for the last time. Unfortunately, he was then injured and his average declined steadily the rest of the year, reaching .294 by the end of the year. He played in 123 games and stole 30 bases and his injury may have cost the Nats the pennant, as they were barely nosed out by the Detroit Tigers on the last day of the season.

Won 100 Yard Match Race

In 1946, he was traded to the Cleveland Indians for long ball hitter Jeff Heath. The change of scenery did not help Case, as his batting average nose-dived to .225 in 118 games. He did, however, recapture his stolen base crown that year with 28 thefts. In Cleveland owner Bill Veeck's first promotion, George raced former Olympic champion Jesse Owens and lost. While in Washington that year, a match race with the Senators' Gil Coan was arranged. Four Amateur Athletic Union (AAU) timers clocked Case in 9.9 seconds for 100 yards over Griffith Stadium turf as he easily beat Coan. Both were running in full baseball uniform. George was nearly 30 years old at the time.

The Senators reacquired Case for the 1947 season but he was used sparingly, appearing in only 36 games, hitting a lowly .150 and stealing only five bases. This ended George's major league playing career.

Baseball Coach at Rutgers U.

After leaving major league baseball, Case served as baseball coach for Rutgers University for 11 years. When Washington acquired an American League expansion franchise in 1961, new manager Mickey Vernon brought Case back to the Senators as their third base coach. He remained with the club until Vernon was replaced in 1963 and then served one year (1968) as a coach for Calvin Griffith's Minnesota Twins.

As a young athlete, Case was recognized for his basketball prowess and was offered scholarships to 27 colleges. It was at Peddie Prep that he discovered his first love—baseball. And, what a great competitor he was!

Case died January 23, 1989 in Trenton, New Jersey at the age of 73.

Post-World War I, 1920-1945
Outfield

John Thomas Stone

(Johnny, Rocky)

BL TR 6' 1" 178 lbs.
B. Oct. 10, 1905, Mulberry, TN.
D. Nov. 30, 1955, Shelbyville, TN.

	Y	G	AB	R	H	2B	3B	HR	RBI	BB	SO	SB	BA	SA
Was.	5	556	2066	358	655	122	55	32	351	247	133	21	.317	.476
Life	11	1200	4494	739	1391	268	105	77	707	463	352	45	.310	.467

Nats' outfielder Johnny Stone is running on a cold spring training day.

Johnny Stone, the hard-luck outfielder, had his major league career curtailed after 11 seasons because of advanced tuberculosis. Batting over .300 in seven if his 11 seasons, the stylish left-handed batter was among the top dozen hitters in the American League while he was playing. The "picture player" could hit, run, throw and field with the best of them. He was a manager's dream, quietly and efficiently making his contribution as a "team" player.

Hits Safely in 34 Consecutive Games

Johnny broke into the minors with Evansville of the Three-I League in 1928, hitting .354 in 75 games. The Detroit Tigers brought him up to the parent club late in the same season and in 26 games he hit for the same average. He played in 26 games for the Tigers in 1929, his average dropping to .260. He won a regular job in 1930, however, when he hit .313 in 128 games, his first full year in the big leagues. During the season, Stone hit safely in 34 consecutive games, which at the time tied him with George Sisler for the fourth longest American League streak.

Stone made almost 600 plate appearances in 1931 and batted .327, driving in 76 runs and slamming 10 home runs, 11 triples and 28 doubles. Despite an average that dipped below .300 (.298), Johnny had his most productive season for the Tigers in 1932. His slugging average was .486 and he drove in more than 100 runs (108) for the only time in his career. He also registered career records with 106 runs scored and 17 home runs; in addition, he laced 35 doubles and 12 triples.

Traded from Tigers to Senators

In 1933, with 574 plate appearances in 148 games, Johnny's average dipped to .280. On May 30, however, he hit two home runs and four doubles in a doubleheader. He was the first player to have six extra base hits in a doubleheader without extra innings (a number of players have since tied him). After the season, Stone was traded to the Washington Senators for outfielder Goose Goslin and pitcher "General" Alvin Crowder who had been giving Nats' manager Joe Cronin some discipline problems. The hard-luck Stone, instead of playing for a pennant contender in '34 saw the Senators plummet all the way to seventh place, while Goslin and Crowder played vital roles on Tiger teams that won American League championships in '34 and '35 and a World Series victory in the latter year.

At the start of the '34 season, the rather good-looking, streamlined and dependable Stone was the only outfielder assured of a starting spot in the lineup. He was inserted in the lineup as the clean-up hitter and in the first of four consecutive .300 seasons in a Washington uniform, he hit .315. In 1935, he hit for about the same average (.314) and he connected for a career high 18 triples. On June 16 he added eight hits (2 triples, 2 doubles and 4 singles) in a doubleheader to go along with four hits from the previous day.

1936 Best Career Season

Stone's 1936 season was by far the best of his career. He hit .341, had a slugging average of .545, drove in 90 runs, had 15 homers, 11 triples, and 22 doubles and scored 95 runs! His final full year with Washington was in 1937 when John again had a great year, hitting .330, driving in 88 runs and garnering 33 doubles.

TB Ends Career in 1938

The fateful year was 1938. Beginning in spring training, Johnny showed signs of the dreaded tubercular disease. Although his form was still good, he was unable to make good contact with the ball. With his average dropping to .244 in 56 games, Clark Griffith sent him off for a complete physical examination. When the fearful disease was confirmed, the shocking revelation ended his baseball career at age 31. After months at Saranac Lake, New York, Stone was able to recover from the illness, despite one lung being punctured, due to his strong constitution and indomitable will.

Clark Griffith paid Stone's full salary in 1938 and helped in other ways. In addition, a "Johnny Stone Day" was held on September 17, 1939 in honor of Johnny. Club president Clark Griffith and Tiger's president Walter O. Briggs presented him with a check for $3,400 to pay off the mortgage on Stone's 88-acre farm in Tennessee. Further, 10,000 fans contributed almost $5,000 to help their stricken player.

After his playing days were over, Stone served as a scout for Detroit for a time before his untimely death of a heart attack at his home in Shelbyville, Tennessee at the age of 50.

CHAPTER FIVE

Post-World War II Era, 1946-1960

Introduction

Washington's worst twentieth-century teams played during this period. Teams finished in the first division only once (fourth place), while ending up next to last or in the cellar nine of 15 years. Their winning percentage was only .416. There were, however, two Hall of Famers who played for the Nats during that time, Early Wynn and Harmon Killebrew. Wynn, a 300-game winner, launched his career with Washington, while Killebrew saved his best years for the Minnesota Twins. Mickey Vernon and Eddie Yost were also among the fan's favorites.

Since Mickey Vernon was selected for the all-time team, the only other eligible full-time first baseman during the period was Julio Becquer. Rather than pick fancy fielding but weak-hitting Julio, I decided to shift Roy Seivers from the outfield to first base since he spent a lot of time at each position. This enabled me to field a stronger lineup by inserting Jim Busby into the outfield with Jim Lemon and Gil Coan.

Leaving Eddie Yost off of the all-time team was a hard thing to do, since it was a toss-up between he and Ossie Bluege. Ossie was the superior fielder and he outhit Eddie with a lifetime average that was about 20 points higher. Nevertheless, it was difficult to discount Yost's remarkable on-base percentage and his superior power. If Yost was selected, there was no obvious choice for the period All-Star team whereas Buddy Lewis played some fine third base during the same period as Bluege.

Clint Courtney, Harmon Killebrew, Jim Lemon, Camilo Pascual, Pete Runnels, Roy Sievers, Chuck Stobbs and Eddie Yost were all members of this Senators' 1956 team.

The rest of the selections were relatively easy to make. Here is the lineup:

Post-World War II Era, 1946-1960 All-Star Team

Right-Handed Pitcher:	Early Wynn
Left-Handed Pitcher:	Chuck Stobbs
Relief Pitcher:	Dick Hyde
Catcher:	Clint Courtney
First Base:	Roy Sievers
Second Base:	Sherry Robertson
Third Base:	Eddie Yost
Shortstop:	Pete Runnels
Outfield:	Jim Lemon
Outfield:	Gil Coan
Outfield:	Jim Busby

A summary of team performance during the period follows:

Post-World War II Era, 1946-1960

Washington Nationals
American League
8 Team League

Year	Finish	Games	Won	Lost	Pct.
1946	4	154	76	78	.494
1947	7	154	64	90	.416
1948	7	153	56	97	.366
1949	8	154	50	104	.325
1950	5	154	67	87	.435
1951	7	154	62	92	.403
1952	5	154	78	76	.506
1953	5	152	76	76	.500
1954	6	154	66	88	.429
1955	8	154	53	101	.344
1956	7	154	59	95	.383
1957	8	154	55	99	.357
1958	8	154	61	93	.396
1959	8	154	63	91	.409
1960	5	154	73	81	.474
Totals - 15 Years, 15 Teams		2307	959	1348	
Averages	7	154	64	90	.416

Post-World War II Era, 1946-1960
Right-handed Pitcher

Early Wynn

(Gus)

SW TR 6'0" 200 lbs.
B. Jan. 6, 1920, Hartford, AL.
D. April 4, 1999, Venice, FL.
Hall of Fame 1971

	Y	W	L	PCT	ERA	G	GS	CG	IP	H	BB	SO	SHO
Was.	8	72	87	.453	3.94	191	168	92	1267	1359	460	386	9
Life	23	300	244	.551	3.54	691	612	290	4564	4291	1775	2334	49

Early Wynn notches his 300th victory July 13, 1963 for Cleveland against Kansas City.

Next to Walter Johnson, the durable Early Wynn was probably the greatest pitcher who ever toiled on the mound for the Senators. In an active career spanning four decades, Wynn notched 300 major league victories, only the ninth pitcher of the twentieth century to accomplish the feat. Thus, he joined the legendary Grover Cleveland Alexander, Lefty Grove, Johnson, Christy Mathewson, Kid Nichols, Eddie Plank, Warren Spahn and Cy Young in that elusive club. Unfortunately for Washington, Wynn did not reach stardom until after the Senators traded him to Cleveland in 1949. Playing eight years, mostly with weak Washington teams, he compiled a losing record of 72-87.

Signed by Washington's Clyde Milan

When the Alabama boy was only 16, he saw an advertisement in the *Sporting News* about a free baseball school to be conducted by the Nats' Chattanooga farm club in Sanford, Florida, so he made a timely visit there. The fastballing young kid with the cutoff blue jeans and worn-out glove quickly impressed coach Clyde Milan who talked Early's mother into permitting him to sign a professional contract. He played for the Sanford team the first year and then was promoted to Charlotte in the Piedmont League where he played in 1938-40. In 1941, he was sent to Springfield of the Eastern League. While in the minors, he was brought back in the fall to the parent club for brief stints. In 1939, he started three games losing two but completing one. In 1941, it was a different story, as he completed four of five games started, and won three and lost one, with an ERA of 1.58. He had made the big time!

When the chunky, copper-complected kid (Wynn was one-eighth Cherokee Indian) first arrived on the scene, he had only his sneaky fastball and a little wrinkle curve. All business and a careful student of the game, Early quickly added to his repertoire. To complement his fastball, Wynn came up with three curves. One thrown at full speed would snap off the plate, the second thrown a little more slowly would drop sharply when it reached the batter and the third was a slow, wide-breaking curve. He also learned the value of the slow change-of-pace pitch while in the minors and he developed a pitching philosophy, which stood him in good stead throughout his career. He usually fed a lot of junk pitches to the good hitters and relied on his fastball to handle the majority of batters.

Known as a "Mean" Pitcher

He believed that control and confidence was essential for a pitcher. He credits Coach Benny Bengough with improving his control. Benny spotted Early watching his feet instead of the catcher's glove during his delivery. Wynn also learned quickly to control his fiery temper. He was an imposing figure on the mound with a "mean" look that struck fear in opposing hitters. If pitchers on the other team were throwing at his hitters, they could expect prompt retaliation from Early.

Early loved the game and wanted to play every day. He was a switch hitter and he played the outfield some while in the minors. In his early days with the Senators, he pleaded, to no avail, with owner Clark Griffith to let him play the outfield when he wasn't pitching. He was, however, used as a pinch hitter 90 times from 1943-55 in recognition of his hitting ability. He was able to clout 17 home runs during his career.

Wynn's first full season was 1942, when he appeared in 30 games, winning 10, losing 16 and completing 10. Wynn became a workhorse for the Senators, leading the league in games started in 1943 with 33. Half of his eight Senators seasons were winning years, although '43 was one of his best when he posted a 10-12 won-lost record with an ERA of 2.91. The following year, however, he led the league in number of losses with 17. His last good year with the Nats was in '47 when he managed 17 wins and 15 losses and an ERA of 3.64. The Senators lost the services of Wynn in 1945 and half of 1946 when Early was in the United States Army.

Bad Trade Sends Wynn to Indians

Wynn was a staunch supporter of Clark Griffith and he resented those who called him "tightwad," maintaining that Griff had always treated him fairly and that Early owed him a lot. "Bad blood" between Wynn and manager Joe Kuhel during the '48 season put the handwriting on the wall however. Griff was gradually turning over the reins of his club to his nephew, Calvin Griffith, at the time. Clark took the blame for it, but it was Calvin who engineered one of the worst Washington trades ever. Calvin sent Wynn and former batting champion Mickey Vernon to the Cleveland Indians for pitchers Joe Haynes, Ed Klieman, and first baseman Eddie Robinson.

Early pitched for Cleveland for nine consecutive seasons and only in his last year of the stretch (1957) did he fail to post a winning year. In that year, however, he led the league in games started with 37 and strikeouts, 184. He also gave up more hits, 270 than any other league hurler. In four of those seasons, he won 20 games or more. He became an integral part of one of the best pitching rotations ever, sharing starts with Bob Feller, Bob Lemon and Mike Garcia.

Loses Only Start in 1954 Series

Early was 23-12 in 1952 despite the fact that he gave up more walks than any other pitcher in the league. His best year with the Indians was 1954, when he led the league with 23 wins and had only 11 losses. He also led the league in games started with 36 and in innings pitched with 270. He played a major role in earning the Indians a spot in the World Series that year. Wynn lost his only start in the Series, a heartbreaking 3-1 loss due to Dusty Rhodes' heroics. With the Indians during that period, he also led the league in 1950 with an ERA of 3.20 and in 1951 with 34 starts and 274 innings pitched.

He loved playing for general manager Frank Lane and manager Al Lopez, so it didn't surprise anyone when the pair obtained Early for the Chicago White Sox in 1958 after they switched from Cleveland to Chicago. Wynn pitched well for the Sox from 1958 to 1962. His best year was 1959, when he led the league again in wins with 22, games started with 37, and innings pitched with 255. He also walked 199 batters to lead the league in that category.

While with the White Sox, he was a league leader in 1959 when he whiffed 179 batters and in 1960 when he recorded four shutouts.

Wins Cy Young Award in 1959

His Cy Young Award-winning '59 season helped capture the flag for the White Sox and Wynn was honored when he was given the starting assignment in the first game of the World Series. Early responded by combining with Gerry Staley to shut out the Los Angeles Dodgers 11-0. Wynn went seven innings. Early also was given starts in games four and six, but he was roughed up both times in short stints, taking the loss in game six, the final game.

Near the end of the 1962 season, the aging and portly Wynn had posted 299 major league victories. But, victory number 300 proved to be elusive. He failed three times before the end of the year, losing a heartbreaker to the New York Yankees in 10 innings. The White Sox released him at the end of the season.

Notches 300th Win

The Cleveland Indians gave him another chance when he was signed in June of '63. It took him five tries with the Indians before he was able to best the Kansas City A's 7-4, despite lasting only five innings. In the process of attempting to win number 300, Wynn also broke Bob Feller's major league record of 1,764 walks when he finished with 1,775.

Wynn, while a Florida resident, continued to be associated with the game after his active playing days ended. He was a coach for Cleveland from 1964-66 and for the Minnesota Twins from 1967-69. While with Washington, he married a local girl. Wynn worked as a newspaperman, radio announcer and salesman, and had a variety of interests. A man with a keen sense of humor, he was able to mimic Nick Altrock's clown act perfectly. But, baseball fans everywhere will remember that when Wynn took the mound in a game, he was nobody's clown. Sportswriters didn't forget it either when they voted him into the Hall of Fame in 1971.

Post-World War II Era, 1946-1960
Left-Handed Pitcher

Charles Klein Stobbs
(Chuck)

BL TL 6' 1" 185 lbs.
B. Jul. 2, 1929, Wheeling, WV.

	Y	W	L	PCT	ERA	G	GS	CG	IP	H	BB	SO	SHO
Was.	8	64	89	.418	4.16	278	152	41	1193.2	1287	380	550	7
Life	15	107	130	.451	4.29	459	238	65	1920.1	2003	735	897	7

Nats' hurler Chuck Stobbs posing with the Griffith Stadium bleachers and center field flagpole in the background.

Despite his many accomplishments, Chuck Stobbs is best remembered for serving up to Mickey Mantle a 565-foot home run that nearly cleared the left field bleachers at Griffith Stadium. Only the old football scoreboard above the bleachers kept the missile from leaving the park.

$30,000 Red Sox Bonus Baby

Stobbs was a high school phenom in three sports at Granby High in Norfolk, Virginia. In his junior and senior years, his teams won state championships in football, basketball and baseball. As a member of the Norfolk American Legion team, Stobbs hurled his team to three consecutive state championships. Chuck fanned all nine batters he faced in an all-American high school classic in New York's Yankee Stadium. Just appearing in the hallowed Stadium was Stobbs' greatest thrill in baseball. As a result, he was given a $30,000 bonus to sign with the Boston Red Sox and sent to the minors with the Lynn, Massachusetts club of the New England League in mid-summer 1947. Before the year was out, Boston called up Stobbs to the majors where his record was 0-1 in four games.

He remained with the Red Sox the following year (1948) but saw limited action. Appearing in only six games, he was not the pitcher of record in any. The next three seasons he pitched very well with the Red Sox with winning records of 11-6 in '49, 12-7 in '50 and 10-9 in '51. But, in each instance, his earned run average was over four. He pitched in 102 games total for the Bosox before he went to the Chicago White Sox for the 1952 season. Although he had one of the best ERAs of his career (3.13 in 38 games) that year, he was only able to win seven games while losing 12. Chuck was with Chicago only one season before moving along to the Senators in 1953. It was in that year on April 17 that Mickey Mantle hit his mighty blast off of Stobbs as the Yankees beat the Senators 7-3.

"Junk" Ball Pitcher for Senators

Stobbs relied mainly on an assortment of six "junk" pitches when he came to the Senators. Once in a while he would intersperse a fastball to keep the hitters off balance. The first two years with Washington ('53 and '54), he was named as a starter and was over .500 at 22-19. In 1955, he was used mainly in relief and in 41 games was only 4-14 with a 5.00 ERA.

Chuck's Best year (1956)

The following year (1956) proved to be Chuck's best. By early September, he had won 15 games and manager Chuck Dressen gave him plenty of starts in an effort to notch 20 wins. Instead he finished with a record of 15-15 and an ERA of 3.60. His marked improvement that year was partially due to a new pitch in Stobbs' inventory. Manager Dressen recognized that Chuck had a natural delivery for a screwball, so Stobbs learned to throw one.

Losing Streak Ends at 16

Little did anyone suspect that his best season was to be followed by his worst. In 1957, the hard-luck left-hander led the league with 20 losses, the first Nat to lose that many since Walter Johnson posted a 25-20 record in 1918. He lost 16 straight games from September 5, 1956 to June 21, 1957, when he was able to beat the Cleveland Indians 6-3 on seven hits. On that date, 3,200 rabbit's feet were distributed to Griffith Stadium fans and others brought their favorite good luck charms to help break the spell. One young lady brought a voodoo kit to stick pins in a doll representing the Cleveland Indians. Stobbs even changed his uniform number from 18 to 13 that night and he went to the mound with a silver dollar presented to him by Nick Altrock, the Nats' coach emeritus. Chuck had been ineffective except for his first starting assignment of the season when he lost a tough one to the New York Yankees 2-1. He did manage to win eight games but his ERA was 5.68.

Never with a pennant contender, Stobbs got his chance in 1958. Although he continued to be ineffective for the Senators, the St. Louis Cardinals of the National League gambled on him by purchasing him in July to help in their expected pennant chase. Unfortunately for Chuck, they fell short that year. He appeared in 17 games with the Cards and posted a 1-3 record. After the season, the Senators' picked him up again.

For the last three years of his career, he was used primarily in relief. In 1959, he worked in 41 games and had his best ERA of 2.98 but was only 1-8. He posted one more good year with the Nats in '60 when he was 12-7 with an ERA of 3.32. His last year in '61, he was with the same club but unfortunately it was now the Minnesota Twins, since Calvin Griffith had fled the city of Washington. Pitching in 24 games, he was 2-3 with an ERA of 7.46.

Following his major league career, Stobbs had jobs in sports broadcasting and coaching. He was an assistant to former Senator Steve Korcheck at George Washington University and later replaced him as head baseball coach when Korchek left to become a part of the Kansas City organization. He also served as a minor league pitching coach for the Kansas City and Cleveland clubs.

Excellent Control Pitcher

One thing in particular stands out when one examines Stobbs' major league pitching record. Chuck was a control pitcher! During his career, he had more strikeouts than walks (897 to 735). His strikeout to walk ratio was especially good while pitching for Washington (550 to 380).

Stobbs was inducted into the Virginia State Hall of Fame in 2002.

Post-World War II Era, 1946-1960
Relief Pitcher

Richard Elde Hyde

(Dick)

BR TR 5' 11" 170 lbs.

B. Aug. 3, 1928, Hindsboro, IL.

	Y	W	L	PCT	ERA	G	GS	CG	IP	H	BB	SO	SHO	SV
Was.	5	16	12	.571	3.41	154	2	0	277.1	255	124	129	0	23
Life	6	17	14	.548	3.56	169	2	0	298.1	273	137	144	0	23

Reliever Dick Hyde received the American League "Sophomore of the Year" award for his 1958 performance.

Right-hander Dick Hyde graduated from the University of Illinois and began his professional baseball career in 1948 with the Class D Concord, New Hampshire Team in the New England League. He spent three years there, appearing in 71 games and winning 14 while losing 19.

Korean War Interrupts Career

His baseball career was interrupted in 1951 and 1952 because of the Korean War and his military service. He returned in 1953 and became a part of the Washington Senators organization. Optioned to AA Chattanooga, Tennessee of the Southern League, he appeared in only one game before being sent to the Class B farm club in Charlotte, North Carolina. In 31 games, he won nine and lost eight with a respectable earned run average of 3.32.

The following year ('54) he was promoted to Chattanooga again and did not do well in the higher classification league, going six and 14, with an earned run average of 5.43. The 1955 season saw him with Chattanooga again where he showed much improvement. In 53 games, he was 8-6 with an excellent ERA of 2.32. That year he reached the parent club briefly, when he worked in three games for the Senators with no decisions and an ERA of 4.50.

Dick spent one more year with Chattanooga (1956) before making the majors on a full-time basis in 1957. He had his best year in the minors, winning 15 and losing only six in 54 games with an ERA of 3.98.

Submarine Reliever for Nats

Hyde came to the Nats in 1957 with an assortment of pitches. A submariner, his curveball broke up and his fastball sank. He also had a screwball in his repertoire. Except for two starts that year, Dick was used exclusively in the majors as a relief pitcher. Hyde enjoyed moderate success his first season with a 4-3 record and an ERA of 4.12.

A.L. Sophomore of Year in '58

It was 1958, however, that brought Dick into the limelight. That year, he was a key factor in 29 of the Senators' 61 wins, almost half of them. His ten wins in a relief role led the league in that category. Although he did not pitch enough innings to qualify for the earned run average title, his mark of 1.75 was the lowest in the league and lowest for the Senators since Walter Johnson's 1.49 back in 1919. His won-loss percentage of .769 was tops in the American League and he finished second in the league with 18 saves. He closed out 44 of the 53 games he appeared in. The 30-year-old right-hander, who worked in a service station during the off season, was voted the American league's "Sophomore of the Year" award by the Baseball Writer's Association of America. He received 46 of 96 votes.

The Yankee's ace reliever, Ryne Duren, had to undergo a knee operation at the conclusion of the '58 season, so naturally the New York Yankees became interested in Hyde. George Weiss, Yankee general manager, was reported to have offered Jerry Lumpe and Tom Sturdivant for him at one time. But, colorful manager Casey Stengel nixed the deal, preferring to see how Duren's knee responded the next year in spring training.

Shoulder Injury Ends Career

Unfortunately for the Senators, Dick hurt his pitching shoulder in '59 and was never able to regain his form. Doctors at Johns Hopkins Hospital in Baltimore, Maryland diagnosed the injury as "a relaxed capsule in the right shoulder joint," for which there was no corrective procedure. The Nats tried to trade him to the Boston Red Sox in June when he and Herb Plews were traded for pitcher Murray Wall and infielder Billy Consolo. When the Red Sox learned of Hyde's sore arm a few days later, they voided the pitcher exchange part of the deal and Dick was returned to the Senators. He finished the season 2-5 in 37 games with an ERA of 4.97.

In his final year with Washington (1960), Hyde played in only nine games and was 0-1 with a 4.15 ERA before being sold to the AAA Miami, Florida club on July 3rd. In 20 games with them, he was 0-5 with an ERA of 5.29.

The next season, 1961, proved to be his last in the majors when the Baltimore Orioles put him on their Rochester, New York farm club's roster and he was brought back to the majors once more when Baltimore recalled him for 15 games. Dick was 1-2 with an ERA of 5.57 before he was given his unconditional release. After his release, he did a little scouting for the Orioles in the Central Illinois area for a brief period.

Hyde cherishes the memories of his six years in the majors and indicates that striking out Ted Williams twice in the same year was a highlight for him. A new change up that he developed did the trick both times.

One wonders what might have been, if Hyde had not contracted the sore shoulder and he was able to pitch like he did in 1958!

Post-World War II, 1946-1960
Catcher

Clinton Dawson Courtney

(Clint, Scrap Iron)

BL TR 5' 8" 180 lbs.

B. March 16, 1927, Hall Summit, LA.

D. June 16, 1975, Rochester, NY.

	Y	G	AB	R	H	2B	3B	HR	RBI	BB	SO	SB	BA	SA
Was.	5	473	1392	145	375	64	9	23	181	123	72	1	.269	.378
Life	11	946	2796	260	750	126	17	38	313	264	143	3	.268	.366

Clint Courtney swinging the bat during spring training.

Clint Courtney, better known as "Scrap Iron," was a short, squat, feisty catcher on the major league scene in the '50s and early '60s. The scrappy, outspoken Courtney may have been best known for his fights with New York Yankee infielder Billy Martin. They first came to blows early in Clint's major league career in July 1952 and it resulted in a $100 fine and a three-day suspension for the backstop. The second altercation touched off a free-for-all after Courtney spiked Yankee shortstop Phil Rizzuto. That time it cost Clint $850, an American League record at the time.

Scraps began his major league career with those same Yanks in 1951, playing in only one game and going zero for two at the plate. With Yogi Berra firmly entrenched as their catcher, Courtney was dealt quickly to the St. Louis Browns where he immediately saw a lot of action. Catching over 100 games each year in 1952 and 1953, he was an immediate success. In the earlier year, he led all American League catchers in fielding percentage with .996, hit a solid .286 with 50 RBI and five home runs. He was named the *Sporting News*' "Rookie of the Year" for his performance.

Although his average dropped 35 points the next season his energetic handling of pitchers pleased the fans. When pitchers needed a "wake-up call," Scraps would fire the ball back to them with a velocity only exceeded later by Paul Casanova of the expansion Senators. On July 16, 1953, Clint was one of three Brown players who hit consecutive home runs in the first inning of their 8-6 win over the Yankees, tying a record.

Unassisted Double Play

When the Browns were moved to Baltimore in 1954, Clint went along. Again he caught over 100 games while regaining his batting form, hitting .270. He connected for the first home run hit in Baltimore's Memorial Stadium on April 15, 1954. Also on June 6 of that year, Courtney pulled off an unassisted double play as the Orioles beat the Yankees 7-5. To top off his fine year, he went five-for-five on August 29 to help beat the Nats 5-0.

He went to the Chicago White Sox in 1955 for 19 games and

then he was picked up by the Senators for the remainder of the season. He had his best year at the plate that year, playing in a total of 94 games and batting .309.

In Bitter Salary Dispute

Although he was a favorite of Washington fans and enjoyed some of his best seasons there, he sometimes found himself in a storm of controversy. Scraps was upset frequently because the Washington managers, especially Chuck Dressen, preferred to let Ed Fitzgerald or Lou Berberet handle the pitchers. In only one of his five seasons with Washington did Clint catch more than 100 games. In 1957, Courtney was fined $200 by Dressen for insubordination and Chuck even tried to get rid of him to the Cleveland Indians.

In his first full year with the Nats, 1956, he hit an even .300 and about one-third of his hits were for extra bases. As a result, he and owner Calvin Griffith were in a bitter wrangle over his salary for 1957. Courtney remained at his ranch at Coushatta, Louisiana as a holdout, seeking a $3,000 raise. He had 900 cattle and eight race horses on the ranch. The argument did not endear Courtney to the Washington management.

Despite his problems with the Senators, he remained with them for another three seasons. Clint was permitted to catch only 59 games in '57 and his average fell to .267. His most active year with the Nats was in 1958 when he caught 128 games and led the American League catchers with 64 assists and 17 double plays. His batting average, though, fell again, this time by 16 points. In 1959, his last year in Washington, he only caught 53 games and his average dropped to .233 so he was traded to the Baltimore Orioles for the 1960 season in a deal which brought infielder Billy Gardner to Washington.

First Catcher with Eyeglasses

Courtney was the first major league catcher to wear eyeglasses while catching and batting. Apparently there was no serious problem caused by their use. While with the Orioles, manager Paul Richards designed a larger catcher's glove for Clint to handle Hoyt Wilhelm's knuckleball. In 28 innings the other Oriole catchers had 11 passed balls but the first time he used the glove, Courtney didn't let any pitches get away from him with men on base. He caught 58 games that year but his average dipped again to .227.

In his final season in 1961, he was with the Kansas City A's as well as Baltimore for a total of only 23 games. He averaged .261 in 46 trips to the plate.

Managed in Minors

After completing his major league career, Clint managed in the minors, including teams with Durham, North Carolina and San Antonio, Texas. Unfortunately, his last stop was with the Richmond, Virginia Braves of the International League. He took over the job in the middle of 1973 and built up a very close relationship with his players. All of his players were stunned on June 16, 1975, when the team was in a Rochester, New York hotel. Talking baseball with one of his players at 12:30 A.M., Courtney suddenly keeled over and he died shortly thereafter in a nearby hospital of a heart attack.

Scrap Iron went out probably the way he wanted it, "talking baseball." He was a contact hitter who loved the game. Throughout his major league career, he never had his strikeouts exceed his walks in any season!

Post-World War II, 1946-1960
First Base

Roy Edward Sievers

(Squirrel)

BR TR 6' 1" 195 lbs.
B. Nov. 18, 1926, St. Louis, MO.

	Y	G	AB	R	H	2B	3B	HR	RBI	BB	SO	SB	BA	SA
Was.	8	901	3159	488	837	135	22	184	585	448	428	8	.265	.496
Life	17	1887	6387	945	1703	292	42	318	1147	841	920	14	.267	.475

Roy Sievers is showered with gifts by fans on "Roy Sievers Day," September 13, 1957.

Roy Sievers was the most prolific home run hitter of the original Washington Senators. Harmon Killebrew hit more homers during his career but not as many as Roy in a Washington uniform. Only the mighty Frank Howard of the Senators' expansion franchise hit more while playing with Washington. Roy hit 180 home runs while playing with the Nats and added another four in a brief stint with the expansion club near the end of his career. He smashed a total of 318 homers playing for four clubs: the St. Louis Browns, Senators, Chicago White Sox and Philadelphia Phillies.

Rookie of the Year in '49

Roy was a quiet, well-liked, and popular ballplayer who rarely displayed any anger. Seldom did he even question an umpire's call. Unfortunately, he was beset by injuries throughout his career; however he was able to accomplish a great deal despite his bad luck. He was signed by the St. Louis Browns and won "Rookie of the Year" honors in 1949, playing outfield and third base. He hit .306, clubbed 16 homers and drove in 91 runs in 140 games to earn the honor. The following year ('51), however, his performance dropped markedly as his average dipped to .238 and his home run and RBI output dropped to 10 and 57 respectively. As a result, he saw only limited service with the Browns in 1951 and in 1952, playing part-time in the minors both years.

Chronic Dislocated Shoulder

The fateful day was August 1, 1951. While playing for San Antonio of the Texas League against Dallas, Roy dove for a fly ball and tried a football-like shoulder roll to recover. It didn't work and he came up with a chronic dislocation of his right shoulder. Though the injury threatened his career, Dr. Bennett, the famous Baltimore surgeon, operated on the shoulder and gave him a reprieve. From then on, Roy had to be extremely careful with his throwing, since Dr. Bennett had warned that Roy was just one throw away from ending his career. As a result, the Browns moved Sievers to first base in 1953 and he was able to make somewhat of a comeback, hitting .270 in 92 games but not many extra base hits were delivered.

Breaks Senators' HR Record

The shoulder gradually became stronger and, fortunately for the Senators, he was traded to them by his club (even up fór Gil Coan) in 1954, the first season the Browns became the Baltimore Orioles. Playing with Washington the next six years, he enjoyed the best years of his career, averaging 30 homers and 100-plus RBI a year during the period. Returned to the outfield and installed immediately as a regular by the Nats, Sievers slammed 24 home runs (a new Washington record) and drove in 102 runs, despite hitting for only a .232 average. On May 5, Sievers drew a bases-loaded walk in the bottom of the ninth to give Washington a 1-0 win over the White Sox.

In 1955, he lifted his batting average to .271, came through with 25 homers, (breaking his Senators record), and had 106 RBI. He broke his home run record again in '56 when he slammed 29. His RBI production fell a little, but he still managed to drive in 95 runs, although his average slipped to .253.

Best Year in 1957

Sievers' banner year came in 1957, however. Returning to the .300 level for the first time since his rookie year, he posted a .301 average, led the league in home runs with 42, RBI with 114 and total bases with 331. The latter was a new club record, breaking Goose Goslin's mark of 329 established in 1925. His RBI crown was the first by a Senator since the Goose won it in 1924. His great season earned him third place, behind Mickey Mantle and Ted Williams, in the voting for the American League "Most Valuable Player" award. He was also runner up to Bobby Shantz for the "Comeback of the Year" award. It was believed by some that Roy deserved both awards.

Hits Homers in Six Consecutive Games, Ties Record

During the latter half of the season, Sievers went on a magnificent home run binge. He hit 10 home runs in the space of 17 games. And, six of them came in consecutive games, tying the American League record held by Ken Williams of the 1922 St. Louis Browns and Lou Gehrig of the 1931 New York Yankees. In fact, he homered on seven straight playing dates, missing only in the first game of a doubleheader on the last date. He still hit seven in eight games. Sievers, displaying his characteristic humility, credited new manager Cookie Lavagetto with improving his hitting by moving him forward in the batter's box.

Sievers was Vice President Richard Nixon's favorite Senator. The Nats were enmeshed in a 12-game losing streak when Nixon was returning from a trip to Russia. He called ahead and told Roy, Bob Allison, Jim Lemon and Harmon Killebrew to meet his plane at Andrews Air Force Base. They were the first to greet him on his return. He chastised them for their performance and said that he would be going to Griffith Stadium in the next day or two to get them back on the right track. Unfortunately, they lost even with the vice president in the stands.

A crowd of 17,826, including Nixon, turned out to honor Roy on September 2, 1957 on "Roy Sievers Night." He was presented with a station wagon, a thousand dollars, a tape recorder and a mink stole for his wife. Emotionally overcome by this expression of appreciation, Roy was unable to finish his prepared speech. He did respond later with two base hits, much to the delight of the fans.

Sievers gave the Senators another solid year in 1958 when he hit .295, lashed out 39 homers and drove in 108 runs. But, the injury jinx hit Roy again in 1959, as he was hampered by a series of injuries. He still managed to chalk up 21 home runs but he drove in only 49 runs while his average dipped to .242. He was used mostly at first base and, in fact, he never played much outfield again.

The last place Senators reluctantly traded the likable Sievers to the Chicago White Sox just before the start of the 1960 season. In return, they obtained needed catching (Earl Battey) and first baseman Don Mincher plus $150,000. Roy played quite a bit for the White Sox that year and in 1961, and he proved to be a good investment for them. Each year he hit .295, hit over 25 home runs and drove in more than 90 runs. On July 19, 1960, the Boston Red Sox snapped Roy's 21-game hitting streak, the longest of any player that year. On May 18, 1961, Sievers was one of four batters fanned by Ryne Duren in the seventh inning, tying a major league record. Del Rice the Angel's catcher was charged with a passed ball and an error, enabling one of the strikeout victims to reach base.

Ends Career with Expansion Senators

Chicago traded Sievers to the Philadelphia Phillies of the National League in November 1961 for pitcher John Buzhardt and infielder Charlie Smith. Roy also played a lot for the Phils over a two and one-half year period. In '62, he was in 144 games with a .262 average, 21 homers and 61 RBIs. In 1963, he appeared in 138 games, hit 19 home runs and drove in 43 base runners. While with the Phils, Roy connected for a pinch grand slam home run. He and the mighty Jimmie Foxx were the only players to hit grand slams in each league as pinch hitters.

After playing in 49 games in 1964 and hitting only .183, the Phillies sent him back to Washington with the expansion franchise in a conditional deal. At the time of the trade, Roy was suffering from a leg injury. He stuck with the Senators despite the injury but he hit only .172 in 33 games with them. The Senators gave him his unconditional release in 1965, after appearing in only 12 games and hitting just .190. In November of that year, the Cincinnati Reds signed him as batting coach but he served with them for only the 1966 season.

Harmon Killebrew tied Siever's seasonal home run record with 42 in 1959 and Frank Howard of the expansion Senators set the Washington record of 48 in 1969. Roy made the American League All-Star squad three times as a Washington Senator in 1956, 1957, and 1959 and once with the Chicago White Sox in 1961.

Sievers did not single out any event that gave him his biggest thrill but he was just very thankful that he was able to put on a major league uniform for 17 seasons! Roy had no connection with professional baseball after his retirement other than participating in an occasional old timer's game. He did, however, work for the Yellow Freight Trucking Company from 1970-1976.

Post-World War I Era, 1946-1960
Second Base

Sherrard Alexander Robertson
(Sherry)

BL TR 6' 0" 180 lbs.
B. Jan. 1, 1919, Montreal, Canada
D. Oct. 23, 1970, Houghton, SD.

	Y	G	AB	R	H	2B	3B	HR	RBI	BB	SO	SB	BA	SA
Was.	9	554	1447	192	334	52	18	26	146	181	223	31	.231	.346
Life	10	597	1507	200	346	52	18	26	151	202	238	32	.230	.342

Sherry Robertson (right) shown with rival George Myatt in spring training camp on March 20, 1946.

The most maligned ballplayer in Washington Senators history was Sherry Robertson. He had the misfortune of being the nephew of owner Clark Griffith. The poor fellow had to endure the boos of many Washington fans for a decade. Yet, to his credit, this underrated Senator was able to stick in the majors for that length of time.

He was the son of a former Montreal player, Jimmy Robertson, who was given a trial by Clark Griffith in the early 1900s when Clark was manager of the Chicago White Sox. Griffith married Jimmy's sister a few years later. When the elder Robertson died, Griffith took his six children under his wing and adopted two of them, Calvin and Thelma. She became the wife of former Senators pitcher, Joe Haynes, and another sister, Mildred, became the wife of Hall of Famer Joe Cronin. Calvin was trained as an executive and later replaced Clark as President of the Washington Nationals.

To avoid accusations of nepotism, Clark traded Cronin and Haynes to other clubs and they were with other clubs for most of their careers. But, this was not true with Sherry who spent almost his entire big league career with Washington.

Long Ball Hitter

Sherry was a star athlete with Washington's Roosevelt High School and later with the University of Maryland. He broke into organized ball with the Senators' Class B farm team in Charlotte, North Carolina. He became an immediate sensation with his long ball hitting and he led the league in home runs and runs batted in. His brother, Calvin, was running the Charlotte club and he had to fine Sherry $10 for not sliding on a close play at the plate that cost Charlotte the game. Sherry also played for the Springfield, Massachusetts team of the Eastern League.

On the strength of his minor league showing, he was brought up to the parent club in 1940. He appeared in only 10 games, hitting just .212. In 1941, he was in just one game with no hits in three trips to the plate. He played a lot more in '43, batting .217 in 59 games. His early days with the Nats were a disaster both at bat and in the field. In one of his early appearances at shortstop, he misjudged a Joe DiMaggio bases loaded pop-up with two out in the ninth inning to let a potential victory slip away. Similar miscues and an anemic batting average (around .200) allowed the fans to get on him without mercy.

In Navy in World War II

Fortunately for him, World War II intervened and navy man Robertson was in Hawaii with other big leaguers entertaining the servicemen with their skills. Playing for the Kaneohe Klippers, Sherry held his own with the other big leaguers and most observers believed that he would be ready to blossom on his return to Washington.

Robertson was much improved in his fielding when he returned in 1946 and with his power at the plate he was always dangerous. He was never able, however, to hit for average. He failed in a try as the Nats' regular third baseman and, although he had other chances to win a regular position, he was a utility man for most of his career. Sherry played in 95 games in '47, hitting .233 and raised his average to .246 in '48.

Played Better on Road

Understandably, Sherry played much better on the road, away from the pressure provided by Griffith Stadium fans. His greatest thrill was belting a home run off Ernie Bonham in Yankee Stadium to give Washington a rare twin-bill victory over New York. When the Nats went on their famous 1949 road trip and reeled off nine straight victories, Sherry batted .367 and hit four home runs. As Robertson and the team paraded down Pennsylvania Avenue, one banner appeared saying "No More Raspberries for Sherry." Unfortunately, the prophecy went unfulfilled.

1949 Was Best Year

Sherry's best year was 1949 when he appeared in 110 games (the only time he played in over 100 games in his 10 seasons with the Nats), batted .251 and had 31 extra base hits, including 11 home runs. The following year (1950), he hit for his highest average (.260) but he did not play as much appearing in 71 games. In his last full year in a Senators uniform, he hit only .189. In May 1952, after playing in only one game as a pinch runner, he was plucked off of the waiver list by the Philadelphia Athletics and he wound up his major league career with them that season hitting only .200 in 44 games.

"Don't worry, be happy" was a philosophy of Robertson's. He had the real secret of living and he was glad to share it with everyone. The late Billy Martin is quoted as saying "He had a wonderful outlook on life, always cheerful and happy."

After his playing career was over, he joined his brother, Calvin, in the operation of the Minnesota Twins. Sherry eventually became vice president and farm director.

On the way home from a hunting trip in South Dakota with Martin, Twins outfielder Bob Allison and scout Angelo Guiliani, he apparently suffered a heart attack while driving and was killed when his car left the road and struck a tree. He was only 51 years old.

Post-World War II Era, 1946-1960
Third Base

Edward Frederick Joseph Yost

(Eddie, the Walking Man)

BR TR 5' 10" 170 lbs.

B. Oct. 13, 1926, Brooklyn, NY.

	Y	G	AB	R	H	2B	3B	HR	RBI	BB	SO	SB	BA	SA
Was.	14	1690	6011	971	1521	282	50	101	550	1274	705	58	.253	.367
Life	18	2109	7346	1215	1863	337	56	139	683	1614	920	72	.254	.371

Eddie Yost shown diving for the ball during spring training.

Eddie Yost was a fixture on the Washington baseball scene for 14 of his 18 big league years. Rightfully nicknamed "the walking man," Eddie led the American League in drawing bases on balls six times during his career. When he retired from active playing, Eddie had accumulated 1,614 walks and only Babe Ruth, Ted Williams and Mel Ott had drawn more during their careers. No other player with less than 200 career homers has drawn that many bases on balls. Yost also led third basemen in putouts, a major league record eight times at the time of his retirement in '62. He had played a major league record 2,008 games and held American League records for assists and chances at third base, too. Yost was the ideal leadoff man, reaching base almost every other time he stepped to the plate, as attested by his .473 on-base percentage. He was also a baseball "iron man," playing in 838 consecutive games, second only to Lou Gehrig's 2,130 until Cal Ripken appeared on the scene.

Never in Minor Leagues

Eddie is a member of a select group of ballplayers who never spent a day in the minor leagues. In his day, only one in 45 was in that category. He turned down opportunities to sign with the New York Yankees and Boston Red Sox because he wanted to go to college. He accepted, however, Washington's offer of a $2,000 bonus because they also offered to pay the $600 tuition necessary to attend New York University in the off season. His father had to sign for him because he was only 17 years old at the time. Scout Joe Cambria, noted for his signing of Cuban players, observed Yost rap out three hits and handle 14 chances at shortstop flawlessly while playing sandlot ball in Orange, New Jersey. When Eddie hit a home run the next day, Cambria quickly offered him the contract. He was able to play in only seven games that year (1944), rapping out two singles in 14 trips to the plate.

The following year and for most of 1946, Yost was in the navy. Fortunately he was sent to upstate New York with a number of other professional players, including catcher Mickey Owen and pitcher Jim Konstanty. He was able to learn a lot about baseball while there.

When he returned to Washington in late '46 after his discharge from the Navy, he found that Cecil Travis had also returned from the service and was a fixture at third base. Realizing that he needed a lot more seasoning, he pleaded with owner Clark Griffith to send him to the minors. Since major league clubs were required to keep returning servicemen on their roster, Clark suggested that Eddie write a letter to Commissioner Happy Chandler and request an exception. While Chandler was sympathetic to Yost's predicament, he refused the request not wanting to set a precedent. It was lucky for the Senators that he did because Travis' feet, that had been frozen during the "Battle of the Bulge," would not support him and 1947 was his final active year.

Schooled in Fielding 3B by Bluege

The Nats' manager that year was one of the greatest fielding third basemen of all time, Ossie Bluege. Due to Travis' condition, Bluege gave a daily crash course for Yost on the intricacies of playing the third sack. Eddie was a willing and apt student. They would arrive at the park at four or five o'clock in the afternoon and work tirelessly before each night game. This wore Yost to a frazzle by the end of the year, but it provided the foundation needed to make him an excellent third baseman. Eddie was particularly adept at coming in quickly on bunts or slow rollers and firing underhanded to first base to nab the runner. He also was outstanding in starting double plays "around the horn."

Installed as Regular at 3B

He was installed as the Senators' regular third baseman before the end of the 1947 season and held the post until he was traded to the Detroit Tigers in 1959. Although he didn't hit much in '47 (.238), '48 (.249) or '49 (.253), he had gained the confidence to play the position and battle opposing pitchers on even terms.

At first, he was a dead pull hitter and many of his fouls were just outside the left field foul line. But, when Bucky Harris became manager of the Nats in 1950, he taught him to go with the outside pitch to right field. This enabled him to boost his average more than 40 points.

The Walking Man

At the plate, Eddie had a keen eye and he was always aware of the strike zone. He seldom offered at pitches outside the zone and he had a knack of fouling off pitches until he either walked or got a pitch he wanted. Under Harris in 1950, he learned to wait out the pitchers, drawing 141 walks, just three less than the league leader, Eddie Stanky. It was the first of eight seasons during his career in which Yost drew 100 or more walks. He enjoyed his best season ever, hitting .295 by waiting for the "fat" pitches after getting the pitcher behind in the count. He was also involved in 35 double plays, two more than the National League record for third basemen but five short of Harland Clift of the St. Louis Browns in 1937.

Yost had another fine year in '51, when he hit .283 and registered a .424 slugging average. He led the league in the number of doubles with 36. In 1952, he was on the American League All-Star Team; however, Eddie dropped 50 points on his batting average to .233 when he slumped during the latter part of the season.

Amazing Consecutive Game Streak

In June 1949, Eddie suffered 11 fractures of his right ankle while sliding into second base against the Cleveland Indians. Amazingly, he returned to the lineup on July 6 and began his remarkable consecutive game string. The streak continued until May 13, 1955 when Eddie asked manager Chuck Dressen to remove him from the lineup. Dressen reluctantly complied. Yost had tonsillitis and was running a 102-degree fever. Eddie had been in for just one play the previous night and his doctor had given him permission to do the same thing again. His pride, however, bowed to integrity and a high personal standard when he made his request to the manager.

Yost had one close call during his streak when Boston Red Sox pitcher, Russ Kemmerer felled him with a fastball which struck him behind the left ear. Eddie never lost consciousness, but he bled profusely and was carried from the field on a stretcher to Georgetown University Hospital, where he remained overnight for observation. He was back in the lineup the next day, however.

"Eddie Yost Day"

September 16, 1953 was proclaimed "Eddie Yost Day" at Griffith Stadium. With Yost's parents in attendance, the handsome bachelor was presented with a new car and showered with other gifts by appreciative Washington fans. He rewarded the fans with a fine season, batting .272 and leading the league in bases on balls with 123.

Yost led the league in 1954 in the number of games played, was second in drawing walks with 131 and hit .256. When his streak was broken in 1955, he was only able to play in 122 games and hit .243. For each of the five years prior, he had played in more than 150 games. In '56, he drew 151 walks, establishing a career record and leading the league. Demonstrating his "iron man" qualities again that year, he played in 152 games and hit .231.The next season (1957), Yost drew less than half the number of walks as in the previous year while playing in only 110 games and hitting .251. His average dropped to its lowest point in the 12 years he played as a regular when he hit only .224 in 134 games in 1958.

Traded to Tigers

Eddie was traded to the Detroit Tigers at the end of the year along with Rocky Bridges and Neil Chrisley for Reno Bertoia, Ron Samford and Jim Delsing. He gave the Tigers two fine years in '59 and '60, playing in over 140 games each year and hitting .278 and .260. He led the American League both years in drawing walks and he also was the league leader in runs scored in 1959 with 115. He hit a career high 21 homers the same year.

He was drafted by the Los Angeles Angels in the expansion draft and wound up his career with them in 1961 and 1962 hitting .202 and .240. He had been hoping to be drafted by the expansion Senators, but general manager Ed Doherty lost the coin toss. He was used sparingly by the Angels who were in a youth movement.

Eddie was a class guy on the field and off of it. A devout Catholic, his long time roommate with the Nats, Gil Coan, recalls that Yost made a point of attending mass regularly, whether the team was at home or on a wearying road trip.

Managed Expansion Senators for One Game

The persistent Yost took more than a decade to accomplish his educational goals, gaining a B.A. in Physical Education and a master's degree in Recreation from New York University. The longtime bachelor later married and is a devoted family man. He stayed close to baseball after retirement from active play, serving as a coach for the Los Angeles Angels, Washington Senators, New York Mets and Boston Red Sox. With his educational background and diamond skills, one wonders why he wasn't given a chance to manage in the big leagues! He was, however, called on to manage the Washington Senators on May 22, 1963 after Mickey Vernon had been let go by the management. His tenure was the all-time shortest when Gil Hodges replaced him after one game, a loss.

Post-World War II Era, 1946-1960
Shortstop

James Edward Runnels

(Pete)

BL TR 6' 0" 170 lbs.
B. Jan. 28, 1928, Lufkin, TX.
D. May 20, 1991, Pasadena, TX.

	Y	G	AB	R	H	2B	3B	HR	RBI	BB	SO	SB	BA	SA
Was.	7	921	3356	431	921	125	42	18	355	413	341	15	.274	.353
Life	14	1799	6373	876	1854	282	64	49	630	844	627	37	.291	.378

Playing for the Red Sox, Pete Runnels tags out Washington's Bob Allison on September 16, 1960.

Pete Runnels was one of the better hitters of his era, a line-drive spray hitter who could hit to all fields. When he first arrived on the big league scene, the left-hander was strictly an opposite field hitter. He was a "singles" hitter, a throwback to the days of Wee Willie Keeler. He led the American League in batting on two occasions and on another he battled Ted Williams to the final day of the season before losing out.

After coming out of Rice Institute, Pete was playing Class D ball in Texas when he was discovered by one of Washington's best scouts, Joe Cambria. Clark Griffith paid $12,500 for him in 1949 and after serving an apprenticeship with the Nats' Chattanooga team where he hit .356, he was brought up to the Senators for part of the 1951 season. Runnels was a versatile infielder, seeing duty at first base, second base and third base as well as short, and he even played the outfield once.

A Regular with the Senators in 1951

Runnels became a regular during the '51 season and hit a respectable .278 in 78 games, and in his first full year he upped his average seven points, hitting .285 in 152 games. That season, he also led all American League shortstops with 314 putouts. The next two seasons '53 and '54 he dropped to .257 and .268, still primarily playing shortstop. He did finish second in the league with 15 triples in '54. In 1955, he was shifted to second base and he regained his batting eye, hitting .284. The next year (1956), he had the first of a half-dozen .300 seasons, registering a .310 average. This was his best year with the Senators and he divided his time between first and second bases when in the field.

Traded to the Red Sox

Inexplicably, his average dropped 80 points in 1957—his last season with the Nats. When Calvin Griffith traded Pete to the Boston Red Sox for Albie Pearson and Norm Zauchin, he did not make one of his better deals. Zauchin was never able to make the big time and the Senators only got one good year from Albie, while Runnels gave Boston five straight .300 seasons. Pete had made a number of friends among the fans during his seven years in Washington and they were sorry to see him move on to the Red Sox.

Pete was always a quiet, self-effacing gentleman, and a rather colorless performer, who went about his duties without fanfare and without complaining. The Texan was willing to play anywhere on the field if it would help his team. His major weaknesses were a lack of power and a throwing arm that was not especially strong.

Runner–Up for Batting Crown

With the Red Sox, Pete reached his peak. Perhaps, his close association with Ted Williams had something to do with it. It was in 1958, his first season with Boston, that Pete took Williams down to the wire for the American League batting championship. Ted carried a three-point lead into the last game of the season against the Senators and he had a double and home run while Pete went 0-4. This enabled Williams to beat out Runnels by six points. Williams captured the title by batting .636 during the final series against Washington. Runnels finished with a .322 average and was second in the league with 103 runs scored.

Pete Charges Mound During Scuffle

Earlier in the season, the usually docile Runnels touched off a mob scene when he charged the mound and his friend, Camilo Pascual, after being decked by a head-high fastball. In the scuffling, Pascual suffered a slight spike wound while being restrained by Coach Bob Swift. Fortunately there were no serious injuries from the melee.

Pete continued his hot hitting for the Red Sox in '59 when his batting average was over .300 again with a .314 mark. His on-base percentage of .415 was second in the league and he was also runner-up with 95 walks. In a game on August 14, Pete was walked twice in the same inning as the Red Sox defeated the Yankees 11-6.

Captures Batting Title

He did capture the batting crown in 1960 with a .320 average. On August 30, Pete went six for seven as Boston edged Detroit in 15 innings in the first game of a twin bill. His fifteenth inning double knocked in the winning run. He collected three more hits in the nightcap victory. With nine hits in the doubleheader, Runnels tied a major league record. It was most unusual but the Red Sox did not plan to play the batting champion regularly during the following 1961 season. Pete, however, changed that with his bat and soon worked his way back into the lineup for 143 games. That year, his .317 average was not good enough to take the batting title but it erased all thoughts in the minds of Boston management of not playing him regularly the next season.

In one game during the season, he hit into a double play while being credited with a single. Against the Minnesota Twins, with one out and a runner on second base, Runnels poked a ground ball past the pitcher, which was backhanded behind the bag by the second baseman. He flipped it to third and the runner was caught and tagged out in a rundown and when Pete attempted to take second base he also was gunned down.

Regains Batting Crown

In 1962, Runnels regained the batting crown with his best average ever, .326. This was his last season in the American League. It is unusual for a batting champion to be traded before the next season but that's exactly what happened to Pete. The Red Sox traded him to the Houston Colts for outfielder Roman Mejias. Runnels wound up his career with Houston, playing in 124 games in 1963 but hitting only .253. He was used only sparingly his final year (1964), appearing in 22 games and hitting a measly .196.

For a two-time batting champ, Pete played in relative anonymity. But, this underrated ballplayer earned the respect and admiration of many Washington and Boston fans as well as his teammates! Runnels was selected for the American League All-Star squad three times and in the July 30, 1962 game he was one of three members of the team to homer in their 9-4 victory over the National League.

Pete was called on to manage the Boston Red Sox for 16 games during the 1966 season. He died at the age of 63 in Pasadena, Texas.

Post-World War II Era, 1946-1960
Outfield

James Robert Lemon

(Jim)

BR TR 6' 4" 200 lbs.

B. Mar. 23, 1928, Covington, VA.

	Y	G	AB	R	H	2B	3B	HR	RBI	BB	SO	SB	BA	SA
Was.	7	767	2769	369	741	91	33	144	451	289	603	12	.268	.480
Life	12	1010	3445	446	901	121	35	164	529	363	787	13	.262	.460

Jim Lemon homers against the Yankees on May 13, 1960 but the Senators lose 7-3. Bob Allison offers congratulations.

Jim Lemon was a tall, free swinging, long ball hitter for the Senators for seven years. From Covington, Virginia, Lemon played the outfield for the local Westvaco team until he was signed in 1948 by the Cleveland Indians when he was 19 years old. He was a minor league slugger and when he slammed 39 home runs and drove in 119 runs for Oklahoma City by mid-August 1950, he was promoted to Cleveland. In 12 games, however, he hit only .176. Because of the Korean War, Uncle Sam grabbed Jim and he played and managed at Fort Meade, Maryland for two seasons. In 1953, he returned to the Indians for a brief stint of 16 games, hitting .174.

Clouts 4 Homers in Minor League All–Star Game

After seeing no action with the Indians in 1954, he was acquired by the Senators in May, but due to the fact that manager Bucky Harris had an over-abundance of outfielders, including Roy Sievers, Jim Busby, Clyde Vollmer, Tommy Umphlett and Tom Wright, he saw limited service his first two seasons. He managed to get in 37 games in '54, hitting .234 but only 10 games in'55 when he batted .200. He spent part of his time with Chattanooga the Nats top farm club in the Southern Association. On July 19, 1955 in the league's All-Star contest, Lemon clouted four home runs to lead his team to victory over the first-place Birmingham Barons 10-5.

He came into his own in 1956, however, as the Senators' regular left fielder, playing in 146 games and hitting .271. He walloped 27 home runs and tied for the American League lead in triples with 11. Demonstrating that he had a fine arm, too, he led the league outfielders in double plays with six.

Slugs Three Homers in Griffith Stadium Game

Late in the year, with President Eisenhower in the stands, Jim set a club record by smashing three consecutive homers into the left field bleachers in one game. His hits came off New York Yankee pitcher, Whitey Ford and he was only the second player to ever hit three homers in that location. Joe DiMaggio accomplished the feat when he put all three of his homers into the bleachers earlier. After the game, the president called Jim over to give him special congratulations.

Lemon led the league in another category in '56, strikeouts. Unfortunately, he whiffed 138 times, surpassing Larry Doby's major league record of 121. The free swinger managed to cut down on the number of strikeouts after that, but he did lead the league again in '57 and '58 with 94 and 120 respectively. Washington fans loved to see Jim attack the ball, reminiscent of former Senators great, Goose Goslin, who put every ounce of energy into each swing. In 1957, Lemon had his best season average-wise when he hit .284 with 17 homers.

The following year ('58), Jim cracked 26 home runs, although he hit none in his last 38 games because of constant pain in his left knee, which denied him, leverage. It also affected his hitting as his average dropped to .246, the lowest average of his career when playing full time.

Hits Two Homers in One Inning

After surgery on his knee during the winter, Jim came back strongly in 1959, clouting 33 homers, driving in 100 runs and lifting his average to .279. In September, he tied two major league records when he smacked two home runs in one inning and drove in six runs in a 10-run third inning, as the Nats pasted the Boston Red Sox 14-2. The second homer was delivered with the bases loaded. It was the first time in history that a Washington player had hit two home runs in one inning.

The next year (1960), in his final season with Washington, Lemon produced a personal record high 38 homers (Mickey Mantle won the crown with 40) while again knocking in 100 runs. Twenty-four of his 38 home runs were hit in spacious Griffith Stadium. His batting average fell only 10 points to .269, despite the fact that he was hitting with more power.

Injured Shoulder Ends Career

After the team was moved away to Minnesota, Jim was unable to do as well. His trouble began when he suffered a torn muscle in his shoulder. As a consequence, he lost strength in his arm and was not able to regain his long-ball power. His average dipped to .258 in 1961 and he was able to hit only 14 home runs. In '62, he appeared in only 12 games, spending most of the season on the disabled list. He hit only .176 in 17 trips to the plate.

Although he had surgery to repair the torn muscle, he could not make a successful comeback in 1963, playing with three teams. In seven games with the Minnesota Twins, he hit .118, in 31 games with the Philadelphia Phillies, mainly as a pinch hitter, he hit a creditable .271, but he finished his playing career with the Chicago White Sox hitting .200 in 36 games.

Jim liked the Washington area, so after his playing days were over, he moved there and bought a restaurant in suburban Maryland. This, despite the fact, that he signed a contract as a coach for the Minnesota Twins for three years. He served in that capacity from 1965-67.

Manages Expansion Senators

George Selkirk, the expansion Senators' general manager, hired Lemon to manage the team in 1968 after Gil Hodges left the post to manage the New York Mets. He was given a two-year contract but when the Senators finished last with a 65-96 record, Jim's contract was bought up and he was replaced for the 1969 season. A number of key injuries and the loss of ace reliever Darold Knowles adversely affected the team's performance.

Lemon continued his association with professional baseball as a coach for the Minnesota Twins for the 1981-84 seasons and then he worked with various minor league clubs from '85-'96.

Jim was inducted into the Virginia State Hall of Fame in 1988.

Post-World War II Era, 1946-1960
Outfield

Gilbert Fitzgerald Coan

(Gil)

BL TR 6' 0" 180 lbs.

B. May 18, 1922, Monroe, NC.

	Y	G	AB	R	H	2B	3B	HR	RBI	BB	SO	SB	BA	SA
Was.	8	733	2451	335	621	80	42	36	246	203	345	70	.253	.364
Life	11	918	2877	384	731	98	44	39	278	232	384	83	.254	.359

Gil Coan (in uniform) catches President Truman's "opening pitch" and returns it for autographing.

Gil Coan was the most promising rookie ever to arrive on the Washington baseball scene! Unfortunately, he was never able to realize the high expectations held for him. Joe Engel, the Senators' chief scout who discovered so many great ballplayers declared, uneqivocally, that Coan was the best of them all. To put this high praise in perspective, Goose Goslin, Sam Rice, Bucky Harris, Ossie Bluege, Joe Judge, Fred Marberry and Earl McNeely were all dispatched to the Senators on Engel's recommendatiòn and formed the nucleus of the Nats' 1924 and 1925 championship teams. In addition, he sent Joe Cronin, Buddy Myer, Joe Kuhel and Cecil Travis who were all on Washington's 1933 American League pennant winners. Buddy Lewis was another of Engel's discoveries.

Minor Leaguer of the Year

In 1944, Coan dropped out of Brevard Junior College in North Carolina to sign a professional contract with the Kingsport, Tennessee Class D club of the Appalachian League. Married early to his childhood sweetheart, they must have struggled to make ends meet on the $175 a month he was given to sign. Playing the outfield for Kingsport he did so well, hitting .367, that he was promoted to Washington's top farm club, Chattanooga of the Class AA Southern Association in July. He became the club's regular right fielder before the end of the season and caught the eye of management when he hit for a .340 average. The next year (1945), he was voted "Minor Leaguer of the Year" by the "*Sporting News*" when he led the league in seven categories, including a .372 average, 201 hits, 40 doubles, 28 triples and 55 stolen bases.

Brought Up to Senators' in '46

With these credentials Clark Griffith didn't hesitate to promote him to the parent club for the 1946 season. With his solidly built six foot, 180 pound frame, classic swing, power and blazing speed, he was given a "can't miss" label. He was reportedly faster than George Case, having scored from second base on bunts a half-dozen times and from first base on an infield out. His only drawback seemed to be the thumb on his left hand. Gil lost the top joint through surgery because of a serious infection.

Although Griff wanted Coan installed as the regular center fielder, manager Ossie Bluege used an outfield of Jeff Heath, Stan Spence and Buddy Lewis in 1946. He was given a chance in July to show management what he could do, and for a ten-day period he came through for the Senators. Starting before the home crowd for the first time on July 14, Coan went five for nine in a doubleheader as the Senators won both games from the St. Louis Browns. Three of his four outs were hard hit line drives. On July 18, Gil's inside-the-park home run in the eighth inning enabled Senators pitcher Dutch Leonard to shut out the Detroit Tigers 1-0 and on July 23 he ruined the Tiger's Hal Newhowser's bid for a shutout by scoring Washington's only run.

He was returned to part-time duty, however, and was never able to regain his minor league form. It was soon apparent that he had been brought up too soon. He appeared in only 59 games that year and his batting average was a lowly .209. So in 1947, he was optioned back to Chattanooga where he again burned up the Southern Association, hitting .340. Brought back to Washington in September, he again raised hopes when he hit .500 in 11 games.

Coan, himself, admitted that he had been brought up too early and in addition he was hampered the first two years with infected feet and a strained muscle in his right side. With many of the outfielders from the previous year traded away, it seemed that Coan was now ready for stardom in 1948. Although he appeared in over 100 games each year, Gil again disappointed everyone in '48 and '49, hitting only .232 and .218 respectively. In 1948, however, he did finish second in the league with 23 stolen bases.

Hits Stride in 1950

It was not until 1950 that Coan found himself, thanks to the tutelage of the savvy Bucky Harris. Harris encouraged him to hit to all fields and to stop trying to pull everything to right field.

Used primarily against right-handed pitching, Coan hit .303 and rapped out 28 extra base hits. This, despite the fact that he fractured his skull, sliding into second base and missed six weeks of the season. After returning from the hospital, he put together a 16-game hitting streak. He also hit two grand-slam home runs within a five-day period early in the season. The first was off of St. Louis Brown pitcher Ned Garver and it enabled the Nats to score a 4-3 victory, while the second one was hit against Cleveland Indian ace Bob Lemon giving the Senators a 10-5 win over the Tribe.

Coan Mainly Responsible for Sweep of Yankees

Trying to prove that the 1950 season was no fluke, Coan repeated his .303 batting average in 1951, appearing in 135 games and registering his best year with 163 hits, 25 doubles, seven triples and nine home runs. He scored 85 times and drove in 62 runs. He deserved to be selected as an all-star that year but Casey Stengel left him off the team. Gil got sweet revenge when the Senators travelled to New York for a three-game series in July. In the first game of a July 4 doubleheader, Coan collected three hits including two home runs as he drove in six runs in the Nats' 9-6 win. In the nightcap, Gil drove in the winning run as the Yankees went down to defeat. The next night he hit another home run and a double as the Senators swept the series. He completed his eight-year career with Washington in '52 and '53 when his batting averages tailed off to, first .205 and then to .196.

Traded to the Baltimore Orioles before the start of the 1954 season, Coan made a gallant last comeback, hitting .274 in 94 games. But, in 1955 during the season, he was sent to the Chicago White Sox and then to the New York Giants of the National League. He was unable to do well with any of them, hitting .238 with the Orioles, .176 with the White Sox and .154 with the Giants.

The 32-year-old outfielder reached the end of the trail in May of 1956 when the Giants farmed him out to Minneapolis. Although Detroit wanted his services as a pinch hitter for 1957, Gil decided he would rather return home and spend more time with his family.

He was used in only four games in '56, mainly as a pinch runner. When he returned home he coached baseball for his alma mater, Brevard, for two years, 1957 and 1958.

Loses Match Race to George Case

The hard-luck player, whose career was marred by several major injuries, including a broken arm, a broken leg and a skull fracture, did give Washington fans a great measure of hope as well as two solid seasons. One of the highlights of his career was a match race of 100 yards with Cleveland speedster, George Case. Case came out of the starting blocks like a bolt of lightning and it took Coan 60 yards to pull even, but the extra effort caused Gil to break stride and Case won handily. They received $500 each for their efforts.

His most embarrassing moment occurred in a game at Yankee Stadium when Yankee star, Mickey Mantle smashed a drive into deep left centerfield. Coan chased the ball down and as he was ready to fire it back toward the infield, the ball slipped out of his hand and fell back behind him. Meanwhile, Mickey easily circled the bases for an inside-the-park home run.

After his association with baseball ended, he invested in a local insurance firm, dabbled in real estate and finally settled down as a full-time farmer.

Post-World War II Era, 1946-1960
Outfield

James Franklin Busby

(Jim)

BR TR 6' 1" 175 lbs.
B. Jan. 8, 1927, Kenedy, TX.
D. July 8, 1996, Augusta, GA.

	Y	G	AB	R	H	2B	3B	HR	RBI	BB	SO	SB	BA	SA
Was.	4	481	1917	232	539	80	20	21	223	116	171	40	.281	.377
Life	13	1352	4250	541	1113	162	35	48	438	310	439	97	.262	.350

Jim Busby, with his bat, poses for a photograph before a night game.

The best years (1952-1955) of Jim Busby's baseball career were spent in a Washington uniform. With the Nats, Jim put 19 extra percentage points on his career .262 batting average and added 27 points to his career-slugging average of .350. He collected about half of his total base hits and extra base hits while only with the Washington club about one-third of the time.

The light-hitting Busby stayed in the majors because of his slick fielding abilities. He usually patrolled center field and with his natural speed, covered considerable ground in flagging down potential base hits. He was an early sensation as a base stealer, and while pitcher Allie Reynolds was wrong in declaring Busby "better" than George Case at the art, he was a dangerous threat to steal. Three times, he was among the leagues' top five base stealers. Like Case, he was extra-quick in getting a break for the bag and in gaining full speed.

Quaterbacked Texas Christian U in 1945 Cotton Bowl

Busby starred in baseball and football while attending Texas Christian University and, as quarterback, led the 1944 Horned Frogs to the January 1945 Cotton Bowl against Oklahoma A & M. After a brief stay in the U.S. Army, he played his first professional baseball with Muskegon of the Central League and later played with Waterloo of the Three-I League and Sacramento of the Pacific Coast League. While with Sacramento in 1950 Jim hit .310, scored 76 runs and only made two errors in 300 outfield chances. That was enough to earn him a spot in the big leagues with the Chicago White Sox before the end of the year. He appeared in 18 games for them but hit only .208.

1951 All-Star for Chisox

In 1951, Busby demonstrated that he was major league caliber. He hit .283 and proved to be a terror on the base paths with a career high 26 steals, second in the league. Opposing base runners learned early that they could not take liberties with Jim's arm when he chalked up a career high 16 assists. In what amounted to his rookie season, Jim was selected for the American League All-Star Team. When he began the 1952 season in a protracted slump for the first 18 games (hitting .144), Washington was able to trade for him. He only hit .244 for the Nats that year while playing in 129 games, but he did lead all American League outfielders with 472 putouts.

1953: His Best Year for Senators

Jim hit the pinnacle of his career in 1953 and 1954 with the Senators. He tallied career marks in '53 in batting (.312), slugging percentage (.415), RBI (82), doubles (28) and triples (7). In 1954, he led all American League outfielders in number of games (155) and putouts (491), and with a career high 628 trips to the plate he registered 187 hits and 83 runs both career highs. He almost topped the .300 mark again with a batting average of .298.

Hits Grand Slams in Consecutive Games

When his average dropped to .230 in 49 games the next year, Busby was sent back to the White Sox for whom he hit .243 in 99 games the rest of the '55 season. He was given a change of scenery in 1956 when the Cleveland Indians obtained him, but he was only able to hit .235 in 135 games. He did, however, smash a career high 12 home runs for them and two of them were grand slams in back-to-back games, enabling him to join only three other American Leaguers in the feat, namely Babe Ruth, Jimmie Foxx and Bill Dickey, a select trio.

Despite this display of power, he was dealt to the Baltimore Orioles after 30 games in 1957 (hitting just (.189), and by hitting .250 for the Orioles he was able to raise his seasonal average to .239. Busby was able to lead all American League outfielders in fielding percentage that season with .983. His batting average was about the same in 1958, but that was not indicative of his value to the team. Playing in the outfield in 103 of the 113 games played,

Jim committed only one error. But, sportswriter Phil Wood uncovered a remarkable statistic: the Orioles were 0-42 in games without Busby in the lineup. It is ironic that one of the recognized managerial geniuses, Paul Richards, was evidently unable to recognize that the Orioles were unable to win that year without Busby!

The Boston Red Sox took a chance on him in 1959 but in 69 games he hit a lowly .235. So after appearing as a defensive replacement in just one game in 1960, he was returned to Baltimore where he hit .258 in 79 games. His average was exactly the same in 75 games in 1961, as Jim said goodbye to the American League at season's end.

Ends Career in NL

When the National League expanded, Busby was drafted by the Houston Colt .45s for the 1962 season. But after only 15 games and a .182 average, Jim was given his unconditional release.

For a number of years, Jim remained in the game, coaching for his old skipper, Paul Richards, at Baltimore, Houston, Atlanta and Chicago. Later he retired to his home in Millen, Georgia. Jim died of a heart attack in University Hospital in Augusta, Georgia on July 8, 1996.

CHAPTER SIX

Expansion Era, 1961-1971

Introduction

Surprisingly, the Expansion Era teams provided the best baseball for Washington fans since 1945, although it was nothing to write home about. Playing at a .418 clip, they managed to land in the basement only three of the eleven years and even were able to make the first division in 1969.

Stocked with some of the other team's rejects and managed by former Senator Mickey Vernon, the new team bade a fond farewell to one of the league's best ballparks, Griffith Stadium, at the close of the 1961 season. Moving to a new stadium in 1962, built primarily for football fans, the Senators performed for a decade before one of the owners, unpopular Bob Short, whisked them away to Texas. Sad times have endured to this day, as Washington fans have been limited to rooting for the nearby Baltimore Orioles or watching a few scattered exhibition or old-timer's games.

Just as Walter Johnson was the idol of earlier Senators fans, a new idol emerged during this period: a gentle giant named Frank Howard. No one on the Washington scene ever blasted such prodigious home runs as Howard. Seats were painted in the upper deck where his mighty blasts had landed. Howard bemoaned plans to take the team west, and to the delight of faithful fans, he homered in his final game at Robert F. Kennedy Stadium.

Bernie Allen, Ed Brinkman, Paul Casanova, Mike Epstein, Frank Howard, Darold Knowles, Ken McMullen, Camilo Pascual and Del Unser all played for this 1969 Nats' team.

Slick-fielding Eddie Brinkman and Paul Casanova, as well as pitchers Camilo Pascual and Darold Knowles also played here during the period. Selections for the team were relatively easy, except for the outfield. It was difficult to leave outfielder Don Lock off the team with his consistent fancy fielding and his occasional bursts of power and the same goes for Fred Valentine who was the club's most valuable player in 1966. The team follows:

Expansion Era, 1961-1971 All-Star Team

RightHanded Pitcher:	Camilo Pascual
Left-Handed Pitcher:	Claude Osteen
Relief Pitcher:	Darold Knowles
Catcher:	Paul Casanova
First Base:	Mike Epstein
Second Base	Bernie Allen
Third Base:	Ken McMullen
Shortstop:	Eddie Brinkman
Outfield:	Jim King
Outfield:	Chuck Hinton
Outfield:	Del Unser

A summary of team performance during the period follows:

Expansion Era, 1961-1971

Washington Senators
American League
10 Team League — 1961-1968
12 Team League—1969-1971

Year	Finish	# Games	Won	Lost	Pct.
1961	9 (Tie)	161	61	100	.379
1962	10	161	60	101	.373
1963	10	162	56	106	.346
1964	9	162	62	100	.383
1965	8	162	70	92	.432
1966	8	159	71	88	.447
1967	7	161	76	85	.472
1968	10	161	65	96	.404
1969	6	162	86	76	.531
1970	9	162	70	92	.432
1971	11	159	63	96	.396
Totals - 11 Years, 11 Teams		1772	740	1032	
Averages	9	161	67	94	.418

Expansion Era, 1961-1971
Right-Handed Pitcher

Camilo Alberto Pascual

(Luis, Little Potato)

BR TR 5' 11" 185 lbs.

B. Jan. 20, 1934, Havana, Cuba

	Y	W	L	PCT	ERA	G	GS	CG	IP	H	BB	SO	SHO
Was.	10	84	111	.431	3.89	321	223	60	1601.1	1530	558	1142	18
Life	18	174	170	.506	3.63	529	404	132	2930.2	2703	1069	2167	36

Manager Chuck Dressen names Camilo Pascual as the starting pitcher for opening day April 14, 1956.

Walter Johnson was the fastest pitcher to wear a Washington uniform (and with little doubt the fastest ever) but Camilo Pascual was probably the Senator with the best curve ball. The quiet, serious Cuban spent 18 years in the majors, dazzling hitters with his remarkable curve, sneaky fastball and tantalizing change of pace, despite recurring arm trouble.

Discovered by Senators Scout Joe Cambria

As with many other of the Senators' Cuban players, Camilo and his brother Carlos were discovered by scout Joe Cambria. Carlos' career was brief, pitching in just two games for the Senators in 1950. Cambria mistakenly sent Camilo to the states as an infielder. But, he was quickly sent to the mound while in the minors with Geneva, New York, and Big Spring, Texas. Washington brought him up in 1954 with high expectations. These were not realized for some time, however. He was unable to maintain his composure early in his career and would get upset when teammates made errors or opposing batters were able to hit him hard. He was only 28-66 his first five years with the Nats as a result. His 18 losses in 1956 and 17 losses in 1957 were the second most in the league. Although he was 8-12 in 1958, his ERA was a respectable 3.15 and that was the first of eight straight years in which his ERA was below 3.50.

Best Year for Nats Was 1959

In 1959, however, he finally blossomed into the pitcher that had been envisioned. By his own admission, this was his finest year. Playing with a last place club that finished last in hitting and last in fielding, Camilo fashioned a 17-10 record with a 2.64 earned run average, the best by a Senator in 31 years. He led the American League that year with 17 complete games and six shutouts. His 185 strikeouts (second in the league) were the most by any Washington pitcher since Johnson posted 188 in 1917. Adding a wicked sidearm curve, controlling his temper, gaining experience, improving control and getting plenty of rest between starts all contributed to his success. In his final season in Washington ('60), he had another winning year at 12-8 with an ERA of 3.03.

Hits Peak with Twins

Unfortunately for Washington fans, Pascual recorded most of his victories while in Minnesota, after the original Senators were moved. His first season in Minnesota (1961) was a losing one, though; he was 15-16 with an ERA of 3.46. He did pitch in the second All-Star game that year, allowing no hits and notching four strikeouts in three innings. Camilo then recorded two 20 game win seasons back to back in 1962 and 1963 and led the American League in strikeouts for three consecutive seasons in 1961, '62 and '63, recording more than 200 strikeouts each year. He led the league in shutouts in 1961 with eight, and with five in 1962, while also leading in complete games in '62 and '63 with 18 each year. In 1964, he was 15-12 and was runner-up in the league with 14 complete games and 213 strikeouts. After experiencing arm trouble in 1965, he was unable to regain his league-leading form with the Twins, posting only 9-3 and 8-6 winning records in 1965 and in 1966.

Had Winning Seasons with Expansion Senators

Pascual was traded to the expansion Senators in 1967, where he surprised by posting a winning season that year, 12-10 and he then followed that with another one in 1968 at 13-12, with excellent ERAs of 3.28 and 2.69. The latter ERA was his second best for a full season's work, only eclipsed by his 2.46 recorded in 1963 with Minnesota. After posting a 2-5 record for Washington, Cincinnati acquired him in 1969 in the hope that he could help them in their pennant drive. He appeared in only five games with them, however, without being the pitcher of record. With the Los Angeles Dodgers in 1970, he got into only 10 games and again was not the pitcher of record in any. He concluded his major league career in 1971 with the Cleveland Indians. Again used only sparingly, he posted a 2-2 record in 14 games.

Lost Series Game in '65 to Dodgers

Unfortunately, for Pascual and the Minnesota Twins, the only time that Camilo appeared in a World Series was in 1965, the year that he contracted his sore arm. The Series went the full seven games, with the Twins losing out to the Los Angeles Dodgers four games to three. It might have been a different story if the Twins had won the pennant a few years earlier while Camilo was at his peak. As it was, he started only one game of the Series, the third, gave up three runs in five innings and lost the game, as former Senator Claude Osteen shut out the Twins 4-0 on five hits.

Strikes Out 15 on Opening Day, Ties Johnson's Record

One of the highlights of his career was on opening day 1960 before President Eisenhower and a capacity Griffith Stadium crowd. On that day, Pascual tied Walter Johnson's record (established in 1917) by striking out 15 Boston Red Sox batters en route to a 10-1 victory. Ted Williams homered for the only Red Sox run.

Also, earlier in the year, Pascual led his Cuban team to the Caribbean Series championship against Puerto Rico by winning two games, including the clincher.

Pascual was a complete ballplayer with great control, as attested by his remarkable strikeout-to-walk ratio, and probably the finest fielding pitcher of his time. He was a respected hitter and unsurpassed bunter. On August 14, 1960, his grand-slam home run was the difference in Washington's 5-4 win over the New York Yankees in the first game of a doubleheader. At his peak, he was considered by many to be the best pitcher in the American League. Unlike his Cuban counterpart, Pedro Ramos, he was not colorful but his quiet, business-like approach was a credit to the game. Reliever Darold Knowles described Pascual as one of the classiest men he had ever met and Camilo graciously complimented him after every save. Pascual was selected for the American League All-Star Team five times, 1959-62 and 1964.

Expansion Era, 1961-1971
Left-Handed Pitcher

Claude Wilson Osteen Jr.

(Wimpy, Gomer)

BL TL 5' 11" 173 lbs.

B. Aug. 9, 1939, Caney Spring, TN.

	Y	W	L	PCT	ERA	G	GS	CG	IP	H	BB	SO	SHO
Was.	4	33	41	.446	3.46	108	90	28	638	632	180	315	4
Life	18	196	195	.501	3.30	541	488	140	3460.1	3471	940	1612	40

Claude Osteen (2nd from left) is 4-2 winner over the Indians on June 13, 1962. Pictured also are (left to right) Joe Hicks, Ken Retzer and Steve Hamilton.

Claude Osteen moved from Tennessee to Reading, Ohio, near Cincinnati as a teenager where he played high school baseball for three years. In his senior year, his team won the state championship and in the final game, he struck out 20 batters and hit a home run. Big league scouts had been following him for some time but Cincinnati was able to sign him for a modest bonus because they made room for him on their major league roster immediately (1957). He only pitched four innings in three games and despite a nice 2.25 earned run average he was sent down to Nashville of the Southern Association before season's end.

He was outstanding with Wenatchee of the Northern League in 1958 and as a result, he was promoted to Seattle of the Pacific Coast League where he posted a 5-4 record with a 3.08 ERA. After winning eight and losing 12 with them in '59, he was brought up to the parent club in September and saw limited action in two games. He participated in only one game with the Reds in '61 but did very well that year with Indianapolis of the American Association, winning 15 and losing 11 with an ERA of 3.53. Washington, however, was able to obtain him for three games before the end of the year. He was 1-1 with an ERA of 5.00 for the Nats.

Developed Under Pitching Coach Sid Hudson

Wimpy, as he was sometimes called because of his eating habits, had his best years after he left Washington. His stint with the Senators enabled him to learn and develop the art of pitching under the Nats' pitching coach, Sid Hudson. He had losing records his first two full years with the expansion club but it was not entirely his fault as he did not get much run support from his teammates. In 1962 alone, the team was shut out four times while Osteen was on the mound. He combined for 17 wins and 27 losses for the '62 and '63 seasons.

No. 1 Starter for Senators in 1964

But, Claude hit his stride in 1964, when he began a string of 10 consecutive major league seasons of double-digit wins. He was

15-13 with the Nats and had an ERA of 3.33 despite allowing 256 hits in 257 innings, second most in the league. He had become their number one starting pitcher. At the end of the year, however, Osteen was traded to the Los Angeles Dodgers along with infielder John Kennedy and $100,000 for outfielder Frank Howard, Ken McMullen, Phil Ortega, Pete Richert and Dick Nen. While with the Senators, Wimpy displayed a great strikeouts-to-walks ratio, fanning 315 while walking only 180. He also fashioned four shutouts.

Reached Stardom with Dodgers

It was with the Dodgers, however, that Osteen was to reach stardom. Inserted into a starting rotation, which included the likes of Sandy Koufax and Don Drysdale, he played a major role in the Dodgers' '65 and '66 pennant-winning seasons. Osteen was superb, pitching much better than his 15-15 record in 1965 would indicate. His ERA was under 3.00 for the first time in the majors at 2.79 and during the year he pitched a one-hitter. More importantly, he was virtually impossible to hit in the World Series, hurling seven scoreless innings in Game Three. The Dodgers were reeling after two losses to the Minnesota Twins and it was Osteen who came through with the needed clutch performance, giving him his greatest thrill in the majors. Los Angeles went on to win in seven games. Claude was undefeated against the Twins during his career with a perfect 5-0 record.

Loses Game 3 of Series in 1966

Osteen was 17-14 in 1966 with a 2.85 ERA as the Dodgers repeated as National League champions. Drysdale and Koufax failed to win in the first two Series games, as in the previous year. The team's opponent that year was the Baltimore Orioles and it fell on Claude's shoulders again to avert disaster in Game Three. He pitched his heart out, gave up only one run in seven innings, but lost to Wally Bunker's shutout of Los Angeles. The Orioles went on to sweep the Series.

Claude had acquired a new nickname, "Gomer," because of

his resemblance to television star "Gomer Pyle." Gomer was an even 17-17 in 1967, led the league in the number of hits allowed (298 in 288 innings) but was second in shutouts with five. He fell to 12-18 in 1968, the only time he had a losing record in his nine-year stint with the Dodgers. His 18 losses were tops in the league. Los Angeles had fallen on hard times and was not to win another flag while Osteen was with the club.

20 Game Winner in '69 and '72

That didn't stop Claude from recording one of his two best seasons in '69 as he reached one of his most coveted goals, 20 wins. He was 20-15 with a 2.66 ERA and he posted career highs in starts (41), complete games (16), innings pitched (321) and strikeouts (183). His seven shutouts were again second in the league. Unfortunately, the 293 hits allowed were the most permitted in the league.

Gomer had a total of 30 wins and 25 losses in 1970 and 1971 but his ERA rose above 3.00 again with 3.03 (in 1970) and 3.51 (in 1971). In '70, his four shutouts enabled him to be runner-up in the league for the second consecutive year. He hit the 20 win plateau again in 1972 with a mark of 20-11 and set career marks in winning percentage (.645) and ERA (2.64).

Nineteen seventy-three proved to be his last with Los Angeles despite a fine year in which he posted a 16-11 record and an ERA of 3.31. He was dealt to Houston for the 1974 season and was traded to St. Louis before the end of the year. He combined for a 9-11 record with a 3.80 ERA.

He was back in the American League in 1975 with the Chicago White Sox who used him extensively. He started 37 games but completed only five and finished with a 7-16 record. Claude was enjoying a fine Spring training in '76 and was slated to pitch the opener for Chicago when club president, Bill Veeck made a surprise visit to the camp and Osteen was released before the start of the season. This ended his playing days.

Won Nearly 200 Games in Career

Osteen won nearly 200 games (196), lasting seven innings per start on the average. He was named to three All-Star teams, 1967, 1970 and 1973. He was the winning pitcher in the 1970 game when he pitched three shutout innings. He threw two more scoreless innings in the '73 contest.

After his playing days were over, he served as the pitching coach or scout for a variety of major and minor league teams, including the Philadelphia Phillies, Baltimore Orioles and Los Angeles Dodgers.

Expansion Era, 1961-1971
Relief Pitcher

Darold Duane Knowles
(Darold)

BL TL 6' 0" 190 lbs.
B. Dec. 9, 1941, Brunswick, MO.

	Y	W	L	PCT	ERA	G	GS	CG	IP	H	BB	SO	SHO	SV
Was.	5	20	27	.426	2.36	229	1	0	373.2	319	159	268	0	60
Life	16	66	74	.471	3.12	765	8	1	1092	1006	480	681	1	143

Reliever Darold Knowles apparently got a third strike with that pitch.

Darold Knowles performed his magic as a left-handed relief pitcher for 16 years in the majors. As a "closer" for eight different teams, Knowles appeared in 765 games all told, averaged only about an inning and one-half a game, while posting an ERA of just over three runs a game. He labored five seasons for the Nats, making the most appearances (71 games), posting an ERA of 2.04 and notching 27 saves in 1970. Incredibly, he set an American League record for reliever's losses that year with 14. His best earned run average was gained in 1972 with the Oakland A's when he recorded a 1.36 and had a 5-1 record with 11 saves.

Traded to Washington for '67–'71 Seasons

Darold broke into the majors with the Baltimore Orioles in 1965 but pitched in only five games and was traded to the Philadelphia Phillies of the National League who used him extensively in 69 games during the '66 season. He was 6-5 with an ERA of 3.05 and 13 saves. He was traded to Washington the following year where he made 229 appearances, almost entirely in relief, from 1967 to 1971.

With the Nats in '67, he played in 61 games with a 6-8 record, gaining 14 saves with an ERA of 2.70. He was only able to get into 32 games in 1968 because of military service, going 1-1 with an ERA of 2.18 and four saves. Restricted somewhat by military duties again in 1969, he was able to appear in 53 games with a winning 9-2 record, 13 saves and a 2.24 ERA. His final full year with the Senators (1970) was by far his best as highlighted earlier.

Appears in All 7 Games of '73 Series

On May 8, 1971, Knowles was traded to the powerful Oakland A's after pitching in 12 games and recording a 2-2 record. There, he was used mainly against left-handed hitters, since the A's already had Rollie Fingers as their great relief ace. This was his best year with the Athletics as indicated earlier but his year was ruined when he broke the thumb on his pitching hand and was not able to pitch in the World Series that fall. Knowles did, however, get his only opportunity to play in a World Series the next year (1973) as the A's repeated as American League champions. He made the most of it, gaining credit for a save in the first game against the New York Mets and notching another save in the seventh and deciding game by getting the final out of the Series. Darold says that the save was the biggest thrill of his major league career, and he became the first pitcher ever to appear in all seven games of a World Series. In his final year (1974) with the A's, his ERA rose above 4.00 (at 4.22) after being under four for the ten previous years.

In 1975, he was traded to the Chicago Cubs for two years, appearing in 58 games each year, winning a total of 11 games and losing 16 while earning 24 saves. Back in the American League with the Texas Rangers in 1977, he had a 5-2 record in 42 games but only four saves. He ended his career in the National League when he was sent to the Montreal Expos in 1978 and then the St. Louis Cardinals in 1979 and 1980. With the Expos, he was 3-3 in 60 games with six saves and with the Cards he was 2-6 in 50 games with six saves.

The slender six footer's formula for success was an excellent fastball, a good slider and a tremendous curve ball. With his pinpoint control, he dazzled opposition hitters, especially left-handers. Somewhat overworked by the Phillies before coming to Washington, manager Gil Hodges designed a successful system for using the likable left-hander. Knowles was seldom warmed up unless he was going to be used in a game and he was normally not used in early game situations and never three or four days in a row.

Activated by Military in '68

Knowles was in a unique situation in 1968 because of his military reserve status. As a member of the 113th Tactical Fighter Wing of the District Air National Guard, he was activated by the U.S. Air Force following the seizure of the United States intelligence vessel, *Pueblo,* by the North Korean communists. For a time, he was permitted to play in home games and in some games in nearby cities, as long as he could report back to Andrews Air Force Base (where he was stationed after activation) in time to execute assigned duties.

He made his last appearance on the mound that year on July 12 before being transferred to Itzuke Air Force Base in Japan for about 10 months. The Senators sorely missed him over that period. He returned to the team in late May 1969 and played the rest of the season. Knowles was probably the most publicized professional athlete to be taken from his job as a result of the crisis.

American League All–Star in 1969

Although just back from the military for less than two months, manager Mayo Smith of the Detroit Tigers selected Darold as a member of the 1969 American League All-Star squad. He was the first reliever to be selected since Eddie Fisher in 1965. Surprised by the honor, Darold pitched before a cheering home crowd and went two-thirds of an inning without any damage. Washington manager Ted Williams thought that he should have been picked again in 1970 but because of his 1-6 record he was overlooked. The Senators that year could not buy a run for him when he was on the mound. The fact that he had saved 14 of the Senators 30 victories and had an earned run average around 2.0 apparently was not enough for selection.

After completing his 16-year active career in the majors, he became a roving pitching instructor with the St. Louis Cardinals for eight years. He then served as a pitching coach in the Phillies organization for 12 years and for the last three years as a coach in the Pittsburgh Pirates organization.

Knowles remembers that his finest hour in a Senators uniform was when he came in for late-inning relief after Frank Howard's homer tied the game against Minnesota and sent it into extra innings. Darold shut the Twins out for ten innings, allowing only three hits and striking out ten.

The high-class Knowles was not only the Nats' best left-handed reliever during the expansion years but was probably the best left-handed relief pitcher in the majors during the period. In fact, he was the best left-handed relief pitcher in Washington Senators history.

Expansion Era, 1961–1971
Catcher

Paulino Casanova

(Paul, Ortiz)

BR TR 6' 4" 200 lbs.

B. Dec. 21, 1941, Colon, Matanzas, Cuba

	Y	G	AB	R	H	2B	3B	HR	RBI	BB	SO	SB	BA	SA
Was.	7	686	2310	183	527	77	12	41	216	81	349	2	.228	.325
Life	10	859	2786	214	627	87	12	50	252	101	430	2	.225	.319

Paul Casanova lunges at Oakland's Larry Bittner and tags him out at the plate on June 4, 1971.

Paul Casanova was selected by the Washington Senators as the expansion team's catcher primarily for his defensive prowess and unflagging enthusiasm for the game. Although his lifetime batting average was only .225, he did hit for power on occasion, and hit as well or better than most of the other catchers on the squad during the period. The Cuban-born, Spanish-speaking Casanova had considerable difficulty breaking into the majors. After earlier spring training trials with the Cleveland Indians and Chicago Cubs, he was out of organized baseball and playing semi-pro ball in New London, Connecticut at two dollars a game while working washing cars and digging ditches.

Cleveland sent him down to Newton, North Carolina of the Western Carolina League after one of his spring training trials in 1960. Paul got as far as Charlotte, North Carolina before exhausting his money. Since there was no bus service to Newton, he took a taxicab and the fare was $19. Unable to pay, he spent the night in jail before the Cleveland organization took care of the problem the next day.

Drafted by Nats in Expansion Draft

Casanova's upbeat attitude and strong arm impressed general manager George Selkirk, so he made Paul one of his draft choices in 1961 and sent him off to the minors for seasoning. While there, he was the All-Star catcher for three years and in late 1965 he was brought up to the Senators for good. He appeared in only five games but hit .308 in 13 at bats.

1967 A.L. All–Star Catcher

Nineteen sixty-six proved to be his best year and he started it off right in his second game of the season when he broke up Fred Talbot's no-hitter in the eighth inning with a mammoth home run. He finished the season with a .254 batting average, 13 home runs, five triples and 16 doubles. Defensively, he led American League catchers by participating in 12 double plays, although he also led the league in number of errors with 12. He followed that in '67 with another fine year, hitting .248 and earning a place on the American League All-Star Team. Again, he led the other league catchers by engaging in 19 double plays. Under the tutelage of manager Gil Hodges, Casanova had matured into a solid major leaguer.

In 1968, however, with Hodges leaving to manage the New York Mets, Casanova seemingly lost confidence in his hitting and his fretting affected his whole game adversely. Things deteriorated so much that he even was sent down to Buffalo to try to regain his form. Finishing the season with Washington, he recorded his lowest average (.196) and he was never able to regain his form, although he was able to provide Washington, and later the Atlanta Braves, a solid defensive performance behind the plate for the next half-dozen years.

Paul appeared in 124 games in 1969 and was behind the plate in 122 of them, leading the league in that category but hitting just .216, although he belted 18 home runs. The following year (1970) he led the league's catchers in double plays for the third time with 12 and he raised his average a few points to .229. In his final year in Washington he was in 94 games and hit .203 with 14 homers.

Traded to Braves

Paul was traded to the Atlanta Braves of the National League after the team was moved to Texas in 1972. In his three seasons there, Paul appeared in 173 games and averaged .210 for the three years. In '72, he hit .206 in 49 games and in '73, his average was a little better at .216. He wound up his major league career in 1974 after his hitting barely reached the .200 level at .202.

Possessed a "Rifle arm"

The stature of the 6' 4" Casanova was compared to that of the great New York Yankee catcher, Bill Dickey. The slender, muscular

Cuban had a rifle arm, throwing out numerous runners with regularity, limiting the running game of the opposition and firing the ball back to the pitcher (according to pitcher Darold Knowles sometimes with more velocity than he threw it) whenever they needed a reminder to "get in the game."

He was an "iron man" performer, oftentimes catching both games of a doubleheader and loving it. Paul was behind the plate for all 22 innings in a game lasting over six hours against the Chicago White Sox. Washington won the game in the bottom of the twenty-second inning when Casanova's single drove in the winning run. It was the longest night game in American League history. Even with two strikes on him, he was noted for swinging from his heels and sometimes connecting with amazing power. He was probably the fastest runner among league catchers and he ran the bases with reckless abandon.

Paul Casanova played the game of baseball as it was meant to be played, with enthusiasm, hustle and genuine joy. This clubhouse leader was an important part of the Washington scene for seven seasons!

Expansion Era, 1961–1971
First Base

Michael Peter Epstein

(Mike, Superjew)

BL TL 6' 3.5" 230 lbs.

B. Apr. 4, 1943, Bronx, NY.

	Y	G	AB	R	H	2B	3B	HR	RBI	BB	SO	SB	BA	SA
Was.	5	514	1587	206	398	49	11	73	212	256	412	7	.251	.434
Life	9	907	2854	362	695	93	16	130	380	448	645	7	.244	.424

The Nats' Mike Epstein has a three-run homer during an eight-run inning against the New York Yankees on March 11, 1968.

The powerful Mike Epstein, a college baseball All-American with the University of California at Berkeley, was a much sought-after bonus baby in the early '60s. The Baltimore Orioles signed him for $50,000 and sent him to Stockton of the California League in 1965 and to Rochester of the International League in 1966. Epstein did not disappoint them, earning "Most Valuable Player" and "Rookie of the Year" honors both years. He also was named "Minor League Player of the Year" by both *Topps* and the *Sporting News* for 1966. Each year, he batted over .300, hit 30 home runs and drove in over 100 runs.

But, there was a major problem. Epstein's position was first base and Boog Powell was a fixture there. The Orioles tried, unsuccessfully, to convert Mike to an outfielder while in the minors and wanted him to return to Rochester for further seasoning. Rather than return to the minors, Epstein quit baseball and returned home and to school.

Traded to Washington by Orioles in '67

He sat out almost two months of the '67 season before the Orioles traded him and Frank Bertaina to Washington for one of the Senators' better pitchers, Pete Richert. Badly in need of a left-handed power hitter to augment Frank Howard, he was welcomed by the Nats with high expectations. Manager Gil Hodges gave him the first base job and in his debut against the New York Yankees, he hit an opposite field inside-the-park home run, the first of his career. He set about trying to prove the Orioles wrong and shortly thereafter he hit a home run against them, and later he hit two against the Los Angeles Angels in one game.

From the moment he arrived, he worked extra hard to improve his batting stroke and his weakness in catching pop-ups, and his attitude impressed management. It was evident as the season wore on, however, that he needed more seasoning. When he was in a slump, he was inclined to sulk. He hit only .226 with nine homers and 29 runs batted in 83 games.

Beats Catfish Hunter with Late Homer

Mike appeared to be back on track the next season (1968) in spring training when he led the club with five homers and 14 RBI. He injured his elbow, however, and was unable to get untracked after the regular season started. Batting only .099 just prior to Memorial Day, he was optioned to Buffalo of the International League to permit him to regain his batting eye. Mike accepted the demotion gracefully and was brought back in just two weeks. Facing Catfish Hunter and the Oakland A's in his first game back, he looked bad in striking out twice but with the score tied 2-2, he delivered a long blast for a game-winning home run. With an altered stance and increased confidence, he was able to hit .270 the remainder of the season and ignite optimism again.

Smashes Three Homers in One Game in '69

Epstein had his finest year in the majors in 1969 under manager Ted Williams' tutelage. He hit for an average of .278 and had career highs with 30 homers, 73 runs, 85 runs batted in, 85 walks, a .414 on-base percentage and a slugging percentage of .511. In May, he equalled a club record by smashing three home runs in one game against the Chicago White Sox and as the on-deck hitter when the game ended he almost had a shot at a fourth. He also was able to overcome his defensive weaknesses, and according to pitcher Darold Knowles, he was a very underrated fielder.

But in 1970, trade rumors were continually flying especially concerning the New York Yankees. It seemed that most observers thought that Frank Howard's best position would be first base and that there would be no room for Mike on the club. Epstein was never able to overcome his tendency to worry too much about his slumps, and as a result his performance in 1970 tailed off when he dropped to .256, with 20 homers and only 56 runs batted in. He struck out a career record 117 times. On June 19, the Senators lost to the Orioles despite Epstein's eight RBI.

Hits 4 Straight Homers over 2 Games for A's

He was traded to the Oakland A's in early May 1971 along with Darold Knowles for Paul Linblad, Don Mincher, Frank Fernandez and cash. On June 16, Mike homered his first two times up against the Senators to give him four straight over two games. Playing a lot of first base for the A's, his performance was about the same as the previous year except that his batting average slipped to .238, while hitting 19 home runs and driving in 60 runs. In the American League Championship Series, swept by the Baltimore Orioles, Epstein played in two games and collected one hit in five trips to the plate.

Blanked in '72 World Series

In 1972, Mike made one last encouraging comeback as he registered a .270 batting average with 26 homers and 70 RBI. His 138 games, 123 hits and 18 triples were career highs. When Oakland defeated the Detroit Tigers in the American League Championship Series, Epstein was in all five games registering three hits in 16 at bats for a .187 average. In the '72 World Series, won by Oakland over the Cincinnati Reds in seven games, Mike appeared in six of the seven games but was blanked in 16 trips to the plate although he did score one run.

He was traded to the Texas Rangers before the '73 season and appeared in only 27 games with a batting average of only .188 before being sent to the Los Angeles Angels where he played in 91 games. Again, his performance was weak that year when he finished the season with an average of .209, with only nine homers and 38 runs batted in.

Nineteen seventy-four was his final year in the big leagues as the Angels released him after he played in only 18 games and hit only .161.

Expansion Era, 1961-1971
Second Base

Bernard Keith Allen

(Bernie)

BL TR 6' 0" 185 lbs.

B. Apr. 16, 1939, East Liverpool, OH.

	Y	G	AB	R	H	2B	3B	HR	RBI	BB	SO	SB	BA	SA
Was.	5	530	1482	126	351	52	11	30	154	172	161	10	.237	.348
Life	12	1139	3404	357	815	140	21	73	351	370	424	13	.239	.357

Bernie Allen collides with outfielder Brant Alyea while catching Cleveland's Chuck Hinton's pop-up on July 8, 1969.

Bernie Allen was one of the most versatile athletes ever to don a Senators uniform. He starred in three sports in high school and college and was named to the High School All-American basketball team. A first string quarterback at Purdue University in 1959 and 1960, he was *Sports Illustrated's* "Back of the Week" for his performance against Wisconsin in 1959. He also led the Boilermakers to a 23-14 victory over top-ranked Minnesota in 1960.

Rookie Season in '62 Is His Best

Upon graduation, he signed a contract to play baseball with the Minnesota Twins, and then spent only one year in the minors with Charlotte of the South Atlantic League in 1961. The following year ('62), he had his best season in the majors, playing virtually every game for the Twins and batting .269. Bernie had career highs in games (159), runs (79), hits (154), doubles (27), triples (7), RBI (64), walks (62), strikeouts (82) and slugging percentage (.403). He also teamed with shortstop ZoiloVersalles as the American League's leading double play makers.

Suffered Serious Knee Injury

In 1963, he suffered a terrible start, hitting only .164 in early June. But, manager Sam Mele stuck with him and by the end of the season he raised his average to .240 in 139 games. Allen's career hit its low point on June 24, 1964. He suffered a serious knee injury playing against Washington when Don Zimmer slammed into him to break up a double play using a clean, hard slide. He was on the disabled list the rest of the year and finished the season with a .214 average in 74 games. Optioned to Denver the following year to play himself back into shape, he was brought back up by the Twins late in the year and appeared in only 19 games hitting .231.

Traded to Senators for '67 Season

Bernie won back his starting position at second base during the spring of '66 but he reinjured his knee in June and his performance tailed off. Nevertheless, he was able to play in over 100 games and hit .238. As the Twin's newly elected player representative, he fell into disfavor with manager Sam Mele and he and pitcher Camilo Pascual were traded to the Washington Senators for the 1967 season.

The Nats acquired Allen somewhat in self-defense. He had batted .296 against them since coming to the majors and smashed nine of his 32 homers against them. He was particularly fond of the Senators' park, hitting seven of the nine there. Bernie apparently won the Nats' regular second base position during spring training, but manager Gil Hodges also later used Bob Saverine, Tim Cullen and Frank Coggins there. Still, Bernie appeared in 87 games despite a lowly .193 average for the year.

One Contact Lens Used

The following year, new manager Jim Lemon used Allen against both right and left-handed pitching and he played in 120 games. Before the season started, Bernie had an eye examination and one contact lens was prescribed. Seeing the ball a lot better, he improved his average 48 points over the previous year to .241. Bernie was also able to improve defensively with the new contact, as he led all American League second baseman with a .991 fielding percentage. His 1969 season was essentially equivalent to his '68 performance, when he played in 122 games and raised his batting average another six points to .247. He was credited with stealing five bases, a career record.

His knee collapsed on him again during spring training of '70, but by the end of May manager Ted Williams declared that: "Bernie Allen has been our most dependable hitter," this after the second baseman drove in the tying runs and scored the winning run in the bottom of the twelfth inning in a wild extra inning game with the Kansas City Royals. He was unable to sustain his performance at the plate, however, and finished the season with a .234 average.

Best Year with Senators Is '71

Bernie had his best year for the Nats during his final season in Washington in 1971, when he hit .266 in almost 100 games and again played excellent defense, teaming with shortstop Eddie Brinkman to give the Senators a solid middle of the infield. His on-base percentage was .359, his best.

Hits Three Homers in Cooperstown Exhibition

When the Senators left Washington for Texas at the end of the '71 season, Allen was traded to the New York Yankees as part of a three-team swap. Bernie had become disenchanted with manager Ted Williams and asked to be traded. Although he hit a disappointing .227 in 97 games his first year with the Yanks, he did perform a few heroics for them during the season. In July '72, Allen cracked a 374-foot homer in the top of the 11th to enable Mel Stottlemyre to edge the Twins 1-0. His performance in a 1972 game, held at Cooperstown as part of the induction ceremonies, will long be remembered. With the Yankees facing the Los Angeles Dodgers of the National League, he became the first player ever to hit three home runs in the annual game. All three of the homers were hard shots that cleared the right field fence.

His final year in the major leagues was 1973 when he split his time between the Yankees and the Montreal Expos of the National League. With the Yanks, he was in 17 games and hit .228; then he closed out his career in Montreal hitting only .180 in 16 games His seasonal average was .206 for the 33 games.

While with the Twins, the quiet-spoken and amiable Allen along with third baseman Rich Rollins operated a franchise of the Napoleon Hill Academy in the Twin Cities. They instructed students on how "to think positively and grow rich," based on 17 principles developed by Hill in 1908. Bernie's adherence to those principles certainly played a leading role in his successful climb to the majors.

Expansion Era, 1961-1971
Third Base

Kenneth Lee McMullen

(Ken)

BR TR 6' 3" 195 lbs.

B. Jun. 1, 1942, Oxnard, CA.

	Y	G	AB	R	H	2B	3B	HR	RBI	BB	SO	SB	BA	SA
Was.	6	767	2820	350	709	97	16	86	327	275	442	15	.251	.389
Life	16	1583	5131	568	1273	172	26	156	606	510	815	20	.248	.383

Ken McMullen being congratulated by Frank Howard after connecting for a grand slam against the New York Yankees on April 12, 1967.

Ken McMullen held down the "hot corner" for the Senators for over five years. The big Californian's physique was more suited to playing first base or the outfield but nonetheless Ken provided the Nats with major league third base play. He proved to be a durable player, averaging 150 games a season for the five full seasons he played in Washington. Pitcher Darold Knowles described him as a "premier professional." Under the tutelage of Coach Eddie Yost, Ken mastered the art of coming in on bunts and making the barehanded throw to first base. Many believed that he was the best in the league at it, even outdoing the great Brooks Robinson. He did not have the quickness of Brooks or the range of some other third basemen, but he was steady, reliable and able to pull off many spectacular plays.

$60,000 Bonus Baby of Dodgers

McMullen was a superior athlete in high school in both baseball and basketball, winning statewide recognition in both sports before being signed for a $60,000 bonus by the Los Angeles Dodgers of the National League. He was optioned to Reno of the California League his first year in professional ball (1961) where he hit .288 with 21 homers and led the league with 107 walks, 200 assists and 22 double plays. Promoted to Omaha of the American Association in 1962, he hit another 21 home runs and batted .282. He appeared in six games with the Dodgers late in the season, compiling a .273 average. In '63, he was with Spokane of the Pacific Coast League until called up by Los Angeles and given a shot at becoming their regular third baseman. He appeared in 79 games but batted only, .236. The next year (1964), he began the season with the Dodgers but was sent back to Spokane after only 24 games because he was hitting only .209. He didn't do much better there, batting .234 in 93 games.

Senators MVP in 1965

McMullen was traded to the Senators for the 1965 season as part of a deal, which brought Frank Howard, Phil Ortega, Dick

Nen and Pete Richert in exchange for Claude Osteen and John Kennedy. He was voted the Senators' "Most Valuable Player" that year as he cracked out 18 homers and finished the season with a .263 batting average in 150 games. He hit a home run on opening day against the Boston Red Sox but then was benched because of a slump. He returned to the starting lineup on May 2, becoming a fixture at the third base position for five years. On August 13, he tied a major league record by starting four double plays against the Baltimore Orioles. On the down side, he led American League third basemen that year with 22 errors but he finished just behind American League leader Clete Boyer in total chances.

He was going great during spring training of 1966; however, he suffered a bone chip in his left thumb sliding into second base in an exhibition game against the Philadelphia Phillies. He missed several games and was forced to use a specially constructed foam rubber guard, which hampered his play. His average nosedived to .233 that year and his home run total dropped to 13. On September 26, 1966 in a game against the Boston Red Sox, he tied the major league record for most assists by a third baseman in a nine-inning game when he made 11 of them.

Has Expansion Club Record 19–Game Hitting Streak

The following year ('67), he was on the way to regaining his form with 60 runs batted in and 15 homers, when a line drive from Bob Allison's bat ripped open the ring finger on his right hand on August 10. The day before, his twentieth inning home run enabled the Senators to beat the Minnesota Twins 9-7. He was out of the lineup for 10 days and he played the rest of the season with a sponge wrapped around the finger. The injury occurred near the end of his 19-game hitting streak, an expansion club record. Hampered by the injury, he finished the year with a .245 average, 67 RBI and 16 home runs. He did, however, celebrate the biggest slugging game of his major league career on August 4 against the California Angels, with two home runs and a double and he enjoyed a fine fielding year, leading American League third basemen with 38 double plays.

1969 Is Finest Season

His 1968 season was essentially the same as in '67 (hitting .248 in 151 games) except that he achieved his highest homer total with Washington, 20. Ken was noted as a clutch hitter and four times that year he was involved in sending over the winning run in extra inning games. But, under the tutelage of manager Ted Williams, McMullen enjoyed his finest season in '69 his last full season with the Senators. Reminding him to hit to all fields according to where the ball was pitched, Ken regained his old form and finished with a .272 average, 19 home runs and a career high 87 RBI. He also led American League third basemen in putouts with 185 and tied Brooks Robinson for the lead in fielding with .976.

Reluctantly, Washington traded McMullen to the California Angels the following year (1970) on April 26 after 15 games to acquire fancy fielding Aurelio Rodriguez and bonus baby Rick Reichardt. The Senators gained two regular players but California obtained Ken to provide more power at the third base position. He did lead American League third basemen in total chances per game that year. Ken hit a career high 21 homers in 1971, but he was never able to play up to his performance in '69 in any of the three years he was with the Angels, hitting .229, .250 and .269 in consecutive years.

Returned to Dodgers in '73

He was back with the Los Angeles Dodgers again for three years from 1973-75 where he was used only sparingly and hit .247, .250 and .239 in a total of 107 games. He did contribute to their pennant-winning season in '74, and his first two hits in 1975 were pinch-hit home runs driving in seven runs. He was signed by the Oakland A's for the '76 season and he appeared in 98 games mainly as a reserve and posted a .220 batting average, leading the league in pinch hits (9 for 31).

McMullen closed out his career as a designated hitter and utility man with the Milwaukee Brewers in 1977, playing in 63 games and hitting .228. Although Ken played for the Nats for only six of his 16 big league years, more than half of his lifetime statistics were generated while playing for Washington.

Expansion Era, 1961–1971
Shortstop

Edwin Albert Brinkman
(Ed)

BR TR 6' 0" 170 lbs.
B. Dec. 8, 1941, Cincinnati, OH.

	Y	G	AB	R	H	2B	3B	HR	RBI	BB	SO	SB	BA	SA
Was.	10	1142	3845	350	868	125	27	31	273	289	573	27	.226	.297
Life	15	1845	6045	550	1355	201	38	60	461	444	845	30	.224	.300

Shortstop Ed Brinkman tags out Boston's Rico Petrocelli on April 14, 1965.

One of the best moves the expansion Senators made was to sign, in 1961, a Cincinnati high school boy named Ed Brinkman for a $60,000-plus bonus. Brinkman was a teammate of record breaker Pete Rose while growing up and in high school. The irony is that it was Eddie, not Pete, who was the standout slugger on the teams. Brinkman hit .460 his senior year with nine home runs, and was 9-0 as a pitcher. His greatest asset was a strong throwing arm. Almost every other major league club was interested in him but he selected Washington because he believed that he would be able to make the majors sooner with an expansion team.

With the Class D Pensacola team in the Florida State League in 1961, Ed hit .290 in 53 games and played third base in four games with the Senators in September, batting .091 in 11 trips to the plate. He was brought up from Raleigh of the Carolina league in mid-season the following year ('62) after hitting .325. He was alternated with Ken Hamlin at shortstop but the Nats soon discovered he was not ready for major league pitching as indicated by his .165 average in 54 games.

Spectacular Defensive Player

He was installed as the regular shortstop in '63 and his spectacular defensive play at shortstop had the league buzzing. His powerful arm enabled him to get the ball to first base quicker than any shortstop in the American League. He had inherited a strong arm from his father, a semi-pro catcher, and developed it as a pitcher in high school. His biggest weaknesses in the field, when signed, were in handling balls hit in the hole between short and third, and his double play techniques. His major weakness, however, was with the bat and in his first full major league season he hit only .228 in 145 games.

The 1964 season was almost a carbon copy of '63, except that he was absent from the lineup more because of his lack of hitting, .224 in 132 games. He experienced a close call in July of that year, when former Senator Camilo Pascual's high fastball hit Brinkman on the helmet about two inches over the left eye and just inches from the temple. Eddie sank to his knees and fell across the plate head first. He quickly recovered, however, and continued in the game.

National Guard Unit Activated

When Jim Lemon became manager in 1966, Ed was coming off his worst year, hitting an anemic .185 in 154 games. Lemon assigned coach Nellie Fox the task of improving Brinkman's hitting. The experiment resulted in some success as Eddie raised his average 44 points to .229, earning him a raise for the next season.

In '67, his hitting fell again to its former level, and in addition, his National Guard Unit was activated because of the Vietnam War. So in 1967, he played in only 109 games, batting .188. There was one bright spot, however, as Ed led all other American League shortstops in fielding with .979. He followed with another poor season in '68, hitting .187 in 77 games.

Ted Williams' Advice Improves Hitting

When Ted Williams arrived on the scene as Washington manager, Ed enjoyed his best seasons. At Ted's request, he choked far up on his new bottle bat handle, took a shorter stride and tried to hit more often to the opposite field on the ground. Waiting longer for the ball and chopping at it raised his average to a respectable .266 in 1969, his best year in the majors and an increase of 79 percentage points. He was named the "Most Improved Senator" by the Washington chapter of the Baseball Writers of America.

Leads A.L. Shortstops in Putouts, Assists and Double Plays

He enjoyed continued success in 1970, compiling virtually the same offensive statistics, hitting .262. But, his most important achievements that year were found in his fielding statistics. Generally recognized for his superior fielding skills, Brinkman put together an extraordinary season to give firm support for those that said he was one of the best fielding shortstops in the majors. He led American League shortstops in three important categories with 301 putouts, 569 assists and 103 double plays.

To the surprise of many, Ed was traded to the Detroit Tigers in 1971 and he remained with them through the 1974 season. He turned in another sparkling performance in the field in '71 as he established a new major league record for shortstops by playing in 56 straight errorless games. He led league shortstops again with 513 assists and in the number of games played (159). Unfortunately for the Tigers, Ed returned to his previous batting form with an average of .228. His home run in the first inning of a game, however, did enable Detroit to become the first team to hit four homers in the first inning of a ball game.

72 Consecutive Errorless Games

It was the same story in 1972, with Brinkman hitting just .203 but making his presence known with the glove. He had a personal best and league-leading fielding average for shortstops of .990, and a league-leading 156 games played. He also broke his major league consecutive errorless innings record, made the previous year, by going from May 2 until August 4 without an error, a total of 72 games. Over the period, he handled 331 chances flawlessly. This held up for 16 years until Kevin Elster of the New York Mets went 88 games without error. This record, however, was made over two seasons, so Ed continued to hold the single season record until Cal Ripken broke it in 1990 with a streak of 95 games. Ripken's string would have ended at 67, however, if the official scorer had not changed his mind about a chance that he originally called an error. Brinkman also established a major league record that year for fewest errors by a shortstop (seven) and he also won the "Golden Glove Award" for shortstops.

In '73, Brinkman didn't miss a game in the 162 game season and he led all league shortstops for the third consecutive year in that category. His average improved 34 points to .237, but Ed continued to struggle at the plate. In his final year with the Tigers (1974), Ed's average dropped 16 points to .221 but he flexed some muscle as he had a career best 14 homers in 153 games.

In 1975, he wound up his career in the majors, playing 28 games for the St. Louis Cardinals and hitting .240, one game for the Texas Rangers with no hits in two at bats and 44 games for the New York Yankees, hitting .175.

Expansion Era, 1961-1971
Outfield

James Hubert King
(Jim)

BL TR 6' 185 lbs.
B. Aug. 27, 1932, Elkins, AR.

	Y	G	AB	R	H	2B	3B	HR	RBI	BB	SO	SB	BA	SA
Was.	7	796	2138	286	511	84	13	89	290	290	294	20	.239	.415
Life	11	1125	2918	374	699	112	19	117	401	363	401	23	.240	.411

*Despite Jim King's third homer of the game,
the Senators lose 5-4 to Kansas City on June 8, 1964.*

On December 14, 1960 the Senators paid $2.1 million for 28 ballplayers in the first ever major league expansion draft. One of the best of the lot was the strong-armed, long ball hitting outfielder, Jim King who served the Nats longer than any of the other draftees, playing for all or part of seven seasons. Although he played in the expansion era, he was a throwback to players of an earlier era. Jim loved every minute of the 17 years he spent in organized ball (six in the minors). King was a manager's dream, usually the first to sign his contracts, never complaining, willing to play hurt and never breaking training rules.

Strong–Armed Outfielder

Playing right field because he had the best arm of any of the expansion Senators, Jim had a large number of assists early in his career, until base runners learned not to take liberties with him. King had almost 700 hits during his big league career and over one-third of them were for extra bases.

Jim broke into the majors with the Chicago Cubs of the National League in 1955 and appeared in over 100 games that year and the next, batting around .250 each year. He was traded to the St. Louis Cardinals for the 1957 season and then to the San Francisco Giants for 1958. With the Cards, he hit a nice .314 in 22 games but with the Giants he fell 100 points to .214 in 34 games. Since he had been used by those clubs only sparingly and had such a disastrous season with the Giants, he was back in the minor leagues for 1959 and'60.

Breaks Vernon's Home Run Record

Rescued by Washington in the expansion draft, he appeared in more than 100 games his first six years with the club (1961-66), the vast majority of the time in the outfield but he also caught in two games and was a reliable pinch hitter. His best year, average-wise, was 1961 when he appeared in 110 games and hit .270. In 1962, he led American League outfielders, participating in four double plays. However, his batting average dropped 27 points to .243, although he was able to duplicate his previous season's output with 11 round trippers. Over five percent of his plate appearances in 1963 resulted in home runs (24), enabling Jim to break Mickey Vernon's Senators record of 20 for left-handed hitters. On August 4, King slugged two homers and a double to lead the Senators over the Red Sox 7-5. His batting average dropped another 12 points to .231 that year, although he recorded his highest slugging average with the Senators at .444.

King was well known as a "spring hitter," and he seemed to have Hall of Famer Warren Spahn's number while playing in the National League, hitting him regularly. In an exhibition game at Pompano Beach, Florida while with the Senators, King smashed a line drive through the box and hit Spahn on the shoulder, causing great concern. Fortunately, the injury was not serious.

Slams 3 Homers in Game

Jim made a comeback of sorts in 1964, despite being bothered by appendicitis, raising his average 10 points to .241 and continuing to show power by blasting 18 homers. On June 8, King experienced one of the highlights of his career when he blasted three solo homers in a losing cause against the Kansas City Athletics and added a fourth the next day as the Nats won 5-1. During the off season, Jim had his appendix removed and manager Gil Hodges planned to give him more rest the next season in an effort to increase his effectiveness.

He could not sustain his performance in '65, however, when he suffered his worst season thus far, his average plummeting to .213. But he continued to demonstrate his power with a slugging percentage of .430. His two-run-pinch home run on May 7 off Mel Stottlemyre enabled the Nats to win the first game of a doubleheader as they swept the Yankees. In his final full season with the Senators in 1966, Jim brought his batting average up to .248, a 35-point improvement over the year before. He continued his long ball hitting and on May 28 hit a grand slam homer off

Red Sox pitcher Dick Radatz as the Nats fell 6-5. King also hit for the circuit in each game on September 15 as the Nats split a doubleheader with the Yanks.

Just prior to the trading deadline in '67, King, the last of the original expansion draftees was traded to the Chicago White Sox for outfielder Ed Stroud. Jim, who had just gone zero for four against the New York Yankees, when told of the trade, was sad and disappointed. He couldn't have been as sad as a number of Senators fans who had grown accustomed to King's hustle and all-out style of play. He had been in 47 games with Washington, hitting .210.

Jim appeared in only 23 games with the White Sox, hitting only .120, before being traded along with Marv Staehle and $10,000 to the Cleveland Indians on July 29 for Rocky Colavito. He appeared in just 19 games the rest of the season, batting .143. His major league career came to an end in November of that year when he was given his unconditional release.

Played "Hurt" Often

Over the years, King played with a "bad body," mainly his knees but also he had trouble with his back, arms, and ankles. One wonders what kind of record Jim would have had, had he been a healthy player!

After leaving the game, he returned to his hometown, Elkins, Arkansas, where he worked for more than 25 years for the Alltel telephone company and then retired full time to his cattle farm.

Expansion Era, 1961-1971
Outfield

Charles Edward Hinton
(Chuck)

BR TR 6' 1" 197 lbs.

B. May 3, 1934, Rocky Mount, NC.

	Y	G	AB	R	H	2B	3B	HR	RBI	BB	SO	SB	BA	SA
Was.	4	545	1961	275	549	83	30	49	217	208	303	92	.280	.428
Life	11	1353	3968	518	1048	152	47	113	443	416	685	130	.264	.412

Washington's Chuck Hinton is tagged out by Cleveland's Woody Held as he attempted to steal second base on September 1, 1964.

Chuck Hinton was a three-sport star in high school and for two years at Shaw University in Raleigh, North Carolina. He was signed to a professional contract by the Baltimore Orioles in 1956 and sent to Phoenix in the minors where he hit .271 in 29 games. His baseball career was interrupted when he served two years in the U.S. Army in 1957 and 1958. He was in the Northern League in 1959 where he led the league in batting (.358), hits (178) and he was named to the minor league All-Star team and given "Rookie of the Year" honors.

Taken from Baltimore in Expansion Draft

After not doing well with Vancouver of the Pacific Coast League the next year (1960), he was sent down to Stockton, California where he led the league in batting (.369), stole 34 bases in 36 tries and was named to the league's All-Star team. Baltimore tried to prevent Hinton from being selected in the major league expansion draft of December 1960 by asking him to fake a shoulder injury. This ploy did not fool the Washington management and they obtained Chuck in the draft.

He started the season with Washington the next year (1961) but was sent to Indianapolis of the American Association for a time and did so well (a .316 batting average in 26 games) that he was brought back up to the parent club, appearing in 106 games and hitting .260 for the year. To give you an idea of what a raw rookie Hinton was, the Senators were playing in Detroit when a Tiger bullpen occupant called for a fly ball Hinton was about to catch. When Chuck stepped aside and let it drop, the Tigers scored the winning run.

Batting Title Challenge Falls Short

Hinton, who had tremendous natural ability, put together his best year in a Washington uniform in 1962. Chuck boosted his average to .310 and hit 17 homers while setting career highs with 151 games, 168 hits, 25 doubles, 75 runs batted in and 28 stolen bases. He had a run at the batting title, trailing former Senator Pete Runnels in early September by only a few percentage points. Runnels finished with .326, however, to win the race. Hinton put together a 17-game consecutive hitting streak that year.

1964 A.L. All Star

Hinton was heading for another banner year in 1963 when he was hitting .340 in mid-May but the flu bug hit him and when he returned to the lineup too early, his average plunged dramatically. Late in the season, he brought it up into the .280s, but then Yankee pitcher, Ralph Terry beaned him and after that he dropped to .268 by the close of the season. He did establish career highs in runs scored (80), triples (12) and walks (64). His fielding improved with a .989 fielding average and career highs in putouts (274) and outfield assists (8).

Chuck began his last season with Washington in 1964 with a .404 average over 25 games. He was selected later as a starter in the outfield for the All-Star game as a result of his first half-season heroics. Unfortunately, he tired as the season progressed and his average fell to .274. He was able to tie his career mark by connecting for 25 doubles. He was traded to the Cleveland Indians at the end of the year for Woody Held and Bob Chance.

Hinton did not play nearly as well for the Indians as he had for the Nats, although he had a career high 18 home runs in 1965 while hitting .255 in 133 games. Chuck was to have two tours with Cleveland, the first from 1965-67. Chuck hit about the same in 1966 (.256) as he did in 1965 and in his final year of that tour his batting average dropped to .245 and he set a personal record when he whiffed 100 times. Hinton was sent to the California Angels for the 1968 season.

Gains Career High .318 Average in '70

That season was a disaster for Hinton whose average dropped to only .195, but despite that the Angels used him in 116 games.

California had seen enough of him and Chuck was dispatched back to Cleveland for a second try with the Indians.

Again, he was with the Indians for a three-year period, 1969-71. In 1969, Chuck raised his average to .245 in 94 games. But, in 1970, Chuck had another banner year when he posted career highs in batting average (.318), on-base percentage (.392) and slugging percentage (.477). It appeared that he was back in form at last.

The opposite was true, though, as once again his average tumbled to .224 in 88 games in 1971, and this proved to be his last year in the majors. During his big league career, Chuck played every defensive position, including catcher, thereby demonstrating his versatility.

While with Washington in the early years, Hinton and two others founded a thriving and lucrative insurance business in Washington, D.C. Chuck made the District of Columbia his home and devoted his time to the insurance firm after retiring from baseball.

Expansion Era, 1961-1971
Outfield

Delbert Bernard Unser
(Del)

BL TL 6' 1" 180 lbs.
B. Dec. 9, 1944, Decatur, IL.

	Y	G	AB	R	H	2B	3B	HR	RBI	BB	SO	SB	BA	SA
Was.	4	581	2119	235	543	56	22	22	158	193	217	31	.256	.335
Life	15	1799	5215	617	1344	179	42	87	481	481	675	64	.258	.358

On October 20, 1980, Del Unser of the Philadelphia Phillies scores the winning run to beat Kansas City in the fifth game of the World Series.

Del Unser was noted for his glove work rather than his prowess with the bat. Although his lifetime major league batting average was only .258, he did register three or four credible seasons wielding the stick, nearly reaching the .300 level toward the end of his 15-year career.

Installed as Regular Center fielder

Despite hitting only .220 and .230 in AA ball, his fancy fielding caught the eye of the Senators and when he led the Florida Instructional League in the fall of 1967, he was brought to the Washington training camp the next spring. With Don Lock gone to the Philadelphia Phillies for more than a year, the center field job was up for grabs and Del made such an impression in camp that he was installed as the regular center fielder when the team began the 1968 season.

He proved to be somewhat of a sensation, although he hit only .230 that year. Unser led the American League outfielders in durability, playing in 156 games and making 22 assists and 10 double plays. He was only two putouts shy in leading that category also. His 635 at bats were more than any of his teammates and established a new record for the expansion Senators.

Manager Ted Williams' "Tips" Raise Average

In 1969, new manager Ted Williams arrived on the Washington scene. Del credits Ted's enthusiasm and knowledge with the 56-percentage point rise in his batting average. Williams did not tinker with Unser's sweet batting stroke but worked on the mental part of his game. He taught him to study the opposing pitcher carefully when not batting and to think in advance what good pitch he might get to hit. In addition to hitting .286, Unser led the league with eight triples, the lowest number ever to lead in that category. Del, unfortunately, was caught stealing 10 times, a league high and he committed 10 errors, the only time he was in double digits during his stay in the majors. He recorded 166 base hits for a career high.

Del's average in 1970 fell almost 30 points to .258 but there was no indication of that in the second game of the season when he drove in four runs in the Nats' 14-4 victory over the Chicago White Sox. On August 14, Unser was the hero as he drove in the winning run in the tenth inning as the Senators subdued the White Sox.

Career High 394 Putouts

In his final year with the Senators (1971), Del again had an off-year at the plate with a .255 batting average but he recorded a fine year in the field with a career high 394 putouts. Unser's two run homer on July 4 gave the Senators' rookie pitcher, Pete Broberg, his first major league victory. Del's 11 stolen bases matched his career high, first attained in 1968, and he drew 59 walks another career high.

When Bob Short took the expansion franchise to Texas in 1972, Unser was sent on to the Cleveland Indians. His average with the Indians dipped again, this time to .232 and he was sent over to the National League to the Philadelphia Phillies in 1973 where the change of scenery seemed to agree with him. He displayed more muscle as he hit career highs in doubles (20) and on-base percentage (.354) while hitting a very respectable .289. He dropped 25 points in 1974 to .264 but still had career highs in RBI (61) and in runs scored (72).

He was traded for the 1975 season to the New York Mets along with Mac Scarce and John Stearns for Tug McGraw and two utility outfielders. With the Mets he found his batting eye again and hit .294. His average seemed to simulate a yo-yo with its up and down tendencies, as Del's average plummeted 66 points to .228 when he split time with the Phils and Montreal in 1976. He had a career high 84 strikeouts but he smashed a career high 12 home runs while recording his best fielding percentage of .990.

3 Consecutive Pinch Homers Ties Record

He continued with Montreal for the next two years ('77 and '78) and his averages were up and down again. In 1977, he hit

.273 in 113 games with 12 home runs but his average fell in 1978 to a dismal .196. He began to do more pinch hitting for the Expos that year but did not do well, garnering seven hits in 58 plate appearances. He improved dramatically in that role when he was returned to the Phillies in 1979, batting .304 as a pinch hitter and tying a major league record with home runs in three straight pinch-hit attempts on June 30, July 5 and July 10. He also registered his highest batting average that year, hitting .298 in 95 games. His slugging average of .482 was his best and his .354 on-base percentage tied the career high mark he made in 1973.

Unser's batting average for 1980 was only .264 but he pinch-hit at a .316 clip as the Phillies went on to win the World Championship that year. Del was two for two in the decisive Game Five of the League Championship Series driving in a run and scoring two, including the game winner in the tenth inning as the Phils edged the Houston Astros to earn a spot in the World Series.

Makes Key Hits in 1980 World Series

In Game Two of the World Series, he hit a pinch double off Kansas City's relief ace, Dan Quisenberry, as an important part of the Phillies' come-from-behind eighth inning winning rally. Again, in a pivotal Game Five, Unser rapped a pinch double off of Quisenberry in the ninth inning to tie the game and later scored the winning run from third base on an infield single.

Del played in only 62 games in 1981 when his average barely was above .150. His last season was 1982 when he failed to get a hit in 14-plate appearances and the Phillies released him. After an absence of two years, he returned to the Phillies as a coach and served in that capacity from 1985-1988.

CHAPTER SEVEN

Special Recognitions

Introduction

A requisite part of a successful major league franchise, in addition to skilled players, is a competent on-field manager. Another is a crafty front office executive who has a passion for winning and can assemble the necessary manpower to realize his objective. An often-overlooked ingredient in winning baseball is the ardent support of local fans, and the media's role in gaining their support is vital. One such medium in the case of the Senators was radio, and another, the local newspapers. Since these were so important to the limited successes enjoyed by the Senators, I believe it appropriate to give special recognition to those who best served in these areas.

Stanley Raymond "Bucky" Harris was far and away the best field manager Washington ever had. Likewise there can be no doubt that Clark Griffith was the top chief executive in the history of the Nats. In bringing vivid play-by-play descriptions of Senators games, Arch McDonald was a local favorite and served to stimulate fan support even in the worst of times. The choice of Arch for special recognition was not as clear-cut as Harris' or Griffith's, since Bob Wolff was also a fan favorite and outstanding broadcaster. There can be no argument, however, with the selection of Shirley Povich as the top sportswriter.

Washington Managers

Introduction

For all but 10 years in the nineteenth century, Washington fans could watch professional baseball in the city for a period of 101 years (1871-1971). Oftentimes, Senators teams did not fare well and as is the current trend the poor manager took the brunt of the blame. It is not surprising then that there were frequent managerial changes, especially in the nineteenth century, when there were 20 different managers for the 19 teams fielded by Washington. There was a lot more stability in the twentieth century, when only 21 different managers were used over a 72-year period.

Washington managers won one World Championship, three American League flags and led teams to 21 first division finishes out of 92 tries. On the other hand, while there were 71 second division finishes, the Nats landed in the basement only 18 times, 19 if you count the one tie-for-last finish.

To select the best Washington manager was a "no-brainer." Stanley Raymond "Bucky" Harris piloted the Nats to one World Championship and a second American League pennant. Under his direction they finished in the first division six times in the 18 seasons he was at the helm. The only other manager to serve more than five years was Clark Griffith in the early days of the twentieth century. He did do a commendable job by piloting the Senators to five first division finishes in nine tries.

Photo of Washington manager Bucky Harris (left) shaking hands with former Senator pilot Joe Cronin prior to a Nats-Red Sox game.

List of Washington Managers

Year	Name	Team Nickname
1871–1872	Nicholas Ephraim "Nick" Young	Olympics
1872	Joseph Wik "Joe" Miller	Nationals
1873	Nicholas Ephraim "Nick" Young	"
1874	No Team	
1875	John Samuel "Holly" Hollingshead	Nationals
	William Robert "Bill" Parks	
1876-1883	No Team	
1884	John Samuel "Holly" Hollingshead	American Assoc.
1884	Michael B. "Mike" Scanlon	Statesmen
1885	No Team	
1886	Michael B. "Mike" Scanlon	Statesmen
1887	John H. Gaffney	"
1888	Walter F. Hewitt	Senators
1889	John Francis Morrill	"
	Arthur Albert Irwin	
1890	No Team	
1891	Samuel W. "Sam" Trott	American Assoc.
	Charles M. "Pop" Snyder	
	Daniel W. "Dan" Shannon	
	Tobias Charles "Sandy" Griffin	
1892	William Harrison "Billy" Barnie	Senators
	Arthur Albert Irwin	
	Daniel "Danny" Richardson	
1893	James Henry "Jim" O'Rourke	Senators
1894-1897	Gustavius Heinrich "Gus" Schmelz	"
1898	Thomas T. "Tom" Brown	"
	John Joseph "Jack" Doyle	
	James Thomas "Deacon" McGuire	
	Arthur Albert Irwin	
1899	" " "	Senators
1900	No Team	

Year	Name	Team Nickname
1901	James H. " Jimmy" Manning	Senators
1902–1903	Thomas Joseph "Tom" Loftus	"
1904	Malachi J. Kittridge	"
1905–1906	Garland "Jake" Stahl	Nationals
1907–1909	Joseph D. "Joe" Cantillon	"
1910–1911	James Robert "Jimmy" McAleer	"
1912–1920	Clark Calvin Griffith	"
1921	George Florian McBride	"
1922	Jesse Clyde Milan	"
1923	Owen Joseph "Donnie" Bush	"
1924–1928	Stanley Raymond "Bucky" Harris	Nationals
1929–1932	Walter Perry Johnson	"
1933–1934	Joseph Edward "Joe" Cronin	"
1935–1942	Stanley Raymond " Bucky" Harris	"
1943–1947	Oswald Louis "Ossie" Bluege	"
1948–1949	Joseph Anthony "Joe" Kuhel	"
1950–1954	Stanley Raymond "Bucky" Harris	"
1955–1957	Charles Walter "Chuck" Dressen	"
1958–1960	Harry Arthur "Cookie" Lavagetto	"
1961–1963	James Barton "Mickey" Vernon	Senators
1964–1967	Gilbert Raymond "Gil" Hodges	"
1968	James Robert "Jim" Lemon	"
1969–1971	Theodore Samuel "Ted" Williams	"

Washington Team Finishes

Period	Number of Teams	First Division	First Place	Last Place
19th Century	21	0	0	6
1901–1919	19	5	0	4
1920–1945	26	14	3	0
1946–1960	15	1	0	4
1961–1971	11	1	0	4
Total	92	21	3	18

All-Time Washington Manager

Stanley Raymond Harris
(Bucky)

Washington manager Bucky Harris on the steps of the dugout.

Bucky Harris was dubbed the "Boy Wonder" when he led a Senators' team that had a losing record the year before to the one and only Washington World Championship in 1924. Clark Griffith had appointed the 27-year-old, with limited major league experience, the playing manager for that season. Griff had hoped that Harris' scrappy, fiery and hustling demeanor would rub off on his teammates, and it did! He commanded respect from such future Hall of Famers as Walter Johnson, Sam Rice and Goose Goslin, despite his young age.

Harris was widely recognized as a smart, clever and innovative manager and no better example of his ability can be demonstrated than in the seventh and deciding game of the 1924 World Series against John McGraw's New York Giants. Harris started right-hander Warren "Curly" Ogden who faced only two batters before giving way to lefty George Mogridge, who had been warming up secretly under the stands. This ploy was used to force manager McGraw to remove left-handed slugger, Bill Terry, from the lineup and this may have been decisive in enabling the Senators to win the extra inning game and the Series!

Bucky's low-key approach and excellent knowledge of the game gained the loyalty of his players and the respect of his peers. But, it still took him another 23 years to win another World Championship, this time, leading the New York Yankees in 1947. He did, however, lead the Senators to their second consecutive American League Championship in 1925.

Rarely Had Talent to Win Big

Unfortunately, Harris rarely had the players he needed to win big. After piloting the Senators from 1924-28, he moved to the Detroit Tigers for four years (1929-33), the Red Sox (1934) and then returned to the Nats for eight years (1935-42). He was appointed manager of the Philadelphia Phillies for 1943 but was fired during the season after 92 games. His players threatened to strike to protest against his firing.

He managed in the International and Pacific Coast leagues for a few seasons before the Yankees hired him for their 1947 championship year. At the end of the 1948 season, the Yankees let him go despite a 94-60 record and a third place finish. He was back with the Senators for his last tour of duty with them in 1950-54.

Managing in 29 big league seasons (18 with the Nats), he collected the two World Championships, three American League pennants, 2,157 wins and 2,218 losses. Only Connie Mack's 2,948 losses were more.

The veteran's committee elected Bucky to the Hall of Fame, as a manager, in 1975.

Washington Presidents and Officials

Introduction

There were 21 different presidents or other officials responsible for the 92 teams fielded in Washington for the period 1871-1971. Some of the officials, like Clark Griffith, Thomas Noyes and the local officials of the expansion club had a genuine interest in giving the Nats' fans winning teams and ones that Washington fans could be proud of. Others, like George Wagner and Bob Short were in it just to make a buck.

Clark Griffith served 36 years as the Nats' top official, while Thomas C. Noyes had the next longest tenure of 15 years. Griffith, however, was the only one who enjoyed a modicum of success as teams during his tenure won a World Championship and three American League pennants. This, plus the fact that the Senators were a first division club almost half of the 44 seasons that Griffith managed or owned the team, makes his selection as the "best official" easy.

List of Washington Presidents or Officials

Year		Name	Team Nickname
1871		Nicholas E. Young	Olympics
1872		Mr. Pike	"
"		Mr. Miller, R. Hough	Nationals
1873		Nicholas E. Young	"
1874	No Team		
1875		D.W. Bruce, A.F. Childs	"
1876-1883	No Team		
1884		L. Moxley	American Association
"		H.B. Bennett	Union Association
1885	No Team		
1886-1887		Robert C. Hewitt	Statesman
1888		"	Senators
1889		Walter F. Hewitt	"
1890	No Team		
1891		H.B. Bennett	American Association
1892-1899		George B. Wagner	Senators
1900	No Team		
1901-1903		Frederick Postal	"
1904		Thomas J. Loftus	"
"		Harry B. Lambert	"
1905-1909		Thomas C. Noyes	Nationals
1920-1955		Clark C. Griffith	"
1956-1960		Calvin R. Griffith	"
1961-1962		Elwood R. Quesada	Senators
1963-1967		James R. Johnson	"
1968		James H. Lemon	"
1969-1971		Robert E. Short	"

All-Time Washington President or Official

Clark Calvin Griffith

(The "Old Fox")

B. Nov. 20, 1869, Clear Creek, MO.
D. Oct. 27, 1955, Washington, D.C.

Washington Baseball Club president and owner, Clark Griffith, sitting at his desk.

Clark Griffith's 44-year association with Washington baseball began in 1912 when he purchased part interest in the club and became its field manager. In 1920, after very successful pitching and managing careers, he purchased a majority interest in the Senators and directed their activities for the next 36 years. Considering his limited financial resources, he did a marvelous job.

The Nats, the Philadelphia Athletics and the St. Louis Browns were the "poor" teams in the American League and they had to concentrate on keeping their franchises solvent and were under considerable handicap when competing with the "rich" owners who could "buy" the talent they needed. While Connie Mack and Bill DeWitt sold their better ballplayers to remain in the black, Clark resorted to clever trades to keep his head above water. While he first earned the label "The Old Fox" because of his pitching style, it was aptly used to recognize his skills in architecting profitable trades.

At the end of the 1914 season, Walter Johnson (the idol of Washington fans) announced that he had jumped to Chicago of the new Federal League. He had accepted an offer of a one-year salary of $16,000 plus a bonus of $10,000. Clark had no such money and pleaded with the other American League owners for help. They agreed to fund the salary but not the bonus. The distraught Griffith received the additional $10,000 from the Chicago White Sox's owner Charles Comiskey after Clark pointed out that Johnson, pitching in Chicago for a rival team, would take many customers from Comiskey's turnstiles.

Shrewd Moves Lead to 3 Pennants

Griff made a shrewd move in 1924 when he chose the "Boy Wonder," young Bucky Harris to be player/manager of his team, resulting in a World Championship that year and an American League pennant in '25. He repeated the formula in 1933 when he named young Joe Cronin as his player/manager and Joe led the Nats to their third American League flag. "The Old Fox's" trading skills were never more evident than when he acquired all six ballplayers Cronin said he needed to win the pennant. Earl Whitehill, Walter Stewart and Jack Russell provided the pitching and Goose Goslin, Fred Schulte and Luke Sewell provided the necessary hitting and fielding for the successful championship drive.

Griffith claimed that he sold only one good player for money and that was his son-in-law, Joe Cronin. When the Boston Red Sox offered $250,000 for him Clark couldn't turn it down, saying that no baseball player was worth that much money.

The Senators played baseball in several different ballparks in the early years but Washington players and fans enjoyed the most beautiful park, built in 1911, and originally known as National Park II but renamed Griffith Stadium in 1920 in honor of Clark. The original National Park was constructed of wood in 1892 but a fire led to a rebuilt steel structure in 1911. It was used through the 1961 season, until D.C. Stadium was ready for play. But, it turned out that Griffith Stadium was far superior for viewing baseball games. Much like Fenway Park and other small, cozy sites, you sat close to the action and felt like you were part of the game.

Griff groomed his adopted son, Calvin, to be his successor. When Clark died of a massive stomach hemorrhage in Washington, D.C., on October 27, 1955, Cal took over the reins of the club, but he couldn't hold a candle to "The Old Fox."

Washington Broadcasters

Introduction

A faithful, loyal and supportive fan base is an essential ingredient of any winning baseball team. A wildly cheering hometown crowd can elevate a player's skill level and spur him to new heights of athletic achievement.

All types of media (radio, television and newspapers) are important elements in creating and maintaining the necessary fan base. When a team is winning, it is not difficult to achieve the foregoing. The challenge comes, however, when teams have losing records and fan support usually diminishes as "fair weather friends" desert the "sinking ship."

The Baltimore Orioles are a prime example of this. Since moving to Camden Yards, they have usually enjoyed capacity crowds as they played winning baseball while feeding on spirited fan support. In their 2001-2002 rebuilding seasons, when wins were hard to come by, the team played before many empty seats for a number of games.

Building and maintaining interest in Washington baseball among local residents was a very difficult challenge. Only the St. Louis Browns and Philadelphia Athletics, among major league franchises, had a similar problem. While sportswriters such as Shirley Povich and television commentators such as Dan Daniels did their part in encouraging fan support, radio was the principal medium and Arch McDonald the most successful in securing and inspiring a generation of ardent Senators supporters. He was unchallenged as the number one Senators fan!

While other radio announcers also provided a positive impact on their audiences, it was apparent that Arch "lived and died" with the fortunes of the team. The unbridled satisfaction he received when the Nats won and the exasperation he projected when the team lost because of a "bonehead" play was transferred to his listeners and inspired fierce loyalty to the team.

I shall never forget the disappointment and anger McDonald felt when center fielder Bingo Binks lost a fly ball in the sun and may have cost the Senators the 1945 American League flag. Arch was greatly disturbed because the Philadelphia center fielder had stopped the game a few minutes before to retrieve his sunglasses from the dugout and Binks had failed to follow suit.

Most hometown fans like a "homer" favoring the local team during the radio broadcasts and there never was an equal to McDonald. Further, his dry humor and superior knowledge of the game, contributed greatly to maintaining and expanding the fan base even through some dark and dreary days of Washington baseball.

All-Time Washington Broadcaster

Arch McDonald

B. 1901 D. October 16, 1960, New York, NY.

Longtime Senators' radio announcer Arch McDonald is in the broadcaster's section of the Hall of Fame in Cooperstown, N.Y.

Bob Wolff had the quality voice, energetic style and accurate commentary, but Arch McDonald had the baseball knowledge, savvy and the homespun humor that made him the darling of Washington baseball fans. The familiar strains of McDonald's theme song, "The Old Pine Tree" promised Senators listeners that a few charming hours of Washington baseball radio coverage was imminent.

McDonald was the "voice of the Senators" for 22 years and his relaxed, easy-going southern style attracted many avid fans to his radio broadcasts. Arch began his broadcasting career with a Senators farm club, the Chattanooga Lookouts and was brought to Washington by Clark Griffith in 1934 to broadcast the action on station WJSV (later WTOP).

Home games were broadcasted live from Griffith Stadium, but Arch was at his best in recreating the action of away games from Western Union telegraph lines. McDonald used his imagination and ingenuity to "fill in the gaps" which were inherent in the concise messages received in the studio. The Arkansas native coined such phrases as "there she goes, Mrs. Murphy"(denoting a home run), "ducks on the pond" (for base runners) and "right down Broadway (for a called strike) in order to embellish his re-creation.

When Peoples Drug Stores, Arch's sponsor, built the "World's Largest Drug Store" in downtown Washington, they reserved space for a glass soundproof studio for McDonald's use in broadcasting away games. People flocked to the store to watch the re-creation as they ate a sandwich or ice cream soda. Arch was at his best when creating suspense for the customers. He used a four-note gong to indicate single, double, triple or home run by striking it one, two, three or four times respectively. If the score was tied and the opposition had the winning run in scoring position, he would raise the mallet as if the game would soon be lost but instead would announce that the opponent had made an out.

Broadcast Yankee Games for One Year

Arch had a one-year break in service when he took a job with a young Mel Allen to do the New York Yankee games. But, the big city was too much for the "ol' country boy" and he returned to Washington to his old job. Walter Johnson had replaced him that year but he was no Arch.

McDonald, in conjunction with Peoples Drug Stores established the "Hot Stove League" for the youth of the city in the '30s. As a charter member, I was privileged to be part of a group of kids who had their picture taken with then manager Bucky Harris.

Later Arch took to the road and was able to give live broadcasts of all Nats' games. His last year doing the games was 1956 when new sponsors did not renew his contract. He continued to do football broadcasts for the Washington Redskins until October 16, 1960 when he died of a heart attack while returning to Washington by train after a Redskins-New York Giant's game.

McDonald was honored by the *Sporting News* as the No. 1 "Sports Announcer of the Year" in 1932, 1942 and 1945. He was the first to win the award three times. The 1932 award was received for broadcasting the games of Washington's minor league affiliate the Chattanooga Lookouts. The latter two were for doing Senators' games. Arch received the ultimate award when he was inducted into the Broadcasters Hall of Fame in Cooperstown, New York, receiving the "Ford C. Frick Award" on July 25, 1999.

Washington Sportswriters

Introduction

The Washington daily newspapers had their considerable effect in recruiting Senators baseball fans from the Capital City populace and from the surrounding areas, and in maintaining a loyal fan base. The printed page was all there was until radio came into its own, late in the first half of the twentieth century. The city of Washington was most fortunate in having a number of fine newspapers distributed throughout the area. These included, among others, the *Washington Daily News, Washington Herald, Washington Post, Washington Star* and the *Washington Times.*

The sports sections of these newspapers employed many fine sportswriters who produced the articles that kept loyal Senators fans and others up to date on the progress of the teams and their players. Their reporting piqued fan interest in the teams and their local baseball heroes, leading to increased attendance at games. Included among the excellent sportswriters were: Bob Addie (*Post*), Lewis F. Atchison (*Post*), Ken Denlinger (*Post*), Richard Dozer (*Star*), John Drohan (*Star*), Paul W. Eaton (*Star*), Bill Fuchs (*Star*), J. V. Fitzgerald (*Post*), William Gildea (*Post*), Burton Hawkins (*Star*), Dick Heller (*Star*), Steve Hershey (*Star*), Jerome Holtzman (*Star*), George E. Minot, Jr. (*Post*), Bob O'Donnell (*Times*), Shirley Povich (*Post*), Milton Richman (*Star*), Robert C. Ruark (*Star*), Morris Siegel (*News*), Francis Stann (*Star*), Marc Stein (*Post*), Denman Thompson (*Star*), Russ White (*Star*) and Merrell Whittlesey (*Star*).

While Burton Hawkins, Francis Stann and Merrell Whittlesey wrote a large number of the articles I used in my research and were assigned to cover the Senators for long periods, there is no doubt that the dean of Washington sportswriters was Shirley Povich.

All-Time Washington Sportswriter

Shirley Povich

Veteran Washington Post sportswriter Shirley Povich was given the J. G. Spink award "for meritorious contributions to baseball writing" at the National Baseball Hall of Fame in 1975.

Without question, Shirley Povich was the dean of Washington sportswriters! For almost three-quarters of a century, Povich wrote more than 15,000 columns for the *Washington Post* readers. Most of these concerned the exploits of the Washington Senators. A native of Maine, he was hired by *Post* publisher Ned McLean in 1923 as a copyboy and he was given his first byline the following year when the Nats won their only World Series Championship.

Shirley became the youngest sports editor of a major United States newspaper when he was given the job at the *Post* in 1926. His unique and famous daily column "This Morning," often filled with brief and pungent observations, was required reading for true Senators fans. Although Povich officially retired in 1977 after 51 years with the paper, he continued to write columns from time to time for the next 25 years. In fact, his last column was written the day before his death.

Ben Bradlee, former executive director of the *Washington Post*, stated that Povich was the reason people bought the paper. The paper was purchased for the sports section. Without exaggeration, he said, "Shirley carried the paper for a number of years."

Gains National Recognition

Povich was not only recognized as a superior local sportswriter but also he gained national recognition as one of the best. In 1975, he joined such legendary sportswriters as Grantland Rice, Ring Lardner and Damon Runyan in an exclusive club when he received the J. G. Spink Award at the National Baseball Hall of Fame induction ceremonies. The award is given to a baseball writer "for meritorious contributions to baseball writing." Although not officially inducted into the hall, the recipient is presented a certificate during the ceremonies and is given permanent recognition in the "Scribes and Mikemen" exhibit in the Library of the National Baseball Hall of Fame.

Shirley Povich passed away on June 4, 1998 in Washington, D.C.

GLOSSARY OF BASEBALL TERMS AND ABBREVIATIONS

Abbreviations

For Batters:

Y = Year
G = Games
AB = At Bats
R = Runs Scored
H = Hits
2B = Doubles
3B = Triples
HR = Home Runs
RBI = Runs Batted In
BB = Bases on Balls (Walks)
SO = Strikeouts
SB = Stolen Bases
BA = Batting Average
SA = Slugging Average
TB = Total Bases

For Pitchers:

Y = Year
W = Wins
L = Losses
PCT = Winning Percentage
ERA = Earned Run Average
G = Games Pitched
GS = Games Started
CG = Complete Games
IP = Innings Pitched
H = Hits Allowed
BB = Bases on Balls Allowed
SO = Strikeouts
SHO = Shutouts
SV = Saves
H/9IP = Roughly, Hits Allowed Per Game
BB+H/9IP = Walks plus Hits Allowed Per Game

For all players:

BR = Bats Right-handed
BL = Bats Left-handed
TR = Throws Right-handed

TL = Throws Left-handed
SW = Switch Hitter
B = Born
D = Died

Definition of Terms

Assist = Help from a fielder putting an offensive player out.
At Bat = The offensive team's turn to bat the ball and score.
Balk = An illegal act by the pitcher.
Ball = A pitch outside the strike zone.
Bases on Balls = (Walks), four balls and the hitter advances to first base.
Base = One of four stations to be reached in turn by the runner.
Baseball = The spherical ball thrown by pitchers and hit by batters.
Bases Loaded = Runners at each base.
Bat = Instrument used by the hitter while batting.
Batting Order = The order in which offensive players take a turn at bat.
Breaking Ball = An off-speed pitch that curves.
Bullpen = Area designated for pitchers to warm-up.
Bunt = A batted ball tapped slowly within the infield.
Catcher = Player receiving the pitch while stationed behind home plate.
Change Up = A slow-pitch thrown with the exact arm action as a fastball.
Choke-Up = Gripping the bat up on the handle away from the knob.
Closer = Relief pitcher who specializes in pitching the last few outs of the game.
Complete Game = Pitching the entire game.
Curve = A pitch that can move in many directions as it approaches the batter.
Designated Hitter = Player who bats in the pitcher's spot in the line-up.
Diamond = The infield playing surface.

Double = A hit that enables the batter to reach second base.

Double Play = Any defensive play that results in two base runners called out.

Doubleheader = Two games played by the same teams on the same day.

Dugout = Enclosed seating facility for the team.

Earned Run = A run scored without benefit of a defensive error.

Error = A defensive mistake that benefits the batter or base runners.

Fast Ball = A straight pitch thrown by the pitcher as hard as possible.

Fielder = Any defensive player.

Fly Ball = Batted ball that goes high in the air in flight.

Forfeited Game = A game ended by the umpire with the offended team winning 9-0.

Grand slam = A home run hit with runners on each base.

Ground Ball = A batted ball that rolls or bounces close to the ground.

Hit = A play in which the batter safely reaches a base after hitting the ball.

Hit and Run = The batter swings at the ball while the base runner attempts to steal.

Home Plate = The fourth station to be reached by the runner.

Home run = A long ball hit by the batter entitling him to advance four bases.

Infield = Area ninety feet square with the corners being the four bases.

Infielder = Fielder who occupies a position in the infield.

Inning = A period of play where each team bats until three outs are recorded.

Knuckleball = Thrown with a special grip, the ball's movement is unpredictable.

Line Drive = A hard hit ball hit in the air at a low trajectory.

Line-up = A team's batting order and fielding positions.

Mound = Hill the pitcher stands on while pitching.

No hitter = A game in which the offensive team does not reach a base via a safe hit.

Passed Ball = A pitched ball missed by the catcher allowing a runner to advance.

Perfect Game = Game in which the pitcher does not allow any batter to reach base.

Pinch Hitter = A hitter who substitutes for another player and takes his turn at bat.

Pop-Fly = A high, but short, fly ball which usually is caught in or near the infield.

Putout = When a fielder receives the ball and a batter or runner is out as a result.

Relief Pitcher = The pitcher replacing the starting pitcher or another reliever.

Run = Score obtained as a result of a base runner crossing home plate.

Runner = An offensive player who is advancing toward, or returning to any base.

Runs Batted In = Runs scored by teammates as a result of a batter's performance.

Sacrifice Fly = Fly ball that advances a runner after it is caught.

Safe = When the umpire signals that a runner is entitled to the base he is trying for.

Save = Credited sometimes when a relef pitcher keeps his team's lead until the end.

Shortstop = Defensive player positioned between second and third bases.

Shutout = A game in which one team doesn't score any runs.

Sinker = A fast pitch that breaks downward as it reaches the plate.

Slider = Appears to be a fastball until it breaks sharply as it reaches the plate.

Southpaw = A left-handed pitcher.

Spitball = Illegal pitch in which a foreign substance causes it to act unpredictably.

Starter = A pitcher who begins and ends the game or is replaced by a relief pitcher.

Steal = Attempting to advance a base between pitches.

Stolen Base = Successfully advancing a base between pitches.

Strikeout = Out recorded by obtaining three strikes on the batter.

Strike Zone = The area over home plate that defines a called strike.

Strike = If a batter swings and misses, fouls the pitch or it is taken in the strike zone.

Switch-Hitter = Player who is able to bat right-handed or left-handed.

Tag = A batter or runner is touched with the ball by a defensive player.

Triple = A hit enabling the runner to safely reach third base.

Two Base Hit = A hit enabling the runner to safely reach second base.

Walk = The batter is awarded first base after the pitcher delivers four balls.

Wild Pitch = A pitch so far from the strike zone that the catcher cannot block it.

CREDITS FOR USE OF BASEBALL CARDS AND PHOTOGRAPHS

Page #15—Photo—Copyright Washington Post; reprinted by permission of the D.C. Public Library.

Page #17—Photo—Author's Collection.

Page #21—Card—T.C.M.A. Ltd., 1975
Card—1961 Topps Chewing Gum

Page #29—Card—Goudey Gum Co., 1933.
Photo—Copyright Washington Post; reprinted by permission of the D.C. Public Library.

Page #34—Card—Goudey Gum Co., 1933.
Photo—Property of the Minnesota Twins, reprinted by permission.

Page #39—Card—1940 Play Ball, Gum Inc., Phila., Pa.
Photo—Copyright Washington Post; reprinted by permission of the D.C. Public Library.

Page #43—Card—Bowman Gum Division, Phila., Pa., 1955.
Photo—Property of the Minnesota Twins, reprinted by permission.

Page #47—Card—1935 Diamond Star, National Chicle Co., Cambridge Mass.
Photo—Property of the Minnesota Twins, reprinted by permission.

Page #51—Card—T.C.M.A. Ltd., 1975.
Photo—Property of the Minnesota Twins, reprinted by permission.

Page #56—Card—1935 Batter-up.
Photo—Copyright Washington Post; reprinted by permission of the D.C. Public Library.

Page #60—Card—Goudey Gum Co., 1933.
Photo—Copyright Washington Post; reprinted by permission of the D.C. Public Library.

Page #66—Card—DeLong Gum Co., 1933, Boston, Mass.
Photo—Copyright Washington Post; reprinted by permission of the D.C. Public Library.

Page #72—Card—1960 Topps Chewing Gum.
Photo—Author's Collection

Page #76—Photo—Copyright Washington Post; reprinted by permission of the D.C. Public Library.

Page #77—Card—1955 Topps Chewing Gum.
Photo—Property of the Minnesota Twins, reprinted by permission.

Page #84—Photo—National Baseball Hall of Fame Library Cooperstown, N.Y.

Page #86—Photo—The Society for American Baseball Research, Cleveland Oh.

Page #90—Photo—National Baseball Hall of Fame Library Cooperstown, N.Y.

Page #94—Photo— National Baseball Hall of Fame Library Cooperstown, N.Y.

Page #97—Card—Library of Congress Prints and Photographs Division, Lot 13163-05, no. 251.
Photo—National Baseball Hall of Fame Library Cooperstown, N.Y.

Page #102—Photo—Copyright Washington Post; reprinted by permission of the D.C. Public Library.

Page #105—Photo—National Baseball Hall of Fame Library Cooperstown N.Y.

Page #109—Photo—National Baseball Hall of Fame Library Cooperstown N.Y.

Page #113—Photo—National Baseball Hall of Fame Library Cooperstown N.Y.

Page #116—Photo—National Baseball Hall of Fame Library Cooperstown N.Y.

Page #120—Photo—National Baseball Hall of Fame Library Cooperstown N.Y.

Page #125—Card—Library of Congress Prints and Photographs Division, Lot 13163-02, no. 37.
Photo—National Baseball Hall of Fame Library Cooperstown N.Y.

Page #131—Photo—Copyright Washington Post; reprinted by permission of the D.C. Public Library.

Page #133—Photo—National Baseball Hall of Fame Library Cooperstown N.Y.

Page #137—Card—1961 Fleer.
Photo—National Baseball Hall of Fame Library Cooperstown N.Y.

Page # 141—Photo—National Baseball Hall of Fame Library Cooperstown N.Y.

Page # 144—Card—Library of Congress Prints and Photographs Division, Lot 13163-30, no. 192.
Photo—National Baseball Hall of Fame Library Cooperstown N.Y.

Page # 148—Card— Library of Congress Prints and Photographs Division, Lot 13163-18, no. 381.
Photo—National Baseball Hall of Fame Library Cooperstown N.Y.

Page #152—Card—Library of Congress Prints and Photographs Division, Lot 13163-30, no. 198.
Photo—National Baseball Hall of Fame Library Cooperstown N.Y.

Page #155—Card—Library of Congress Prints and Photographs Division, Lot 13163-27, no. 49.
Photo—National Baseball Hall of Fame Library Cooperstown N.Y.

Page #158—Card—Library of Congress Prints and Photographs Division, Lot 13163-18, no. 379.
Photo—Copyright Washington Post; reprinted by permission of the D.C. Public Library.

Page #162—Card—BG-18 Blankets, 1914.
Photo—National Baseball Hall of Fame Library Cooperstown N.Y.

Page #166—Card—Library of Congress Prints and Photographs Division, Lot 13163-17, no. 51.
Photo—Property of the Minnesota Twins, reprinted by permission.

Page #170—Card—Library of Congress Prints and Photographs Division, Lot 13163-18, no. 468.
Photo—National Baseball Hall of Fame Library Cooperstown N.Y.

Page #175—Photo—Author's Collection

Page #177—Card—1939 Play Ball, Gum Inc., Phila., Pa.
Photo—Original Photo by C. M. Conlon, N.Y.

Page #181—Card—T.C.M.A., 1975.
Photo—National Baseball Hall of Fame Library Cooperstown N.Y.

Page #185—Card—Goudey Gum Co., 1933.
Photo—Author's Collection, Courtesy Jack Russell.

Page #191—Card—T.C.M.A., 1975.
Photo—Property of the Minnesota Twins, reprinted by permission.

Page #195—Card—Goudey Gum Co., 1933.
Photo— Property of the Minnesota Twins, reprinted by permission.

Page #200—Card—The Sporting News Publishing Company, 1991.
Card—T.C.M.A. Ltd., 1975.

Page #205—Card—1941 Play Ball, Gum Inc., Phila., Pa.
Photo—Copyright Washington Post; reprinted by permission of the D.C. Public Library.

Page #209—Card—1939 Play Ball, Gum Inc., Phila., Pa.
Photo—Copyright Washington Post; reprinted by permission of the D.C. Public Library.

Page #213—Card—Goudey Gum Co., 1933.
Photo—Copyright Washington Post; reprinted by permission of the D.C. Public Library.

Page #217—Card—1941 Play Ball, Gum Inc., Phila., Pa.
Photo—Courtesy of George Case III.
Page #222—Card—Goudey Gum Co., 1934.
Photo—Copyright Washington Post; reprinted by permission of the D.C. Public Library.
Page #227—Photo—National Baseball Hall of Fame Library Cooperstown N.Y.
Page #229—Card—Topps Chewing Gum, Co., 1956.
Photo—Copyright Washington Post; reprinted by permission of the D.C. Public Library.
Page #234—Card—Topps Chewing Gum, Co., 1954.
Photo—National Baseball Hall of Fame Library Cooperstown N.Y.
Page #238—Card—Topps Chewing Gum Co., 1958.
Photo—Copyright Washington Post; reprinted by permission of the D.C. Public Library.
Page #242—Card—Topps Chewing Gum, 1953.
Photo—Copyright Washington Post; reprinted by permission of the D.C. Public Library.
Page #246—Card—Topps Chewing Gum Co., 1956.
Photo—Copyright Washington Post; reprinted by permission of the D.C. Public Library.
Page #252—Card—1950 Bowman Gum Inc., Phila., Pa.
Photo—Copyright Washington Post; reprinted by permission of the D.C. Public Library.
Page #256—Card—Topps Chewing Gum Co., 1956.
Photo—Copyright Washington Post; reprinted by permission of the D.C. Public Library.
Page #262—Card—Topps Chewing Gum Co., 1953.
Photo—Copyright Washington Post; reprinted by permission of the D.C. Public Library.
Page #267—Card—Topps Chewing Gum Co., 1960.
Photo—Copyright Washington Post; reprinted by permission of the D.C. Public Library.
Page #271—Card—1953 Bowman Gum, Inc., Phila., Pa.
Photo—Courtesy of Gil Coan.

Page #276—Card—1955 Bowman Gum, Inc., Phila., Pa.
Photo—National Baseball Hall of Fame Library Cooperstown N.Y.

Page #281—Photo—National Baseball Hall of Fame Library Cooperstown N.Y.

Page #283—Card—Topps Chewing Gum Co., 1960.
Photo—Copyright Washington Post; reprinted by permission of the D.C. Public Library.

Page #287—Card—Topps Chewing Gum Co., 1962.
Photo—Copyright Washington Post; reprinted by permission of the D.C. Public Library.

Page #292—Card—Topps Chewing Gum Co., 1971.
Photo—CopyrightWashington Post; reprinted by permission of the D.C. Public Library.

Page #296—Card—Topps Chewing Gum Co., 1967.
Photo—Copyright Washington Post; reprinted by permission of the D.C. Public Library.

Page #300—Card—Topps Chewing Gum Co., 1968.
Photo—Copyright Washington Post; reprinted by permission of the D.C. Public Library.

Page #304—Card—Topps Chewing Gum Co., 1971.
Photo—Copyright Washington Post; reprinted by permission of the D.C. Public Library.

Page #308—Card—Topps Chewing Gum Co., 1966.
Photo—Copyright Washington Post; reprinted by permission of the D.C. Public Library.

Page #313—Card—Topps Chewing Gum Co., 1964.
Photo—Copyright Washington Post; reprinted by permission of the D.C. Public Library.

Page #318—Card—Topps Chewing Gum Co., 1961.
Photo—Copyright Washington Post; reprinted by permission of the D.C. Public Library.

Page #322—Card—Topps Chewing Gum Co., 1963.
Photo—Copyright Washington Post; reprinted by permission of the D.C. Public Library.

Page #326—Card—Topps Chewing Gum Co., 1969.
Photo—Copyright Washington Post; reprinted by permission of the D.C. Public Library.

Page #332—Photo—Property of the Minnesota Twins; reprinted by permission.

Page #336—Photo—Property of the Minnesota Twins; reprinted by permission.

Page #341—Photo—Property of the Minnesota Twins; reprinted by permission.

Page #346—Photo—National Baseball Hall of Fame Library Cooperstown, N.Y.

Page #350—Photo—Copyright Washington Post; reprinted by permission of the D.C. Public Library.

Front Cover—Photo—Copyright Harris and Ewing; Property of the Minnesota Twins, reprinted by permission.

Back Cover, Top—Photo—Property of the Minnesota Twins, reprinted by permission.

Back Cover, Center—Photo—Internet, Worldwide Web. www.cjis.com/central.htm.

Back Cover, Vernon—Card—1963 Topps Chewing Gum.

Back Cover, Lemon—Card—1968 Topps Chewing Gum.

BIBLIOGRAPHY

Interviews

Coan, Gil. July 21, 2001.
Howard, Frank. March 11, 2000 and August 2001.
Hyde, Dick. July 6, 2002.
King, Jim. July 10, 2001.
Knowles, Darold. December 2001 and March 14, 2002
Lemon, Jim. October 2001 and March 2002.
Osteen, Claude. July 1, 2002.
Russell, Jack. March 1990 and February 1991
Sievers, Roy. July 2, 2002.
Stobbs, Chuck. July 6, 2002.
Travis, Cecil. July 1, 2002.
Vernon, Mickey. March 1993 and July 2, 2002.

Archival Sources

Charlottesville Historical Society, Charlottesville, Virginia.
Clearwater Public Library, Clearwater, Florida.
Jack Russell Personal Scrapbook, Clearwater, Florida.
Prince Georges County Public Library, Hyattsville, Maryland.
Library of Congress, Washington D.C.
Martin Luther King Library, Washington, D.C.
Maryland University Library, College Park, Maryland.
National Baseball Library, Cooperstown, New York.
Society for American Baseball Research Library, Cleveland, Ohio.
University of Virginia Library, Charlottesville, Virginia
Washington Historical Society, Washington, D.C.
Washington Star Collection, Martin Luther King Library, Washington, D.C.

Newspapers

Albion Evening Recorder
Baltimore Sun
Boston Globe
Chattanooga Times Monitor
Christian Science Monitor
Clearwater Times
Ft. Lauderdale News and Sun
Johnson City Press-Chronicle
New York Daily Mirror
New York Times
New York World Telegram
Philadelphia Inquirer
Prince Georges Journal
St. Louis Globe
St. Petersburg Times
Spokesman Review and Spokane Chronicle
Sporting News
Sports Collector's Digest
Washington Daily News
Washington Herald
Washington Post
Washington Star
Washington Times
Washington Times-Herald

Books

Auker, Eldon. *Sleeper Cars and Flannel Uniforms.* Chicago: Triumph Books, 2001.

Bealle, Morris. *The Washington Senators.* Washington, D.C. : Columbia Publishing Company, 1947.

Beckett, Dr. James, and others, editors. *Baseball Card Price Guide.* Dallas: Beckett Publications, 1998.

Dewey, Donald and Nicholas Acocella. *Encyclopedia of Major League Baseball Teams.* New York: Harper Collins Publishers, 1993.

Hartley, James R. *Washington's Expansion Senators (1961-1971).* Germantown, Maryland: Corduroy Press, 1998.

James, Bill. *The Bill James Historical Abstract.* New York: Villard Books, 1985.

Kavanagh, Jack. *Walter Johnson: A Life.* South Bend, Indiana: Diamond Communications, Inc., 1995.

Lieb, Frederick. *The Detroit Tigers.* New York: Putnam's, 1950.

Neft, David and others. *The Sports Encyclopedia: Baseball.* Grosset & Dunlap, 1981.

Povich, Shirley. *The Washington Senators, An Informal History.* G.P. Putnam's Sons, 1954.

Reichler, Joseph L., editor. *The Baseball Encyclopedia.* New York: 1985.

Ritter, Lawrence. *The Glory of Their Times.* New York: Morrow, 1966.

Thomas, Henry W. *Walter Johnson, Baseball's Big Train.* Lincoln and London: University of Nebraska Press, 1995.

Thorn, John and Pete Palmer, editors. *Total Baseball.* 2nd ed. Warner Books,1991.

Articles

Addie, Bob. "Big Mac Bad Medicine for Senator Foes." *The Sporting News,* May 14, 1966.

_____. "Epstein Addition to Nat Lineup Takes Heat Off Howard." *Washington Post,* June 17, 1967.

_____. "Killebrew Reflections." *Washington Post,* April 12, 1968.

_____. "McMullen Rips Up Too-Slow Tag as Budding Nat Slugger." *The Sporting News,* June 12, 1965.

_____. "Nats' Beau Ideal—Walloper Jim King." *The Sporting News,* August 14, 1966.

_____. "Nats Cure 2 Pains With One Deal, for Pascual and Allen." *The Sporting News,* December 17, 1966.

_____. "Up With Epstein—Nats Doffing Hats to Hard-Working Slugger." *The Sporting News,* July 15, 1967.

Ainsmith, Edward W. "Biographical Sketch." National Baseball Library, 1964.

Atchison, Lewis F. "And Paddles for Weak Hitters." *Washington Post*, May 31, 1960.

Bailey, Arnold. "The Walking Man." *Sports Collector's Digest*, January 18, 2002.

Bergman, Ron. "A's Land Needed Lefty in Deal With Senators." *The Sporting News*, May 22, 1971.

Boetel, Ray. "An Oldtimer Can Remember Having a Beer with Babe." *Fort Lauderdale News and Sun-Sentinel*, February 8, 1976.

Brown, Doug. "Epstein Deal Gives Orioles Prize Plum." *Baltimore Sun*, June 10, 1967.

Chass, Murray. "Orioles to Epstein: Give Us Break for Year." *Baltimore Sun*, May 15, 1967.

Daley, Arthur. "In Capital Letters." *Sports of the Times*, April 8, 1959.

_____. "Mike Gets His Chance." *New York Times,* June 9, 1967.

Daniel. "King Not Too Speedy, But May Help Giants." *New York World Telegram and Sun,* April 4, 1968.

_____. "Slam Brakes on Busy Busby? Bombers Can Wish." *New York World Telegram*, June 19, 1951.

_____. "Stengel Vetoes Deal for Hyde." *New York World Telegram*, February 19, 1959.

_____. "Veteran Left-Hander Wins Ninth Game Beating Faber." *New York Telegram,* August 21, 1929.

_____. "Yankees Still Trying for Pitcher Hyde." *New York World Telegram*, December 29, 1958.

Denlinger, Ken. "New-Life in the Minor Mode: Howard is No Less a Tower." *Washington Post,* July 29, 1990.

Dozer, Richard. "Richards Boosts Busby as Next Chisox Skipper." *Washington Star,* August 21, 1976.

Drohan, John. "Johnson-Ainsmith Battery." *Washington Star,* March 1932.

Eaton, Paul W. "Morgan, In An Accident, Is Suspended." *Washington Star*, July 10, 1915.

_____. "Ray Morgan Injured." *Washington Star*, April 17, 1915.

Falls, Joe. "Guys with the Dough Don't Even Hit .300." *Knight News Service*, 1977.

Fitzgerald, J.V. "Morgan to Phils by Waiver Route." *Washington Post*, February 1, 1918.

Fuchs, Bill. "Sievers Leaves Wealth of Records for Senators' Sluggers to Shoot At." *Washington Star*, April 4, 1960.

Gammon, Wirt. "Just Between Us Fors." *The Chattanooga Times*, August 19, 1940.

Gildea, William. "Goose Goslin Dies, Nats' Hall of Famer." *Washington Post*, May 16, 1971.

_____. "Goslin Gave Up All Hope 3 Years Ago." *Washington Post*, January 29, 1968.

Good, Rebel. "Mickey Vernon." *Washington Star*, February 27, 1953.

Hapgood, Warren. "Red Sox Taking Yankees." *Washington Star*, July 11, 1939.

Harmon, Pat. "Family, Friends Help Hoy Mark His 90th Birthday." *Cincinnati, Ohio*, May 23, 1961.

Harrison, James R. "Yankees Purchase Zachary, Southpaw." National Baseball Library, August 24, 1929.

Hawkins, Burton. "The Baseball Beat." *Washington Star*, February 23, 1956.

_____. "The Baseball Beat." *Washington Star*, February 28, 1957.

_____. "The Baseball Beat." *Washington Star*, September 5, 1957.

_____. "The Baseball Beat." *Washington Star*, September 15, 1957.

_____. "The Baseball Beat." *Washington Star*, September 27, 1956.

_____. "Baseball Leaders, Fans to Pay Tribute to Vet Before Tilt with A's." *Washington Star*, August 15, 1947.

_____. "Capital's Fans Were Nice to Nice Fellow." *Washington Star*, August 16, 1947.

_____. "Case's Base Running Mark, Club's Close Win Thrill Fans." *Washington Star*, September 15, 1943.

_____. "Case Leads in Grit As Well As in Base Stealing." *Washington Star*, September 27, 1943.

_____. "Coan Brought Up Too Soon, Says Griff." *Washington Star*, August 2, 1947.

_____. "Courtney Going to First Bidder After New Fine." *Washington Star*, May 2, 1957.

_____. "Death of Milan, in Uniform to the Last, Stuns Nats." *Washington Star*, March 4, 1953.

Hawkins, Burton. "Eddie Yost One of Select Few Who Never Played in Minors." *Washington Star,* March 10, 1949.

_____. "George Case Ready to Join Senators' Staff." *Washington Star*, November 30, 1960.

_____. "Griffs Ready to Swap Anybody but Sievers." *Washington Star*, September 30, 1957.

_____. "Harmon Killebrew." *Washington Star*, September 12, 1960.

_____. "How Good Is Pascual?" *Washington Star*, April 3, 1960.

_____. "Lewis Resigns Because of Business." *Washington Star*, February 25, 1950.

_____. "Outfield Job O.K. with Lewis So Long as Pay Is Regular." *Washington Star*, September 18, 1939.

_____. "President Sees Game of Power Won by Yanks." *Washington Star*, September 1, 1956.

_____. Runnels' Fight No Match for Ted's Finish." *Washington Star*, September 29, 1958.

_____. "Senator Welker's Tip Brings Senators First Bonus Rookie." *Washington Star,* June 20, 1954.

_____. "Senators Hope to Sign Young Marberry." *Washington Star*, May 27, 1954.

_____. "Senators Turn Attention to Halting Ted's Streak." *Washington Star,* September 24, 1957.

_____. "Stobbs Will Get Another Chance for 20 Wins." *Washington Star*, September 6, 1956.

_____. "Superstitions, Charms Invoked and Stobbs Ends Losing String." *Washington Star*, June 22, 1957.

_____. "Travis Drafted, Nationals Must Rebuild Infield." *Washington Star*, December 26, 1941.

_____. "Yost, On Streak, Gets Car, Other Gifts Tonight." *Washington Star* September 16, 1953.

Hawkins, Burton S. "Roar of Crowd Now Music to Sherry's Ears." *Washington Star,* March 26, 1942.

Herron, Gary. "Claude Osteen: Still Bleeding Dodger Blue." *Sports Collector's Digest,* December 14, 1990.

Heller, Dick. "Kekich's Pitch to Howard: One for the Road Maybe?" *Washington Star,* October 1, 1971.

Hershey, Steve. "Benched Howard Disillusioned." *Washington Star,* July 9, 1972.

_____. "Stobbs, Baseball Still in His Blood, Accepts Job as Head Coach at GW." *Washington Star*, May 21, 1970.

_____. "Stobbs Now Sports Broadcaster." *Washington Star*, February 19, 1963.

Holster, Tom. "Eddie Foster, King of the Hit and Run." Nats News, 1999.

Holtz, Joyce Kopp. "The Most Unforgettable Character I've Met." *Albion, Michigan,* March 9, 1987.

Holtzman, Jerome. "Busby, Schaefer Add to Chisox 'Old Gang' Look." *Washington Star*, January 17, 1976.

Hunter, Bob. "Lefty Adding New Depth to Mound Staff." *The Sporting News*, May 15, 1965.

Leonard, Dutch as Told to Shirley Povich. "Too Old to Pitch? Don't Make Me Laugh!" *Saturday Evening Post*, July 4, 1953.

Levitan, Linda. "So Near, Yet So Far." *Deaf Life,* Vol. X, Number 3, September, 1977.

Mann, Jack. "How Brinkman Found a Whole New Ball Game." *Baltimore Sun*, December 19, 1979.

McGuire, Jim. "'Deacon' Jim McGuire." *Albion Evening Recorder*, August 2, 1932.

_____."James Deacon McGuire." *Albion Evening Recorder*, November 2, 1936.

Minot, George E. Jr. "Epstein Alters Stance, Attitude." *Washington Post*, August 25, 1968.

_____. "McMullen Faces Struggle to Regain Regular Status." *Washington Post*, March 5, 1967.

Nichols, Max. "Rollins, Allen Place Success in Hands of Positive Thinking." *The Sporting News,* January 1, 1966.

O'Donnell, Bob. "City Senses a Pennant as Nats Win Another." *Washington Times*, 1985.

Overfield, Joseph M. "William Ellsworth Hoy, 1862-1961." *The National Pastime*, Fall, 1962.

Parker, Dan. "Hines' Triple Play." *New York Daily Mirror,* July 25, 1935.

Povich, Shirley. "The Big Train: Always on the Right Track." *Washington Post*, October 17, 1927.

_____. "This Morning." *Washington Post*, August 31, 1946.

_____. "This Morning." *Washington Post*, February 21, 1946.

_____. "This Morning." *Washington Post*, January 12, 1937.

_____. "This Morning." *Washington Post*, July 13, 1945.

_____. "Senators' Bluege, Dead at 84." *Washington Post*, October 16, 1985.

Richman, Milton. "Sherry Had Life's Secret." *Washington Star*, October 27, 1970.

Ruark, Robert C. "Memories of Dutch on Opening Day." *Washington Star*, April 14, 1958.

Rubin, Bob. "Legends That Match the Man." *Spokesman Review and Spokane Chronicle,* April 4, 1991.

Rumill,Ed. "Allen Makes Hodges Play Him Regularly." *Christian Science Monitor*, April 24, 1967.

Schacht, Al. "My Own Particular Screwball." *Washington Star*, April 15, 1955.

Siegel, Morris. "A Belated Tribute to Pete Runnels." *Washington Star*, September 8, 1962.

_____. "Epstein May Be Ready to Live Up to Billing." *Washington Star*, June 29, 1967.

_____. "Hondo Set for Padres." *Washington Star*, March 17, 1981.

_____. "Killer's Homers Mount as Hairline Recedes." *Washington Star*, August 2, 1957.

_____. "Mack Played to Win, Even All-Star Games." *Washington Star*, July 6, 1964.

Stann, Francis. "After 40 Years, Rice Keeps His Series Secret." *Washington Star*, September 27, 1964.

_____. "The Big Guy." *Washington Star*, January 21, 1972.

_____. "Bluege, Overcoming Game Leg of Rookie Days." *Washington Star*, March 13, 1938.

_____. "Cazzie Says Senators Are Making Own Breaks." *Washington Star*, May 5, 1969.

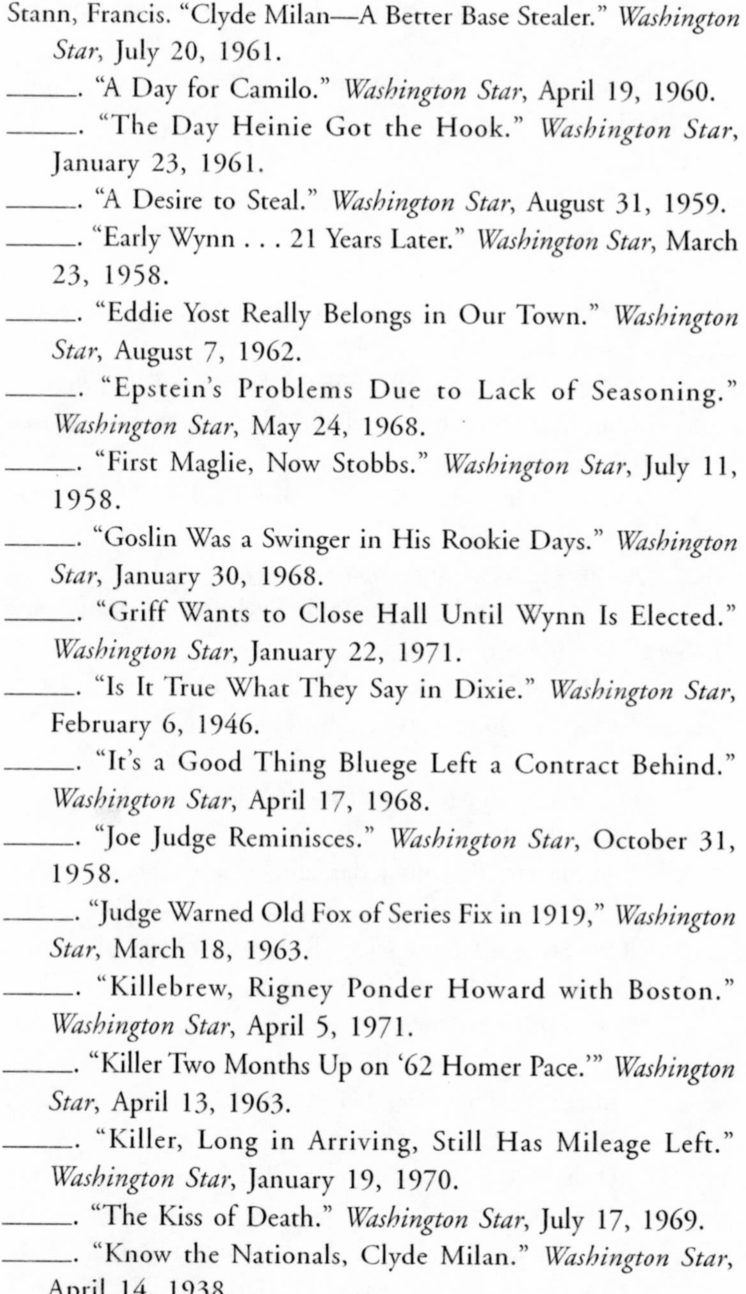

Stann, Francis. "Clyde Milan—A Better Base Stealer." *Washington Star*, July 20, 1961.

———. "A Day for Camilo." *Washington Star*, April 19, 1960.

———. "The Day Heinie Got the Hook." *Washington Star*, January 23, 1961.

———. "A Desire to Steal." *Washington Star*, August 31, 1959.

———. "Early Wynn . . . 21 Years Later." *Washington Star*, March 23, 1958.

———. "Eddie Yost Really Belongs in Our Town." *Washington Star*, August 7, 1962.

———. "Epstein's Problems Due to Lack of Seasoning." *Washington Star*, May 24, 1968.

———. "First Maglie, Now Stobbs." *Washington Star*, July 11, 1958.

———. "Goslin Was a Swinger in His Rookie Days." *Washington Star*, January 30, 1968.

———. "Griff Wants to Close Hall Until Wynn Is Elected." *Washington Star*, January 22, 1971.

———. "Is It True What They Say in Dixie." *Washington Star*, February 6, 1946.

———. "It's a Good Thing Bluege Left a Contract Behind." *Washington Star*, April 17, 1968.

———. "Joe Judge Reminisces." *Washington Star*, October 31, 1958.

———. "Judge Warned Old Fox of Series Fix in 1919," *Washington Star*, March 18, 1963.

———. "Killebrew, Rigney Ponder Howard with Boston." *Washington Star*, April 5, 1971.

———. "Killer Two Months Up on '62 Homer Pace.'" *Washington Star*, April 13, 1963.

———. "Killer, Long in Arriving, Still Has Mileage Left." *Washington Star*, January 19, 1970.

———. "The Kiss of Death." *Washington Star*, July 17, 1969.

———. "Know the Nationals, Clyde Milan." *Washington Star*, April 14, 1938.

Stann, Francis. "Lane and His Track Team." *Washington Star*, July 18, 1955.

_____. "Lewis, Travis, $150,000 Pair Rated Best of 'Kid' Majors, Picked Up By Nats for $100." *Washington Star*, March 19, 1938.

_____. "Looks Easy to Rick." *Washington Star*, February 8, 1963.

_____. "Mister Bread and Butter." *Washington Star*, March 21, 1958.

_____. "Necessity, Not Nepotism, Has Sherry on Spot." *Washington Star*, April 7,1946.

_____. "A New Challenge." *Washington Star*, April 9, 1961.

_____. "One Man's Hobby: Baseball." *Washington Star*, March 17, 1957.

_____. "Pascual Could Be Best of All Cuban Pitchers." *Washington Star*, March 3, 1964.

_____. "A Pair of Aces." *Washington Star*, June 2, 1954.

_____. "Pete Runnels Belongs to Willie Keeler's Era." *Washington Star*, December 5, 1962.

_____. "The Picture Player." *Washington Star*, December 2, 1955.

_____. "Rick, the Quiet Ferrell." *Washington Star*, January 28, 1959.

_____. "Roy Sievers: A Member of the Phillies." *Washington Star*, November 29, 1961.

_____. "Roy Sievers: Perennial Bargain." *Washington Star*, July 15, 1960.

_____. "The Story of Sam Rice, Baseball's 'Man of War.'" *Washington Star*, May 8, 1963.

_____. "Sievers on the Bench." *Washington Star*, September 16, 1957.

_____. "Something That Was Left Behind." *Washington Star*, February 27, 1950.

_____. "Stylish Muddy Was Complete Ball Player." *Washington Star*, November 15, 1963.

_____. "Time When Griff Blew It." *Washington Star*, July 3, 1958.

_____. "Top Finds of 40 Years: Persistent Early Wynn." *Washington Star*, February 11, 1968.

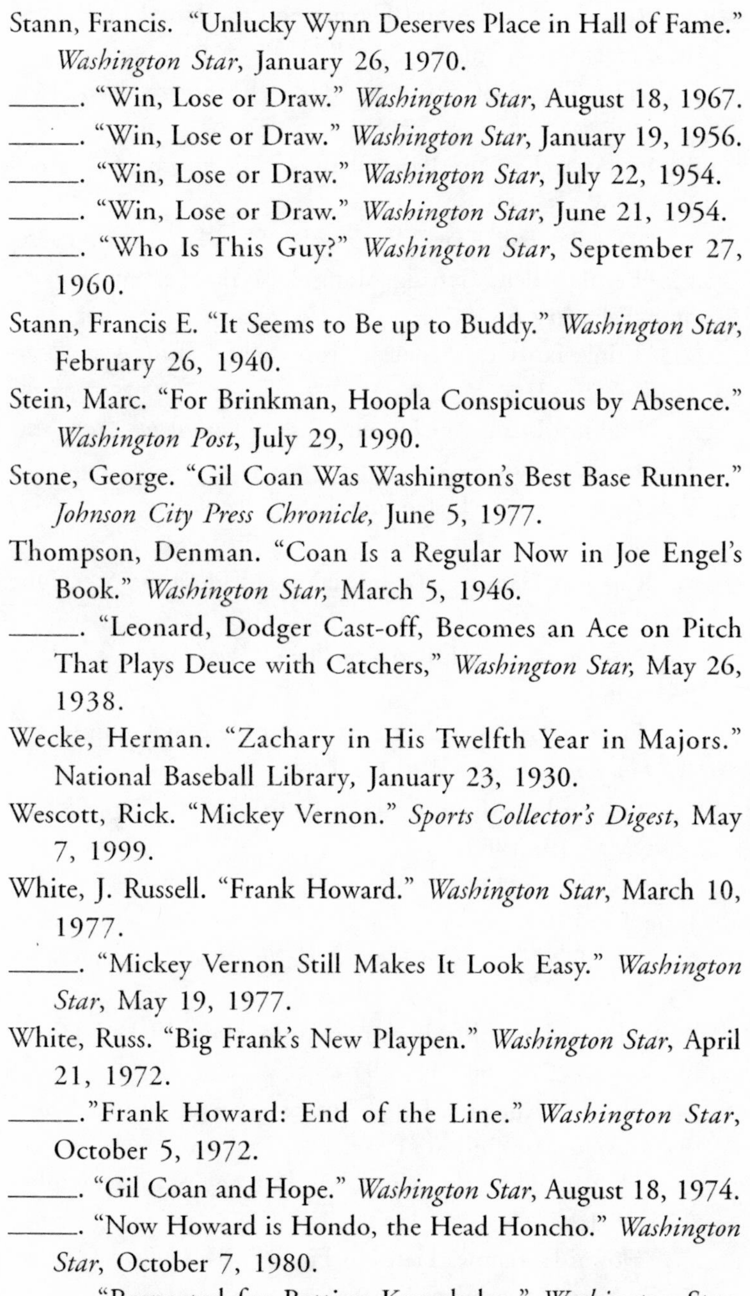

Stann, Francis. "Unlucky Wynn Deserves Place in Hall of Fame." *Washington Star*, January 26, 1970.

———. "Win, Lose or Draw." *Washington Star*, August 18, 1967.

———. "Win, Lose or Draw." *Washington Star*, January 19, 1956.

———. "Win, Lose or Draw." *Washington Star*, July 22, 1954.

———. "Win, Lose or Draw." *Washington Star*, June 21, 1954.

———. "Who Is This Guy?" *Washington Star*, September 27, 1960.

Stann, Francis E. "It Seems to Be up to Buddy." *Washington Star*, February 26, 1940.

Stein, Marc. "For Brinkman, Hoopla Conspicuous by Absence." *Washington Post*, July 29, 1990.

Stone, George. "Gil Coan Was Washington's Best Base Runner." *Johnson City Press Chronicle*, June 5, 1977.

Thompson, Denman. "Coan Is a Regular Now in Joe Engel's Book." *Washington Star,* March 5, 1946.

———. "Leonard, Dodger Cast-off, Becomes an Ace on Pitch That Plays Deuce with Catchers," *Washington Star,* May 26, 1938.

Wecke, Herman. "Zachary in His Twelfth Year in Majors." National Baseball Library, January 23, 1930.

Wescott, Rick. "Mickey Vernon." *Sports Collector's Digest*, May 7, 1999.

White, J. Russell. "Frank Howard." *Washington Star*, March 10, 1977.

———. "Mickey Vernon Still Makes It Look Easy." *Washington Star*, May 19, 1977.

White, Russ. "Big Frank's New Playpen." *Washington Star*, April 21, 1972.

———."Frank Howard: End of the Line." *Washington Star*, October 5, 1972.

———. "Gil Coan and Hope." *Washington Star*, August 18, 1974.

———. "Now Howard is Hondo, the Head Honcho." *Washington Star*, October 7, 1980.

———. "Respected for Batting Knowledge." *Washington Star-News*, August 23, 1974.

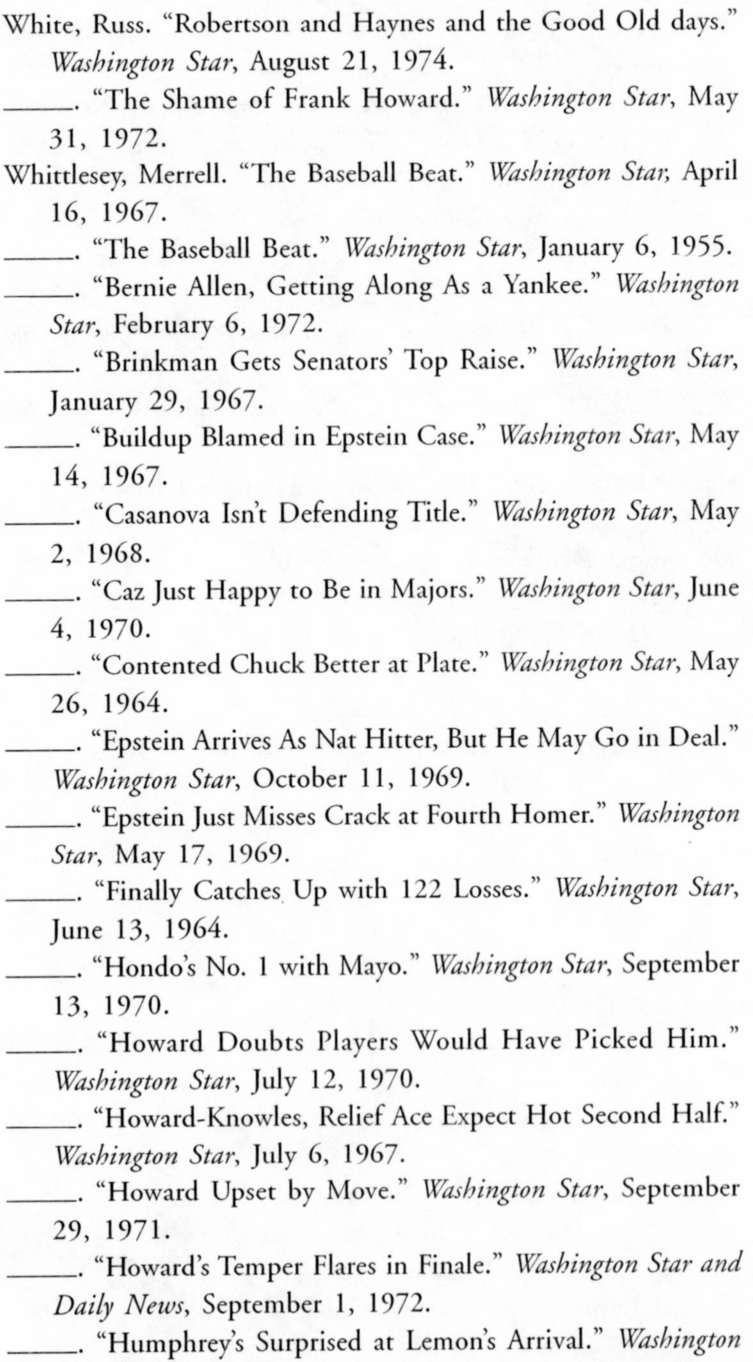

White, Russ. "Robertson and Haynes and the Good Old days." *Washington Star*, August 21, 1974.

_____. "The Shame of Frank Howard." *Washington Star*, May 31, 1972.

Whittlesey, Merrell. "The Baseball Beat." *Washington Star*, April 16, 1967.

_____. "The Baseball Beat." *Washington Star*, January 6, 1955.

_____. "Bernie Allen, Getting Along As a Yankee." *Washington Star*, February 6, 1972.

_____. "Brinkman Gets Senators' Top Raise." *Washington Star*, January 29, 1967.

_____. "Buildup Blamed in Epstein Case." *Washington Star*, May 14, 1967.

_____. "Casanova Isn't Defending Title." *Washington Star*, May 2, 1968.

_____. "Caz Just Happy to Be in Majors." *Washington Star*, June 4, 1970.

_____. "Contented Chuck Better at Plate." *Washington Star*, May 26, 1964.

_____. "Epstein Arrives As Nat Hitter, But He May Go in Deal." *Washington Star*, October 11, 1969.

_____. "Epstein Just Misses Crack at Fourth Homer." *Washington Star*, May 17, 1969.

_____. "Finally Catches Up with 122 Losses." *Washington Star*, June 13, 1964.

_____. "Hondo's No. 1 with Mayo." *Washington Star*, September 13, 1970.

_____. "Howard Doubts Players Would Have Picked Him." *Washington Star*, July 12, 1970.

_____. "Howard-Knowles, Relief Ace Expect Hot Second Half." *Washington Star*, July 6, 1967.

_____. "Howard Upset by Move." *Washington Star*, September 29, 1971.

_____. "Howard's Temper Flares in Finale." *Washington Star and Daily News*, September 1, 1972.

_____. "Humphrey's Surprised at Lemon's Arrival." *Washington Star*, October 17 1967.

_____. "Imagine Senators Without Howard." *Washington Star*,

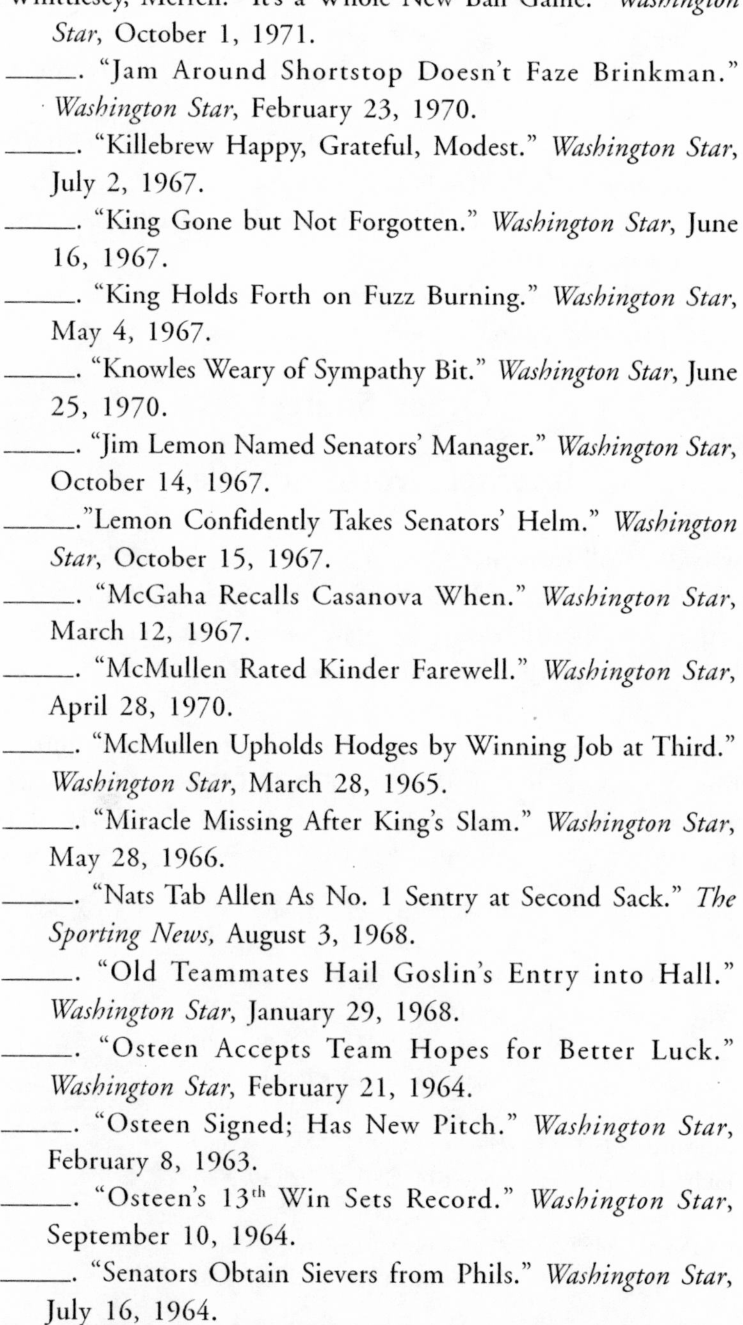

Whittlesey, Merrell. "It's a Whole New Ball Game." *Washington Star*, October 1, 1971.

———. "Jam Around Shortstop Doesn't Faze Brinkman." *Washington Star*, February 23, 1970.

———. "Killebrew Happy, Grateful, Modest." *Washington Star*, July 2, 1967.

———. "King Gone but Not Forgotten." *Washington Star*, June 16, 1967.

———. "King Holds Forth on Fuzz Burning." *Washington Star*, May 4, 1967.

———. "Knowles Weary of Sympathy Bit." *Washington Star*, June 25, 1970.

———. "Jim Lemon Named Senators' Manager." *Washington Star*, October 14, 1967.

———."Lemon Confidently Takes Senators' Helm." *Washington Star*, October 15, 1967.

———. "McGaha Recalls Casanova When." *Washington Star*, March 12, 1967.

———. "McMullen Rated Kinder Farewell." *Washington Star*, April 28, 1970.

———. "McMullen Upholds Hodges by Winning Job at Third." *Washington Star*, March 28, 1965.

———. "Miracle Missing After King's Slam." *Washington Star*, May 28, 1966.

———. "Nats Tab Allen As No. 1 Sentry at Second Sack." *The Sporting News,* August 3, 1968.

———. "Old Teammates Hail Goslin's Entry into Hall." *Washington Star*, January 29, 1968.

———. "Osteen Accepts Team Hopes for Better Luck." *Washington Star*, February 21, 1964.

———. "Osteen Signed; Has New Pitch." *Washington Star*, February 8, 1963.

———. "Osteen's 13th Win Sets Record." *Washington Star*, September 10, 1964.

———. "Senators Obtain Sievers from Phils." *Washington Star*, July 16, 1964.

———. "Senators Saved by Single in 14th." *Washington Star*, September 24, 1968.

Whittlesey, Merrell. "Short Admits Trade's Flaw, but Gets Support." *Washington Star*, May 9, 1971.

_____. "Starting All Over with Big Mike." *Washington Star*, February 28, 1971.

_____. "Ted Convinces Brinkman He, Too, Can Be a Hitter." *Washington Star*, March 17, 1969.

_____. "Wynn Makes Hall After 3-Year Wait." *Washington Star*, January 20, 1972.

Wood, Phil. "Busby Made Orioles A Winner." *Tuff Stuff*, September, 2000.

Other Sources

Internet, Worldwide Web

www.Baseball-Reference.Com
The Baseball On-Line Library, CBS SportsLine, HYPERLINK http://www.Sportsline.com __*www.Sportsline.com*_HYPERLINK http://www.TotalBaseball.com_*www.TotalBaseball.com*_

The following player biographies and statistics were acquired from the above sites on the dates provided below. All statistics were updated via www.baseball-reference.com on July 18 and 19, 2003.

Player	Baseball-Ref	Sportsline	Tot. Baseball
Ainsmith, Eddie	August 14, 2001	July 18, 2001	
Allen, Bernie	August 15, 2001	Nov. 1, 2000	
Altrock, Nick	August 14, 2001	July 18, 2001	
Ayers, Doc	August 14, 2001	July 18, 2001	
Bluege, Ossie	August 14, 2001	July 18, 2001	
Brinkman, Ed	August 14, 2001	Nov. 1, 2000	
Busby, Jim	August 14, 2001	July 19, 2001	
Cartwright, Ed	August 14, 2001		
Casanova, Paul	August 14, 2001	July 19, 2001	
Case, George	August 14, 2001	July 19, 2001	

Player	Baseball-Ref	Sportsline	Tot. Baseball
Coan, Gil	August 14, 2001	July 19, 2001	
Courtney, Clint	August 15, 2001	July 19, 2001	
Cronin, Joe	August 15, 2001	July 19, 2001	Oct. 27, 2000
DeMontreville, Gene	Jan. 18, 2001	Oct. 26, 2000	
Epstein, Mike	August 15, 2001	July 19, 2001	
Ferrell, Rick	August 15, 2001	Feb. 3, 2000	Oct. 27, 2000
Foster, Eddie	August 14, 2001	July 19, 2001.	
Goslin, Goose	August 14, 2001	July 19, 2001	Oct. 28, 2000
Griffith, Clark	August 15, 2001	July 19, 2001	Oct. 28, 2000
Harris, Bucky	August 15, 2001	July 20, 2001	Oct. 28, 2000
Hines, Paul	Jan. 7, 2001	July 29, 2001	
Hinton, Chuck	August 15, 2001	July 20, 2001	
Howard, Frank	August 14, 2001	July 29, 2001	
Hoy, Dummy	Jan. 7, 2001	July 20, 2001	
Hughes, Tom	August 14, 2001	July 20, 2001	
Hyde, Dick	August 14, 2001	July 20, 2001	
Johnson, Walter	August 15, 2001	July 20, 2001	Oct. 28, 2000
Joyce, Bill	Jan. 19, 2001	July 20, 2001	
Judge, Joe	August 14, 2001	July 20, 2001	
Killebrew, Harmon	August 15, 2001	July 20, 2001	Oct. 27, 2000
Killen, Frank	Jan. 17, 2001	July 20, 2001	
King, Jim	August 15, 2001	July 20, 2001	
Knowles, Darold	August 14, 2001	July 20, 2001	
Lemon, Jim	August 14, 2001	July 20, 2001	
Leonard, Dutch	August 14, 2001	July 20, 2001	
Lewis, Buddy	August 14, 2001	July 20, 2001	
Manush, Heinie	August 15, 2001	July 20, 2001	Oct. 26, 2000
Marberry, Fred	August 14, 2001	July 20, 2001	
Maul, Al	Jan. 15, 2001	July 20, 2001	
McBride, George	August 14, 2001	July 20, 2001	
McGuire, Deacon	Jan. 17, 2001	July 20, 2001	
McMullen, Ken	August 15, 2001	July 20, 2001	
Mercer, Win	Jan. 17, 2001	July 20, 2001	
Milan, Clyde	August 14, 2001	July 20, 2001	
Moeller, Danny	August 14, 2001	July 20, 2001	
Mogridge, George	August 14, 2001	July 20, 2001	
Morgan, Ray	August 14, 2001	July 20, 2001	
Myer, Buddy	August 14, 2001	July 20, 2001	
Osteen, Claude	August 14, 2001	July 20, 2001	

Player	Baseball-Ref	Sportsline	Tot. Baseball
Pascual, Camilo	August 14, 2001	July 20, 2001	
Rice, Sam	August 15, 2001	July 20, 2001	Oct. 28, 2000
Robertson, Sherry	August 14, 2001	July 20, 2001	
Ruel, Muddy	August 14, 2001	July 20, 2001	
Runnels, Pete	August 14, 2001	July 20, 2001	
Russell, Jack	August 14, 2001	July 20, 2001	
Schaefer, Germany	August 14, 2001	July 20, 2001	
Selbach, Kip	Jan. 7, 2001	July 20, 2001	
Shanks, Howard	August 14, 2001	July 20, 2001	
Shoch, George	August 14, 2001		
Sievers, Roy	August 14, 2001	July 20, 2001	
Stobbs, Chuck	August 14, 2001	July 20, 2001	
Stone, Johnny	August 14, 2001	July 20, 2001	
Travis, Cecil	August 14, 2001	July 20, 2001	
Unser, Del	August 14, 2001	July 20, 2001	
Vernon, Mickey	August 9, 2001	July 20, 2001	
Wynn, Early	August 15, 2001	July 20, 2001	
Yost, Eddie	August 15, 2001	July 20, 2001	
Zachary, Tom	August 14, 2001	July 20, 2001	

INDEX

ABOUT THE BOOK

Washington Senators' All-Time Greats is one of the first books covering the entire 101-year history of the Senators. For two decades the author conducted interviews and researched the history of the team. Hundreds of players appeared in Washington uniforms over the years and from these Mr. Willis selected an all-time team. In addition, all-star teams from five eras were chosen. Career highlights and statistics are included in each of the sixty-seven mini-biographies; photographs and anecdotes bring the players to life. The author also presents team records and summaries for each year and era, and for the entire history of the Senators. The last chapter of the book honors the best of Senator's managers and owners, and the best Washington play-by-play announcer and sportswriter. Readers are invited to compare their selections with the author's. The book contains a foreword by Senator's great, Frank Howard and is recommended by former Washington stars and managers, Mickey Vernon and Jim Lemon.

ABOUT THE AUTHOR

The author was born (July 5, 1924) and raised in Washington, D.C. in the shadow of Griffith Stadium. He saw his first Senators' game in 1932 and became an avid fan. He is a graduate of McKinley Tech High School, as well as American University, both located in the District of Columbia. In the army during World War II, he later served with the National Security Agency, retiring after thirty-eight years. Since then, he has been a frequent substitute teacher at the Riverdale Baptist School in Upper Malboro, Maryland. In 1986-87, he was a full-time fifth grade teacher there. He is also an active member of the Riverdale Baptist Church. At a ceremony at the Central Intelligence Agency on July 11, 1995, he was honored as one of the "early heroes of Venona" for his work which led to the identification, arrest and conviction of Soviet spies, including Julius and Ethel Rosenberg. He is a member of the Society for American Baseball Research (SABR) and the Washington Baseball Historical Society. For fifty-seven years he has been married to Frances Ladd Willis, and they have three sons and ten grandchildren.

BVG